the Unofficial Guide® to Managing Rental Property

Melissa Prandi, MPM

WILEY

Wiley Publishing, Inc.

Library of Congress Control Number: 2004116111

ISBN: 0-7645-7818-9

Manufactured in the United States of America

10 9 8 7 6 5 4 3 2 1

Book design by Lissa Auciello-Brogan
Page creation by Wiley Publishing, Inc. Composition Services

Acknowledgements

I would like to thank Marilyn Sullivan for recommending me and introducing me to my agent, Marilyn Allen. Things moved right on to my introduction to Roxane Cerda, the friendly senior acquisitions editor at Wiley Publishing, who responded positively, quickly, and in detail, making this experience a positive one. Thank you to my project editor, Tere Drenth, for all your professionalism and commitment to making this an incredible book.

Thank you Ruth Frishman for your sharing and direction at such an early age: You inspired me and made me want to learn just how to do things right. To my good friend Charlie Fagan, for your high level of guidance and ability to direct without saying a word.

Also thanks to Sylvia Hill for her research and technical additions and her upbeat e-mails along the way. A very special thank you to Dana Sansing-Esquibel, Julie DiGiulio, Christine Goodin, Roxie Mikolon, Shawna Shaw, and Natalie Mechetti, my staff at PRANDI Property Management, Inc., for their support and excitement.

Thank you Roy Bohrer and my good friends and members of The National Association of Residential Property Managers (NARPM). Thanks Susan Albern for your contributions and wisdom with Chapter 17. Thanks also to Nancy Kenyon and the staff at Fair Housing of Marin. Thank you to my very good friend Jean Storms of LandlordSource, Inc., for the excellent writing contributions; Judy Cook of Cook & Company, Ltd. I also want to thank Nadeen Green of *Rent Magazine;* John Mangham, the master of the 1031 exchange; Jim McKinney of Professional Publishers for his outstanding forms; and Jeffrey Taylor ("Mr. Landlord") for all your guidance. Thanks also to my close friends for their understanding and encouragement along the way.

Last, but certainly not least, a special thank you goes to Raymond Scarabosio, MPM, for his ever-lasting friendship and support.

Contents

Melissa Prandi, MPM, has been managing residential rental properties on behalf of others for over 20 years. Beginning as a receptionist at G&R Systems, Inc., she quickly learned that property management was the career choice for her, so she obtained her real estate license and became a property manager within that company. After five years, Melissa was given the tremendous opportunity to purchase the company. When she did, she renamed it PRANDI Property Management, Inc., which is currently located in San Rafael, California. Having owned the company for over seventeen years, Melissa specializes in managing single-family homes and smaller residential properties specifically in Marin County, California. She often manages only one or two small properties for a client, perhaps for a personal residence to which they plan to return, and some of these clients have become lifelong friends. Melissa owns and manages her own personal residential and commercial investment properties.

Always interested in being professional and up-to-date, Melissa has earned several designations through the National Association of Residential Property Managers (NARPM). Her personal designations include residential management professional (RMP) and master property manager (MPM), one of less than 100 property management professionals in the United States to have earned this designation. In addition to her personal designations, PRANDI Property Management holds the certified residential management company (CRMC) designation, one of only 19 professional property management companies in the United States to have earned such a prestigious designation.

As well as serving on the National Association of Residential Property Managers (NARPM) national Board of Directors and Executive Committee for nine years, Melissa also served as a national president of NARPM. Her leadership skills and enthusiasm for helping others in the profession still keep her active with national committees and key positions. Locally, she has been chair of the property management committee for the Marin Association of Realtors several times and is currently serving on the board as a director for Fair Housing of Marin. Exemplifying her people skills and being interested in sharing her tips of the profession, Melissa has been the keynote speaker for local, state, and national property management conferences and has written several popular workshops specifically for property managers. She has taught at the local community college and has been featured on a local television news station as a notable professional in her field. Melissa's office is always available to other property managers, and she often shares her forms and procedures with others to enhance the property management profession.

Whether you own a single-family home, a duplex, a triplex, or multiple units, if you rent it out, you're a landlord. And as a landlord, you need good information. This book begins with the basics and takes you through many different steps along the way. Aimed primarily at landlords just getting into the business, *The Unofficial Guide to Managing Rental Property* helps you manage and profit from your investments.

You may be picking up this book with plans to purchase your first rental property. Or perhaps you've suddenly acquired a piece of property that is currently rented or will need to be rented. You may be someone who has, through a series of completely unexpected circumstances, been presented with an opportunity to own a rental property. In fact, many property owners become instant landlords when jobs transfer them out of area.

Believe it or not, many people who purchase and manage their own rental properties enjoy it. So, eventually, you may develop your management business and begin to manage other people's properties in addition to your personal properties. If you choose to go that route and manage properties for other people, you may need a license, depending on the state in which you do business. Because you're going to be held to the highest standards of local, state, and federal laws, you also need to understand the laws about renting property. And regardless of how many properties you manage, your rental property needs to be routinely maintained. This book covers those topics.

Whatever your circumstances, you need to understand the details of property management. This book answers many of your most pressing questions. By picking up this book and reading it, taking notes, applying the systems, and heeding the advice, you will be further ahead than most landlords.

Book description

This book is aimed at individual investors who own properties with four or fewer units and who typically manage rentals part-time. Information to help you maximize the return on your investment includes:

- How to find and finance great rental property
- How to prepare your property for a tenant
- How to effectively market your property
- How to write legal, effective ads that attract good tenants
- How to legally set rental criteria to ensure responsible tenants
- How to find quality tenants and keep them long-term
- How to interview and screen applicants to avoid potentially disastrous tenants
- Where to find forms and letters that help you communicate with current occupants
- How to ensure on-time rent; how to collect late rent
- How to remain aware of new government regulations
- How to stay up to date with fair housing laws
- How to successfully evict delinquent tenants, collect damages, and keep your property intact
- How to hire a professional property manager, should you choose to go that route
- What to look for in that property management company

This book gives you everything you need, in detail, so that you can be the best property manager possible. You find useful tips, as well as methods that are quite simple to implement and that help you manage your property efficiently and effectively.

In order to be a successful investor, you need to have a clear and thorough understanding of your legal rights and obligations as a property manager/owner. You need to have clear and concise policies and procedures in writing, and you need to follow them. Don't make exceptions to your rules. You need to use all the correct legal forms from the application, to the lease, and for the move in and move out process.

This book illustrates how important it is to have good policies and procedures in place in the beginning, before any problem occurs. Remember that most problems occur due to a lack of education and to not following basic steps. When you make an exception to your own policies and procedures, you may find yourself in trouble. Again, treat this like a business. Once you get the hang of it, you can then begin working on the 1031 exchange process (see Chapter 15) and purchase more properties to add to your inventory.

Special features

Every book in the Unofficial Guide series offers the following four special sidebars that are devised to help you get things done cheaply, efficiently, and smartly.

1. **Moneysaver:** Tips and shortcuts that help you save money.

2. **Watch Out!:** Cautions and warnings to help you avoid common pitfalls.

3. **Bright Idea:** Smart or innovative ways to do something; in many cases, the ideas listed here help you save time or hassle.

4. **Quote:** Anecdotes from real people who are willing to share their experiences and insights.

I also recognize your need to have quick information at your fingertips, and have provided the following comprehensive sections at the back of the book:

1. **Glossary:** Definitions of complicated terminology and jargon.

2. **Resource Directory:** Lists of relevant agencies, associations, institutions, Web sites, and so on.

3. **Further Reading:** Suggested titles that can help you get more in-depth information on related topics.

4. **Important Documents:** "Official" forms you need to refer to.

5. **Index**

Getting an Overview of Rental Property Management

PART I

Rental Property Management 101

If you're reading this chapter, you're probably considering purchasing rental property or already own rental property that you want to rent — for any number of reasons. This chapter helps you make the decision to purchase property or help you cope with the decision that has been made for you (if, for example, you inherited property or are renting a house you're having trouble selling).

One thing is for sure — this is not an easy process. You need to treat owning rental property like purchasing a brand-new business that you know nothing about. When you own rental property, there are numerous things you must learn or you will end up in trouble. One idea is to look for a reputable property manager in your area and make an appointment to discuss managing property. As a property manager for others, I often get calls saying, "I don't know anything about renting property, but I'm moving out of the area and don't want to sell."

Chapter 1

> **Bright Idea**
>
> I recommend calling a local property management company and offering to pay a consultation fee. Make a list of questions in advance and spend some time talking about your rental property. By taking the time to get the basics from a professional, you may avoid several mistakes that you would otherwise make.

This is one of my favorite calls. You will likely find that property managers are willing to take the time to discuss the pros and cons with you for the specific type of property and your situation.

You need to be willing to take the time to learn the basics at the beginning and be willing to continue to learn. Know in advance that you'll make your share of mistakes. When you do, get up, dust yourself off, learn from the mistakes, and then swear you will never let those situations happen to you again. This is where joining a group of other property owners or investors — for advice and for moral support — can really pay off.

I have been managing my properties and managing for others 23 years, and I still make mistakes. So I am still learning by reading periodicals, taking courses, and networking.

Understanding the pros and cons

Here's a look at the positives and the negatives of purchasing and managing rental property. If, after perusing these two lists, you decide that property management is not for you, professionals can manage your property for you — see Chapter 17.

Pros of managing rental property

The positive aspects of renting property are as follows; a lot of these apply whether you hire a property management company or not:

- You own your own business.
- You'll never be bored.
- You save the fees charged by a property management professional.

- Technology has made self-managing your properties easier than in the past.

- It's a people business.

- It can be fun and challenging.

- You may enjoy it enough to make it your career and even manage property owned by others.

- After everything is set up properly, it's not a lot of work.

- You have a choice: You can be completely or minimally involved.

- You can see and touch your investment.

- The business provides continual income rather than the one-time income from a sale.

- With creativity, you can purchase with little cash.

- You can keep a home you may want to move back to later (for example, if you're transferred from an area you love).

- Renting properties is usually profitable.

- Renting property provides current or future lodging for your children.

- Buying your first property starts you on your way to purchasing more.

- Property values usually appreciate.

- You diversify your investments.

- There are great tax advantages.

- You can defer capital gains with a 1031 exchange (see Chapter 15).

- It can be a second income.

- It can be a part of your retirement.

- You can use your 401k or other retirement plan to buy the investment property.

- It can be a long-term business.

Cons of managing rental property

You may have days when you question why you purchased rental property and became a landlord. But then, when you arrange an appraisal and find that your property value has gone up, you're probably pleased with the gain in value. The time, money, and effort suddenly are all worthwhile, and you realize that hard work really does pay off.

Keep in mind, however, that managing rental also has a few downsides:

- It takes a lot of time in the beginning to set things up.
- There are many details you need to learn and understand.
- The initial outlay may be greater than with other investments.
- Your property may have a negative cash flow, especially at first.
- Technology is hard to keep up with and takes time.
- Reporting income and expenses on your tax return requires additional time and knowledge.
- There are many local, state, and federal laws.
- You will need to purchase more insurance.
- Like anything, there is always a risk involved.
- You can be sued.
- There are ways you can be taken advantage of.
- The hours are not 9 to 5.
- It is like having a second job, often without vacations.
- Dropping everything to respond to an emergency isn't fun.
- Finding and dealing with contractors can be tricky.
- It is a people business, which means you have to enjoy talking to people.
- You listen to many complaints.

- The market can and does change constantly.

- Things do go wrong with rental property.

You can always hire a professional to rent and/or manage your property. This way you don't have to deal with the emergency call in the middle of the night or all the problems that arise from dealing with different types of people. You let them take on the time-consuming tasks while you receive the income.

> 66 Purchasing rental prop-
> erties allowed me to
> retire a lot earlier than
> I expected. Over time,
> I have made enough
> money to hire a profes-
> sional management
> company, so now I can
> leave town anytime
> I want without the
> worries. 99
> —Chuck P., investor

Overcoming the negatives

To overcome the negative aspects of managing rental property, consider these tips:

- You already know by this point that it takes a lot of time to get started. Just know that and set aside the time. Knowing the time commitment in advance and taking things one step at a time helps you in the long run.

- Minimize or eliminate the risks by investing in setting up your business and tending to the details in the beginning. Also line up and meet with the professionals you will work with (see the "Hiring real estate professionals" section for details).

- Keep your files concise and be sure to keep all paper receipts in your property file (see Chapter 11). In addition, many software programs can assist you with your record-keeping. If you choose to set up your new business on a computer, you may save a great deal of time and effort when filing your tax returns. Invest in a scanner so that all your documents can be accessed online. Get a digital

camera so that pictures of the property can be down-
loaded to your computer and uploaded to your Web site.

- You're on call 24/7 and there are no vacations when you
  self-manage your properties. However, perhaps you can
  occasionally trade with friends who own property by taking
  turns covering for one another while taking vacations.
  In some states, you cannot pay your friends for their time
  unless they have a real estate or property management
  license, but you still have options. I even know people who
  travel in a motor home all year, managing their rental
  properties via e-mail and cellphone, and accessing all
  records and monies online.

- Ask around and do your homework before you hire
  contractors. Most states require a license to do a trade.
  If so, check government Web sites to find consumer
  brochures. You'll probably find some hints and tips on
  what to ask before you choose the right one for you. If you
  have friends who own property, ask them whether they will
  share some of the names of their contractors. And don't
  be afraid to ask friends or other contacts how they're handling their rental properties. Be prepared to hear their
  war stories, though — listen and learn from them, don't
  let them scare you.

- Carry plenty of insurance and be prepared to be sued.
  Make sure you review your insurance annually with your
  agent. Always look at your property from a safety and liability angle.

- Take workshops on how to deal with and listen to all types
  of personalities. Know that managing rental property is
  and always will be a people business.

- Keep up with property-management laws by joining a local
  income property owner's association in your area. Use the
  Internet by searching on "landlord association" and the
  name of your area. Continue to read books and take classes.

- Expect things to go wrong and learn how to be proactive and creative in handling them.

- Keep up with technology.

- Turn negatives into positives and be ready for the next challenge.

Running your business like a business

Whether you've been managing property for years, are just getting started, or are contemplating purchasing your first property, it is a good idea to treat your rental properties like a business. Start with the basics: Choose a name for your business. I suggest that you choose a name that is simple but allows your business to grow, so that you can purchase and rent out other properties under the same name.

I had a client who owned a five-unit Victorian that I managed for years. He purchased the building when his daughter, Sarah, was quite young and named his business Sarah Properties, after her. Not only did this give the business a separate name, but it made it special. The great part of the story is that his daughter is now in college, and I believe the value and equity in the property appreciated enough over the years to help pay for the daughter's college education.

You also need to decide what form you want your new business to take (for example, sole proprietorship, LLC, trust, corporation, and so on). An attorney can give you advice, as can other people who have experience owning and managing properties.

Setting your business up correctly in the beginning means you need to meet with several professional people to gain practical knowledge. Consider meeting with a real estate agent, banker or mortgage broker, accountant, insurance agent, attorney, and (if you want someone to manage your property for you) property manager. See the following section for details.

After you have your new business name, have decided what sort of form your company will take, have met with the

necessary professionals to assist you, there are a few more things
to do:

- **Set up a bank account.** Order preprinted deposit forms
  and a deposit stamp with the new business name. This
  saves you a bit of time in the beginning, but as you accumulate more properties, it can save you massive amounts
  of time and makes your business far more efficient. Seek
  out a bank that has online banking to save money in
  stamps, and even look for one that provides a day-to-day
  tracking of your bank account.

- **Get a P.O. box.** If you don't want your tenants to know
  where you live and don't have a professional office where
  your tenants can mail their rent checks, get a post-office
  box and add a second phone line in your home (or, if you
  have excellent cellphone coverage in your area, get a cellphone dedicated to your business). A separate phone line
  can have an informational voice mail on the outgoing
  message. Also get an e-mail address that contains your
  business name instead of your personal name. Put all of
  this contact information on your new business cards.

- **Set up a Web site.** Keep it simple — you just want a presence on the Internet. You should be able to set up a Web
  site quite simply and affordably; in fact, you may be surprised just how easy it really is to have your own site, which
  can give potential tenants information about your property. I believe a Web site is becoming a critical part of marketing any rental property.

- **Take a class, attend a workshop, or hire a professional to
  teach you the basics to get you started and to keep you out
  of trouble.** There are many fabulous resources out there
  (including this book, I might add!).

- **Plan now to own property long term.** You may not own the
  same property forever, but you should have a plan to purchase property and build your business from there.

Watch Out!

Don't give out your home address and private telephone number. In fact, at some point you may want to consider not being listed in the local phone book. In order to maintain some privacy, keep a separate phone number for your business.

Hiring real estate professionals

One of your most important duties when you're considering purchasing property or have just started managing property is to put together the best team to help you along the way. There are many professionals you need to hire and get to know within your new adventure who can help make you and your new business a success. Take the time to interview and hire people who can help you succeed as a new rental-property owner. Continue to improve and keep up with the details of managing investment properties.

Realtor/broker

Just because you have a real estate sales license or a real estate broker's license doesn't mean you are automatically a Realtor. Realtor is a registered trademark of the National Association of Realtors and it refers to people who are licensed by their states to sell real estate — buildings or land — and who are members of the association.

When hiring someone to represent you in the purchase of your property, it is important to hire a Realtor, preferably one who specializes in the type of property you want to buy. You can dive into more of that in Chapter 3. If you're not sure which Realtor to work with, ask anyone you know who manages rental property.

Establish a relationship with one Realtor when going out to look to purchase any property, including your first investment property. Yet, even with a Realtor on your team, it's up to you to

Bright Idea

Call a friend or acquaintance and ask for recommendations for the professionals they've used in managing their rental property or business. Getting
referrals is the best source you can ask for. If you don't know anyone who
owns rental property, ask among friends, co-workers, and so on.

know what you're looking for when you go out to view rental
properties. Do your homework on your own, look for properties
in the newspaper and on the Web, and have some ideas of the
area and type of property you're interested in.

Banker/mortgage broker

A banker (or mortgage broker) assists you in getting the proper
financing in order to purchase rental property. A banker gets
you the loan from the bank for which he or she works, whereas
a mortgage broker is an independent agent who works with several different financial institutions to find you the best loan possible with terms to meet your needs. Mortgage brokers generally
charge a bit more, through what's referred to as points, which is
usually a fee based on the percentage of the loan.

If you choose to work with a mortgage broker, meet with that
broker prior to making any offers, so that you know where you
stand financially and how you look on paper to a lender, a
process known as pre-qualifying. *Remember:* Many financial institutions have large lending departments, which means you may
never meet the person making a decision to give you a loan.

Insurance agent

The most efficient way to purchase insurance is to have one contact for all your insurance needs. I suggest establishing a relationship with an insurance agent who will not only handle the
insurance on your investment property but also ensure that
everything you own (your primary residence, your automobile,
and so on) has the right amount of coverage.

Bright Idea

Get to know your insurance agent and plan to have all your insurance reviewed each and every year. You need to have more than enough insurance, so look into an umbrella policy, which covers you for an extra one or two million dollars. Mare sure your insurance agent knows about all the properties you own.

Accountant/financial advisor

It is very important to meet on a regular basis with your accountant and/or financial advisor throughout the year to discuss your investment and to be prepared in your tax planning throughout the year. In this way, you can discuss your properties in advance instead of getting surprised when you visit your tax accountant during tax season. Some accountants even have a checklist to help you organize your files and your bookkeeping system.

Sure, you need to have a basic understanding about your investment, but you're not expected to know all the tax laws. That why you hire a good, reliable accountant to take care of your tax needs.

Remember that owning rental property has its tax advantages. You can deduct your purchase costs, your operating expenses, and annual depreciation. (And these tax advantages don't change when you hire a professional property manager.)

Attorney

If you own rental property, I guarantee you'll need the services of an attorney at some point. Typically, you want to meet with an attorney in the beginning to be certain your company is set up properly, and then have him or her on call to assist in legal matters. You may even want to look for a real estate attorney who specializes in evictions.

I found the attorney I use by going to the local county sheriff's office and asking, "Who puts through the most evictions in Marin County?" The first response I received was that they were not allowed to recommend any attorney. I reminded them I was not looking for a recommendation. I was simply asking who puts through the most evictions in our county. They gave me the name, and he has been my real estate attorney for over 20 years. I decided I wanted to hire the attorney who had handled many cases, had a great deal of experience, and had seen it all. And he certainly had a great deal of experience in evictions and in dealing with tenants. He even helped me understand what causes most of the evictions he handles and how to prevent that on my property.

> 66 Going through an eviction can be quite costly and time-consuming. Hire and get a rapport going with an attorney before you run into any problems. 99
>
> —Lisa G., investor

You want to establish a relationship with a real estate attorney in advance of running into problems. Oftentimes, you will find you can pay an attorney for an hour or two of consultation time. If you ask, you may find out that, for example, a group of attorneys is holding workshops nearby or speaking to a group of investors. I know that the local attorneys in my area speak at many different meetings that I attend. If you find and join a local property-owner's group, I can almost guarantee that the group will have an attorney speak at least once during the year.

Property manager

A property manager is a professional who manages investment properties for others; often he or she only manages property and handles rentals. Just because someone is a Realtor does not mean he or she has the expertise and knowledge to manage your property. Go to the National Association of Residential Property Managers (www.NARPM.org) or to the Institute of Real

Estate Managers (www.IREM.org) to find a list of specialized property managers who subscribe to an ethics code. Look for ones who have spent their time and effort in obtaining a certification for themselves and/or for their companies.

Even if you decide to manage your rental property yourself, you should still get to know a local property manager in the area. You find out more about hiring a property-management company in Chapter 17.

Financing properties: Stretching yourself to take that step

The financial part of your new purchase can be a confusing tangle of jargon and paperwork. There is so much to know, so don't try to totally understand it on your own. Your banker or mortgage broker can assist you. Just remember that there are a lot of options out there, so do your homework! Also find out whether the local city, county, or state has any housing programs that can assist you in financing either the purchase or renovation of your property.

Most successful investors have a story of how they had to stretch themselves to get into their first property. Most real estate tycoons can also tell you the story of purchasing their first property and how they personally got started. At any rate, getting started — taking that first step — is the hardest and scariest part, by far. Here's my story:

I remember purchasing my very first home. I had to scrape together every dollar I had. The day of the closing, I was still short by $500 and had to borrow from the Realtor who was representing me! It was a struggle. But then I fixed it up just a small amount, making a few changes to brighten up the inside — getting rid of the pea green and keeping it neutral. Just a few short years later, the property sold for double what I originally paid for it. I moved to a larger home in a nicer area. This was my start in purchasing real estate, and I was only 22 years old!

Years passed, and I was in a comfort zone, living in my larger home and renting office space for my business. I had purchased the property management company where I worked and taken over the lease. Twelve years flew by, and then, all of a sudden, I received a letter from my landlord letting me know that my lease had expired. In addition, my rent went from $1,800 per month to $2,500 in one day. I knew it was time to explore my options. I began to drive around and talk to others to see where I could move and rent more reasonably. I went to see Katherine, a Realtor friend of mine, to show her a flyer I had seen and ask whether purchasing a small office building on the flyer was an option. She immediately showed me a different flyer with information about a property she had for sale that was a much better value but, of course, more money. I looked at the better property with a lot of fear. She encouraged me and worked the numbers, suggesting that I needed to speak to her mortgage broker to make the transaction happen. Reluctantly and fearfully, I met with her mortgage broker, Suzanne, who made it look easy. She asked me lots of financial questions and worked out the numbers, and then told me that it should work out just fine and that I should make an offer on the building. I remember she telephoned Katherine from her office while I was sitting there and told her I was on my way to meet with her to make an offer to purchase the office building.

I met with the Realtor, made an offer, and had it accepted; of course, then I was completely terrified if for no other reason than I had to use my entire savings. During this stressful period, however, I remember a conversation I had with a real estate friend of mine who told me to stretch myself.

> 66 Take a rubber band out of your drawer. Okay, now I want you to stretch it, a little more, but don't let it snap. This should be the way you live your life. 99
>
> —Ralf C., mentor and friend

I purchased the property, moved my business there, and after four years, the property was appraised for double what I paid for it. I had taken a risk, I was scared, but it was one of the best investments I ever made. Ultimately, taking risks and stretching yourself to invest in real estate is a good thing.

You don't have to start big and buy a large building. You can start by purchasing a second home and renting out the home you're currently living in. If you haven't yet purchased real estate, look at buying a duplex or triplex and living in one of the units. This way, you have income, can manage the property, get the tax write-offs, and build equity. You can begin fixing up the property while building the equity and the value is going up.

Maintaining your property

The increase in value comes with time, increased rents, and, perhaps most importantly, the amount you maintain your investment. It is very important to care for your investment and to continue to maintain your property. Not only will that lead to the best appreciation in the value of your property, but the hands-on experience of maintaining and managing your property is a good thing, one that will help you understand property management for many years to come. What you learn will always assist you with investing, managing, and purchasing additional properties. Keep in mind that not all investors can take care of their own property maintenance. Know your limits and know when to hire professionals. (Check out Chapter 6 for more on maintenance.)

 Watch Out!

Don't get too comfortable with your rental property management and let things slide. Many owners think everything is fine as long as the rent check comes in, the bills are getting paid, and they haven't heard from their tenant with maintenance complaints. Instead, be proactive, do your drive-bys, and go in your property at least once a year.

Finding and qualifying great tenants

Finding tenants and keeping them is one of the greatest challenges you face as a rental property owner. The object is to prepare your property, market your property, and attract a qualified tenant who will stay long term. You want a tenant who will move in, take reasonably good care of your property, and pay his or her rent on time. When you get great tenants, you need to keep them happy while collecting your rent (see Chapter 12). Manage your investment and increase your value through smart rental practices.

Expanding your business

After you get your foot in the door with your first investment, opportunities to increase your inventory of rental property will continue to come your way. However, many people have reasons for staying with one rental. Perhaps they don't have time for more, or maybe it is the family home that a member of the family will move into one day. But maybe, just maybe, this one experience will encourage you to invest in more properties. You may find you like being a landlord.

The goal of all investors is to watch their investments increase and to expand their portfolios. As the value of your property goes up, your equity increases and, like many investors, you can use your current real estate (even your personal home) to purchase the next property. Never stop watching the papers and the Internet for investment property that comes up for sale, and stay abreast of the market in the area you're interested in. Keep in constant contact with the Realtor who sold you your first investment property; he or she may know of something new that will be coming up for sale. In the same way, if you use a property manager, tell him or her that you want to know if another client is going to sell a property. You can also get the inside scoop on how good the tenants are and what the condition of the property is. Of course, make sure your property manager is comfortable giving out this information; don't press if he or she isn't.

The market in your area will determine how fast the value of your investment will go up. When you've paid off part of the equity in one property, you can refinance that property to purchase your next property; other times it will make more sense to sell your investment to purchase a larger building. Consider starting by purchasing a second property, either a single-family home or a small rental building. Then fix it up and move on to purchasing your next property. You can continue to do this by keeping up with the market, maintaining your property, and staying in touch with what's happening with rental property and rental prices in your area.

It is important to keep your rental rates as close to the current market as possible. This goes hand in hand with the market value of your investment: So, as the value of the property increases, the rent should increase a similar amount. (Note that most single-family homes are appraised based on comparable homes selling in the area. Multi-unit properties, on the other hand, are appraised based on the rental income and/or the CAP rate, which is the net operating income divided by the sales price.) Before purchasing a multi-unit building, it is a good idea to calculate the break-even rate so you will know what level of occupancy you need to break even with your expenses; an accountant or Realtor can help with this.

Just the facts

- There are many advantages to purchasing rental property.
- Purchasing investment property takes planning and should be a well-thought-out process.
- You're going to make your share of mistakes.
- Set up your rental property management as a business.
- Planning is your key to success.
- Build a team of advisors to help run your investments.
- Knowledge is power. When you don't know the answers, there are plenty of professionals who do.

- The long term goal is to purchase investment property, increase your cash flow, and decrease your expenses.
- Stretch to make that first investment.
- Don't get too comfortable — continue to expand your business.
- Maintain your property.
- Find great tenants.

GET THE SCOOP ON...
Types of tax: federal, state, and local (and what
happens if you don't plan ahead for them) ▪
Hiring a great accountant/financial advisor ▪
Understanding depreciation ▪ Repairing versus
renovating ▪ Deciding between passive and
active ownership ▪ Taking advantage of tax
incentives and deductions ▪ Finding out about
business licenses and permits ▪ Protecting your
investment with insurance ▪ Knowing what type
of insurance to carry ▪ Reducing risk through
preventive maintenance ▪ Reviewing your policies

Taxes, Licenses, and Insurance

Throughout this book, I refer to running your investment properties as a "business." This is the best way to keep everything straight, particularly for meeting local, state, and federal tax obligations and requirements; reporting cash-flow; and paying other bills. If you set your rental property up like a business in the beginning, it will keep you on track as your build on you portfolio of properties.

You have income and expenses that have to be accounted for and tracked, not only for your own benefit but also for your state and federal taxes. You need to calculate your income, less your expenses, to determine whether you have a profit and how much in taxes may be due. (If you have a loss, you should be able to apply it against your income.) Remember that owning investment property provides opportunities and great tax benefits. One of the advantages is your ability to deduct all operating expenses and depreciation from your income while the value of your investment is appreciating over time.

That said, tax laws are much more complicated for a investment property than for a personal residence. The taxation laws are quite different and change often, making it difficult to keep up. For this reason, an important part of owning property is having a great financial planner and a certified public accountant (CPA), both of whom have a great deal of knowledge in real estate.

You want to have a general understanding of the taxes and what is expected, as well as knowledge of different types of insurance available to cover your worst-case scenario. In addition, you need to be sure you're complying with your local government agencies. Some cities or counties require special permits and annual inspections by the city inspector or fire department, for health and safety violations.

In the tax world, there are generally two types of income: ordinary income and capital gains. Ordinary income includes your wages, salaries, bonuses, commissions, dividends, rental income, and interest income. This is taxed at varying rates, depending on your tax bracket. On the other hand, you have to handle the other type of tax, capital gains, delicately, because this is the tax for income that is generated when possessions, including stock and real estate, have been sold for a profit. There are formulas for everything when it comes to ordinary income and capital gains income. You need to be sure you have good records and keep your paperwork organized so that you are ready when you meet with your accountant. I highly recommend you meet with your accountant during the year — don't wait until the year is over and you are there to file your tax return for the previous year. By then, it's too late to make changes, and that could quite possibly cost you money. New tax laws and depreciation schedules change often, and there is no way for you to keep up with everything — nor are you expected to. Take the time to make an appointment for a financial and tax review. Plan ahead and be prepared. Have a tax strategy to help you know when to improve your property and when to sell your investment.

Types of taxes

There are many different types of taxes. There are state and federal taxes, local taxes, in some places, city or county taxes, property taxes, and those lovely business taxes. Consult with your accountant for details, and be sure to check with your city, county, and state to be certain you are complying with all requirements.

State tax

Some states don't have a state tax, which means you're not required to do a state tax return. Check with the state government where your property is located to find out about its taxes. Your accountant may have an office in that state or may have a recommendation of whom to contact to obtain the latest information. Many states have a transfer tax and/or a revenue tax, and that accounts for the bulk of state real estate taxes. When you do your tax return and are in a state that has this type of taxation, your accountant can prepare a form that displays the gross and net revenue generated by your properties and calculate what is due.

Some states impose licensing fees for property owners, like a business license due annually based on the size of your property or the income your properties generate. States may also impose licensing fees for rental property. However, the most common tax comes in the form of an amount based on the income — gross (total), not net (after expenses) — that you've generated.

Federal tax

Federal taxes affect everyone. You are required to file your federal tax return on an annual basis and account for your investment property income and expenses. You may have to pay income tax on net revenue, and that amount may be different from what your friend is paying, based on the structure of your business (see Chapter 1) and the way you have taken possession of your property.

There are many ways to structure the set up of your properties. You can have a corporation, partnership, an LLC, trust, and so on. A good accountant will advise you based on your situation. For example, if your rental property is run as a corporation, your accountant may advise you not to have any income in your account at the end of each year to avoid paying a high rate of corporate tax. (You don't want your corporation to be double-taxed.) You can withdraw the money as income, spend it on improvements to your building, or pay bills. Your accountant knows what is the best for your business.

Property tax

Property tax is usually an *ad valorem* (imposed at a percentage of the value) that an owner of real estate or other property pays on the value of the property. Some state tax is based on the size and use of the land. The taxing authority performs or requires an appraisal of the value of the property, and the tax is assessed in proportion to that value.

A major segment of local and governmental agencies receive a large portion of their operating funds by taxing real estate

 Watch Out!

If you feel the tax agencies have overvalued your property, contact your tax assessor to find out whether you can have your property reassessed. Remember, though, that the market does change, so don't ask for a reevaluation if there's any indication that your property has *increased* in value.

within their jurisdiction. In many circumstances, the property tax increases quite frequently through several special assessment charges based on improvements, voted-in measures, schools, or emergency services. These charges can be a percentage or a flat rate, depending on how it was voted in by the people or governmental agency.

A professional appraiser usually assesses the property at the time you purchase the property. This is to determine the value based on the property and other comparable properties in the area. There are three basic methods of determining the fair-market value of a property: the sales comparison, the cost approach, and the income approach. Both appraisers and tax assessors usually use more than one of the above approaches to be sure the final estimate of value is correct.

Keep in mind that building and land are appraised separately. Most states have systems in place in which a property is reassessed or revalued periodically. Then, the higher your property is valued, the higher the property tax. Property taxes in most states are typically paid twice a year.

Property tax is a large, fixed expense. Even though taxes aren't billed monthly, you should account for them when you are doing your monthly budgeting. Some owners have the taxes and insurance included in their mortgage each month. This is known as an impound/escrow account, and is one way to ensure you have the money for these large sums of money due twice per year. Don't be late with your property tax payments, as the penalties are usually around 10 percent. Several states allow you to charge the installments on a credit card at no additional

 Bright Idea

It is a good idea when purchasing a property to take a good look at the details of the tax bill. All the taxes are broken down in detail. Sometimes, you may see special assessments, such as school bonds. If you don't understand something, don't be afraid to ask.

charge, and if you have a special credit card where you accumulate points or airline mileage each month based on your charges, your points can add up quickly if you pay your property taxes this way.

Many lenders address non-payment of property tax within the loan paperwork and have the ability to recall your loan, making it due and payable immediately if you don't pay your taxes.

Some localities also have personal property taxes. So if you leave a refrigerator, washer/dryer, or other furniture and fixtures in the property, you will have to report these as well. Usually, the best source is to contact the city or county government for a full list of taxes assessed or ask your accountant.

Transfer tax

This tax is generally levied at the time of a property sale. It is usually charged by the city, and the rate varies in each area. This amount is usually taken out and accounted for in the escrow process of purchasing or selling any property.

Depreciation

In calculating your income tax obligation each year, the government allows rental property owners to take a deduction for depreciation. Understand that depreciation is not an out-of-pocket expense you incur. Rather, it is an accounting concept that allows you to deduct normal wear and tear and is a way to shelter income. This is designed to not only help with normal wear and tear but also provide you more cash flow. And it doesn't have to do with the way your building is showing its wear and tear.

 Watch Out!

Depreciation is allowed only on your building, not on the land. The amount of deprecation varies, depending on the type of property and when it was purchased. A good accountant can ensure you get the proper depreciation. This is one expense you want to be sure to write off.

Hiring an Accountant

Hiring a good tax accountant is an important part of the whole picture. You want an accountant who can assist and direct you to maintain good records in order to comply with federal, state, and local tax laws. The accountant also needs to be familiar with real estate law and have a good understanding of all rules and regulations.

What does an accountant do?

- Files all property tax forms with the state and federal government.
- Helps you properly set up your business in the beginning.
- Ensures you're allocating your expenses correctly.
- Correctly handles the depreciation schedule.
- Assists with the disbursement if you have partners or investors involved.
- Writes off repairs and depreciates the major improvements.
- Knows your long-term plans for each investment property.

Like anyone else you hire, request clients' names and telephone numbers so that you can call for references.

One of the most important things is that you feel comfortable with his or her approach, background, and ability to take care of the accounting of and taxes for your rental properties.

Rates of depreciation vary with the class and life expectancy of the asset. For example, a building is depreciated over a long period of time, while a computer is depreciated over only a few years. There are limits set by law as to how long the life expectancy for certain items are. Don't guess or decide on your own how long the asset should last. Talk to your accountant.

Repairs versus renovations

The general rule is that repair expenses are tax-deductible in the year spent, while renovation expenses are spread out over a period of years. In other words, larger items must be depreciated over a period of years, while the smaller items can be fully deducted immediately from that year's tax return.

Passive versus active

It is important to know the difference from the IRS standpoint and for your tax purposes. If you are in the business of real estate and it is your primary career, there are no real restrictions on the dollar amount of losses you can claim and apply against your earnings.

Most people consider their rental property as a secondary career. If this is the case, the IRS has a limit of $25,000 on annual loss deductions. Generally speaking, if you are what some refer to as a silent partner, you are a passive investor. As a passive investor, you can use the depreciation deduction to offset any profit from your property.

You are, by IRS standards, actively involved in the decision-making of your rental property, even if you have a professional management company in place. If you are assisting in making decisions regarding such things as major repairs, final selection of your tenants, or rental amounts, you are considered an active investor.

There are many creative ways to ensure you are getting all the advantages and full write-offs available through your knowledgeable accountant.

Business licenses and permits

Building permit fees are a very popular tax with city government. The charge is usually based on a percentage of the total improvement costs for the new construction.

Business licenses are becoming more common as a requirement for rental properties. In some cities or counties, you need to have a business license for each property you own. They calculate the number of units and the income generated, and charge you either a flat rate per unit or a percentage. This amount is generally due annually. Check with your local city or county offices.

Insurance

If you rent out property, you need a landlord's insurance policy. Often, ordinary homeowner's insurance doesn't cover rental property, even if your own residence is in the same building. As a landlord, you have a substantial investment in the property you rent to others and little control over the physical damage that can happen to it. You need to have high-quality rental property insurance featuring protection against fire, vandalism liability, and most other physical losses. Not only do you need to have insurance against these losses, but you also you need to be concerned about lawsuits and having the proper insurance to cover you to defend yourself and protect your assets.

It is imperative for you to maintain a sufficient amount of insurance that will cover them if anything happens to the rental property. An owner who is not adequately protected can face catastrophic financial problems. Insurance is one of the three major expenses you have as a rental property owner, along with your mortgage and taxes.

Like taxes, insurance is one of your major fixed expenses and is something you must have. You have an option to pay the insurance along with your mortgage in the same way as your taxes, with what is called your impound or escrow account. The amount of the annual insurance is calculated monthly, and you pay that amount when you pay your mortgage each month.

Keep in mind that different insurance carriers offer different types of coverages. You need to shop around or hire an insurance agent who will shop around for you. The agent

Moneysaver

Don't be afraid to get another quote from a different insurance company. When you shop around, make sure you're comparing apples to apples. Insurance varies a great deal, especially in the coverage and in the deductibles. Also make sure you review your insurance coverage with your agent at least once a year.

should take the time to explain the coverage and each detail so you know the advantages and disadvantages.

Include coverage for loss of rental income if your property can no longer be occupied due to a covered loss. For instance, if a pipe breaks and causes so much damage that your tenant has to move out for the repairs to be completed, you want that lost revenue reimbursed to you by the insurance company. In addition, purchase additional coverage for furnishings and appliances that are located at the residence. Your personal property will be insured for the direct physical loss caused by any of the perils (fire, flood) listed in your policy.

Types of insurance

Getting insurance is just as important as getting a good loan, and you need the proper coverage for your situation, something a good insurance agent can help you decide. When you figure out what coverage you need in order to satisfy and comply with your lender, shop around. Make sure that you're comparing apples to apples; for example, be sure that the deductibles are all the same when comparing policies.

- **Fire and liability**   Most lenders require you to carry both fire and liablity insurance for your rental property, as this is their safety net. The insurance is designed to protect both you and the lender in the event of an unforeseen occurrence. If there is a fire in your property, you want the ability to rebuild and restore your property as close to the original condition as possible. Even a small fire can be quite costly. Be sure you have liability coverage as well as replacement coverage. Liability and fire insurance is a must. Period.

■ **Umbrella coverage**   This insurance is also known to some as blanket coverage. It is a very cost-effective way to decrease your risk, and it is designed to supplement your other policies. If you were involved in a large lawsuit that was above and beyond your coverage amount, the umbrella policy would kick in as secondary insurance and your backup. This is also used by owners of condominiums who cannot be covered by the standard fire insurance. In that situation, you must cover yourself for liability, even if the homeowner's association covers the fire insurance.

■ **Flood insurance**   This insurance is needed by more people than you may think. Insurance companies sell this coverage separately from your other insurance and is considered a rider policy. Inquire if your property is in a flood plain at the time you purchase your property (this information is usually disclosed during this time). Most lenders require flood insurance if it is determined that your property is located in a flood plain.

■ **Natural disaster insurance**   Earthquake, wind, hail, and hurricane insurance is another item that is sold separately as a rider to your current policy. This insurance obviously is not needed in all areas and is completely optional. Earthquake insurance is expensive and usually has a very large deductible.

■ **Mortgage insurance**   This is an insurance that pays off the balance of your mortgage in the event that you cannot make the payments for reasons such as a disability or death.

■ **Workers' compensation**   This insurance is necessary if you have any employees, even temporary ones. It is to protect you if an accident occurs in the performance of a maintenance or professional task related to your property, as you could be liable for the person's medical bills and loss of wages. This policy protects your on-site manager (if you have one) and any workers who are on the property. You may think you don't have any employees for your rental properties, but in the eyes of the law you do. That unlicensed and uninsured handyman or a friend who works on your property and receives payment is technically an employee. Workers include the tenant who is showing your vacant unit. If you are hiring licensed workers, verify they are carrying their own worker's compensation policy for their employees.

- **Non-owner auto liability**   This insurance is a very inexpensive policy that will cover you if someone working for you is driving. This coverage protects you from liability for accidents and injuries caused by the employee while working and using his or her own automobile.

- **Building ordinance coverage**   This is an important coverage, as it will protect you in the event your rental property is partially or fully destroyed. It covers the cost of demolition and clean up, along with the increased costs you will incur if the property needs to meet new or stricter building code requirements.

- **Renter's insurance**   This is an insurance paid for by your tenants. It is important to include in your rental agreement an explanation to your tenants that their personal belongings aren't covered by your policy. Most residents have the mistaken impression that an owner's insurance provides coverage for the resident's belongings. Renter's insurance usually covers losses of the tenants' personal belongings as a result of fire, theft, water damage, or other loss. It also provides protection against claims made by injured guests. Be sure to inform your tenants they aren't covered by your policy and encourage (or require) them to obtain their own insurance. Explain the benefits of this coverage and that it is usually quite affordable.

▪ **Home warranty insurance**   This is offered to cover any failures of systems in the property. It usually covers plumbing, electrical, appliances, garage doors, and the furnace. If something breaks, you call the home warranty company to take care of the problem. Of course, many want to be paid for the service call — usually $30 to $40 at the time of service. However, this insurances can help protect you from a large expenditure, like replacing a furnace. If your property has been built in the last five years, this may not be needed. You need to determine how old the systems are.

Reducing risk through preventive maintenance

Why wait for a problem to arise or a lawsuit to hit you? Take the time to walk your properties, take care of your repairs, and have a proactive, preventive attitude. Walk around your properties and look for problems, check lighting, and look at the sidewalks for trip hazards. Look for any physical and health hazards and that potential lawsuit waiting to happen. Quite simply, the cost to take care of repairs and risks will be considerably less costly and time-consuming than any lawsuit, court costs, and medical bills.

Cut your losses before they happen. Make your property safe and avoid going through a stressful and expensive lawsuit.

Reviewing your policy

Don't just pay for the insurance each year. Take the time to review your coverage with your insurance agent. If you have hired an insurance agent, ask him to shop other carriers. Plan to review your insurance coverage the same time each year. Each March, for example, I meet with my insurance agent. I gather all the policies and meet at my office to review everything. Time can lapse quite quickly and before you know it — and usually when it is too late — you find you are underinsured and don't have the proper insurance coverage for today's values. Protect your investment with too much insurance.

Having proper insurance is a very important part of owning rental property.

Just the facts

- Paying taxes, obtaining licenses, and having insurance are a requirement of owning rental property.

- It is important to comply with all federal, state, and local tax and licensing requirements.

- Hiring a good tax accountant will save you more than money.

- Both state and federal tax laws are forever changing.

- It is a good idea to meet with your accountant and your insurance agent at least once a year for an overview and review of your rental property needs.

- Use depreciation to shelter your income.

- Be an active investor to reduce your taxes.

- Insurance is there to protect you and your investment.

- More and more local governments have put a business license fee in place for rental property owners for each property.

- You are responsible to have workers' compensation insurance for anyone you hire who is not an independent contractor carrying his own insurance.

- Renter's belongings aren't covered by an owner's insurance policy. It is a good idea to not only put that in writing but also to encourage (or insist) that your tenants obtain renter's insurance.

- Reduce risk by keeping your property safe.

Acquiring Rental Property

PART II

Purchasing Rental Property

There are many reasons why people become landlords or get involved with renting and managing investment property, and these reasons can be quite simple. Some people get into rental property management knowing there is a great deal of work but hoping for good cash flow and property appreciation (that is, the value increases during the time you own the property).

Others may fall into it, instead of choosing to own rental property. Sometimes, people move out of the area either due to a job or a decision to take a sabbatical for a year or two. They may decide not to sell their home because they have plans to return. In these situations, the home was never meant to be a rental property, but receiving income on the property helps pay the monthly bills.

In other cases, a parent gets older and must move to an assisted living facility. The family doesn't want to sell the home for certain reasons. At this point, they look into renting the home to help pay the parent(s) monthly expenses and thus retain the property for an inheritance.

Ways of acquiring property

The following sections discuss some of the ways you can turn your current home into a rental property.

Job transfer/temporary assignment

Executives and professionals are sometimes transferred temporarily from where they own a home to another city or even another country for a specific amount of time. I know I've worked with many employees who expected to be overseas for about two years and wanted to rent their homes while they're out of the country.

You need to weigh your specific circumstances to determine the best way to proceed. Obviously, if you will be out of state or country, you need to look into a professional property management company. I don't recommend that you rely on a close friend or family member to manage your home while you are away, except as a local emergency contact, but that should be the extent of it. Remember that anything that friend or family member says or does is the same as if it came from you. They may really want to help you, but may not have the time to keep up with the laws and take care of the maintenance. Instead, begin with a consultation with a property manager or rental agent. Find out what the rental value is and what should be done in order to rent the property quickly to a quality tenant.

The best way to rent your home is unfurnished. Renting your property unfurnished is much easier in most markets than renting out your home with all of the furniture inside. Not only are there more people looking for unfurnished properties, but people also tend to stay longer when they bring their own belongings. If you decide to leave furnishings in the property, don't expect that they will be untouched and perfect when you return. A couple years of wear and tear can be a lot depending on the lifestyle of the renters. Sometimes a dish may get broken and your pattern is no longer available — now what?

I know the issue is storage and what you can keep on the property. There are times that owners keep the basement or back-yard storage shed to store items they will not need while they are gone. Lock this area separately and provide a key to your property management company. Remember that this area must be spelled out in the lease as belonging to the owner and will not be a part of the leased property.

If you have many items that you will be leaving, look into storage. There are storage companies that will bring a bin to your driveway, leave it for you to pack, and take it to their warehouse to store. This saves you trips to a storage unit and may be paid for by your company as part of the relocation expense.

Many times, when an employee is transferred by an employer, a great deal of the cost and expenses are taken care of by the company. The items you may want to ask for are property management fees, storage fees, rental allowance if you are called home prior to the end of the lease with your tenant, and some of the expenses required to rent your home. This may include changing locks, cleaning, extra insurance, and so on.

Don't leave anything of great value at the property while it is being rented. Also, when are you being transferred, you need to be sure that you take care of forwarding your mail and changing the utilities. It is a good idea to make copies of the instruction manuals for appliances, equipment, and security systems to leave for the tenants. (If you leave the actual manuals behind, you may find that the manuals get packed with the tenant's belongings when they leave.)

Sometimes, when you are going to be gone for two years, you may think it is better to rent your property for two full years.

I don't recommend that. I like to see the properties rent one year at a time. This way, your property manager can evaluate how the property is cared for after the first year and before offering the tenants a second lease. You may want to consider a month-to-month agreement after the first year in the event your company calls you back early.

As an owner renting your property, you can be quite emotional about your home, so I highly recommend you step back and hire a professional. Keep in mind that some of the precious memories you have aren't acceptable to a tenant. If you have a growth chart for your children on the wall, for example, you may want to take a picture or trace it onto a piece of paper. I knew someone who cut it out, repaired the wall, and stored this memory with their furniture.

This section also applies if you have lost your job locally and have had to leave the area to find a job. If you like your home, you just may make the decision to keep it for a couple of years. You never know if the other job is going to be permanent or you may want to move back someday.

Moving to a nursing home

When a parent gets older, he or she may have to move to an assisted-living facility or a rest home. There are options, and one of them is to rent out the home to assist with the expenses and avoid tax liabilities. To understand these implications, you need to seek the advice of your tax professional. Keeping the home also keeps the inheritance intact and may provide funds for emergencies that are not covered in some other manner.

If the house has never been a rental, you may need some time to remove all of the belongings that have been accumulated over many years. Quite often, the home has not been updated for several years and will need quite a bit of work.

Hire a professional to tell you what needs to be done to get the property ready and to give you an estimate of rental value for expense planning. Being prepared is important, as this is usually a very emotional time for your mother and/or father. If they are able, include your parents in the plans. Have them there when you meet with the property management company and let them be a part of the planning and renting of their home.

I find that you need to be realistic with the time it is going to take and know the direction you need to go to get the property ready. This helps a great deal with the emotional side as well as your long-term planning for renting the home.

Death of a parent

The death of a parent while living in the home is also an emotional time and one that requires you to take some time to decide what the next step will be. Planning and following the similar steps to get the property ready as you would if they were moving to an assisted living home is the way to go, but in this case allow more time. Take things slowly and easily if you can; taking a bit longer helps with the healing as well.

Remember that if someone has died on the property, this must be disclosed to any potential renter.

Property you've tried to sell

If the property you are living in now isn't selling, and you have already committed to purchasing another property, you may consider renting out the property. Sometimes, the market turns around in a year or so or you find that you enjoy having your first home as a rental.

Be sure to meet with your accountant and/or your financial planner to be certain that renting your home is what is best for you at this time.

Don't overcommit; stretch, but not too far. If you calculate that you'll lose money by continuing to try to sell, you may find you would be better off renting the property. The loss may be less than selling the property at a time when the market is down. Normally, the rental market follows the sales market — but not always. So, renting out your present home may make a lot of sense, especially if you are moving around November or December when market values are historically lower than the spring and summer.

Sometimes it is also better to rent six months to a year in the area you are moving to. This allows you to make sure you are buying your new home in the right area.

Purchasing an investment property

When interest rates are low and the stock market unstable, buying an investment property may be a good choice for your financial portfolio. If so, there are items you will want to review before making that purchase. The mantra, "Location, location, location," applies to rental units just as it does to your own home.

Compare property values and rents

Do your homework first. Decide on the area in which you are thinking of purchasing. Speak to other friends, if possible, about their investments: where they own and how things are going. After you decide on an area or at least a county or city, check out the area's property values and compare them against the property you are considering for purchase (before you make an offer and get into contract). You need to check both property values and find comparable rentals in that area. If you see large swings or confusing figures, ask questions. If rents seem very low, find out why.

You also want to check with the Chamber of Commerce or your city planning department to see whether any major changes are in store for the area the property is located in. Just imagine if you bought an investment property and found out a month later that a major freeway was going to go through one block away!

Investigate various loan options

Check all loans carefully to see how they will perform in the future. Many adjustable-rate loans can change the property from a good investment to a bad one if the interest rates sky-rocket. Many investors choose interest-only loans to maximize their return on investment. Be realistic — anything can happen.

Consider the property tax

Often, investors base their purchases on current property tax laws. Then, when they purchase at a higher property value, the taxes increase. Don't get caught in this trap. Find out the state tax laws and possible tax changes, and incorporate the new, projected property tax into your figures.

Take into account supplemental tax

In some states, when purchasing a property, you are responsible for paying a supplemental tax. This is usually a local tax paid to your county tax assessor. In California, for example, you receive a supplemental tax bill to be paid in two payments. The amount due is a percentage of the previous owners' assessed value as compared to the price you paid currently for the property. For example, if the previous owner paid $200,000 and you paid $400,000 for the same property, the property is reassessed, and the new value is the price you paid: $400,000. Your local tax office sends you a supplemental tax bill due in two payments for a percentage of that $200,000 difference. This bill is in addition to your normal property tax bill, but (thankfully) it doesn't exist in some states.

Check on insurance coverage

Just as the tax bill can increase, so can insurance. Additionally, you will want to incorporate a "landlord/rental" policy into your estimates that will give you more protection than the standard homeowner's insurance policy. Don't be alarmed; most landlords' policies are a reasonable fee, although in many states that have seen recent natural disasters, all insurance policies have increased a great deal.

Find out whether there have been any claims in the last three years. Be sure that you are able to get insurance on the property before you close the deal.

Confirm utility costs

Check with the local water, sewer, and garbage companies to see whether the utility companies will bill the tenant. Often, on multiple units, you pay for the water and garbage. Ask for copies from the past year of the renter-paid utilities and for the water and garbage. This will give you a general idea of what to expect for those expenses.

Keep in mind that when the rental property has two units or more, you will be paying the common area utilities, which usually includes the outside lights, sprinklers, and laundry room. Some multiple units have a common water heater and others have a separate water heater in each unit — so be sure you include this cost. Common area heating, air conditioning, and lighting will also be your responsibility. If there is a swimming pool or other facilities, the utility costs will be even higher.

Plan for future maintenance costs

What property you buy will determine what you will have to spend on maintenance. If you have an opportunity to purchase a fixer-upper, you need to obtain realistic estimates. Beware of the trap of not planning for any maintenance, simply because you have purchased a property in excellent condition. Think of your own residence and the time and energy required to maintain that property. There is always something.

If the property has a swimming pool, landscaping, or other facilities, there will be monthly maintenance expenses to pay. Check out home warranty companies. There are some that will cover your property, which relieves you of unexpected expenses and the hassle of finding contractors to take care of the maintenance problems.

Consult your accountant/financial planner and real estate agent

Tax laws can change and your financial picture may change with them. Be sure to talk to people who are well-versed in investment property. Remember, tax laws may change later, but if you choose the right property with the right financing, it will weather the changes.

Inspect the property

Always be sure to perform a thorough inspection of the property before buying. If you cannot personally do this, use someone reliable to do it for you. Hiring a professional inspector to examine the structural and mechanical systems of the property is also a sound investment. Get the facts before signing a long-term commitment and a long-term loan.

When conducting the inspections, you usually need both a pest control and a contractor's inspection. There are a few items that are often overlooked that should also be inspected during your inspection time.

- **The roof**   I would always have a professional roofing company inspect the roof to determine the condition and the estimated life remaining before it will need replacement. This is a large expense and one you should be prepared and budget for. A leaky roof is a major problem itself but also can lead to additional problems down the road. Water can do a great deal of damage to the structure of a building and require major repairs or replacement. The time of year when you purchase a property may make it difficult to look for leaks. Hire a professional to inspect the roof.

- **Chimneys**   Often people forget to have the chimney of the fireplace checked. Buildup of creosote or cracks in the firebox are fire dangers. This can also be an unexpected expense.

- **Pool**   If the property has a pool, have the pool as well as any associated equipment checked and inspected. You need to be certain everything is up to code, as a pool can be a large expense and there are many local and state ordinances that go with having a pool. If the pool is used in a multiple unit setting be certain that all your proper signs are posted along with any required safety equipment.

- **Survey**   Some people have a professional survey performed on the potential property. This way, you know your exact property lines and what is expected of you as the landlord within those boundaries.

- **Engineer's report**   There are times that a prospective owner should get a soil engineer's report, especially with a property located on the side of a hill. This is quite common in California, as well as in other places. An engineer has access to reports that display flood plains, sinkholes, and other geological hazards.

Having all these reports done is not only costly but also takes up a great deal of time. This is for your protection and the long-term maintenance of your investment. Take the time to do the inspections you need to feel comfortable about purchasing the property.

Converting your property into a rental

Not all properties make a good rental. Some may be more suitable than others. All properties can be rented out at some price with a certain amount of risk, but it should always make financial and practical sense. The following sections share a few types of properties that may not make the best rentals.

An outdated home

When a house is newer, very little goes wrong with it and you have very few issues with maintenance and care. When you are dealing with an older home that has not been updated, there can be many problems. Often, in an older home, you or the previous owners have been living there so long that you just "put up with the problems" and never get around to repairing that leaky sink or running toilet. As you can read in Chapter 5, the best time to prepare your property is prior to placing the property on the market for rent and prior to new tenants moving in.

Older homes tend to have more minor and major maintenance issues such as furnace or water heater trouble, inoperable

Moneysaver

You will save money replacing or repairing the older items in your property prior to moving a tenant in rather than waiting until something happens after the tenants move in. At this point, you may not have the time to research the costs involved, because your tenants may be moving in quickly.

appliances with unavailable parts, roof leaks, plumbing problems, cracks and settling, and more. A lot of older homes still have fuses instead of a breaker box. With all the bath and kitchen appliances available today, plus computers and home entertainment systems, the old electrical circuits may not be able to handle the load.

Yes, it is true that these maintenance issues are ones you may feel renters should live with. But when you are living in the property, you can care for things a bit easier and you may even tolerate more. Many owners tend to "make do" with older items in the property. When you are renting, however, you must be sure the property is safe and habitable, as well as maintained to public health and safety standards. You want to be a good landlord and not be known as a slumlord. When tenants are paying market rent, they expect all the appliances and systems in the home to work.

When something major stops working, such as heating or air conditioning, any tenant would expect them to be repaired immediately and that usually makes it more of an emergency and in need of immediate attention. When you lived in the property, you could take the time you need to get estimates and wait a bit longer to make repairs. Not so when renting — you must hurry. Whenever things must be repaired in a hurry, you can usually count on them being more costly. This is true of leaking roofs, electrical systems, clogged toilets in the only bathroom — and it always happens on Friday at 5:00 p.m. or over the weekend, when you must pay a higher hourly rate.

All of these items may make an older home less desirable as a rental, unless, of course, you happen to be handy and you keep your older home very well-maintained, with newer major appliances, newer water heaters, a new roof, and other upgrades throughout.

A house with a pool

Many people think having a pool is an advantage and makes the rental more desirable, but that is not necessarily true. A pool is an additional item to worry about and really is more of a liability. More people don't want a pool than want a pool. Consider the cost of maintaining the pool, the correct operation of pump, and liability of someone getting hurt in and around the pool area.

Keep in mind that having a pool usually means higher insurance rates and higher monthly expenses, too. If you have a pool, you usually include the pool service in the monthly rent.

A high-maintenance home

As a homeowner, you are usually willing to and probably even enjoy spending several hours per week watering the flowers, the roses, and the lawn; weeding the garden; mowing the lawn; picking up the leaves; or fixing little things around the property. I can almost guarantee that your tenants will not want to do this on their time off. I cannot tell you how many times I hear the tennants say how they love to garden and how they would love taking care of the property, and they just never find the time.

Set up the property with irrigation and drip systems and put them on timers. Also hire a monthly gardener and include it when you price the rent. Just know that will be an expense you will have with a larger property and on a large lot or in a multi-unit property with a yard or common area.

 Watch Out!

If you have a swimming pool with your rental, even if it is a single-family home, be sure to check with your insurance company and the local city ordinances and requirements. Many insurance policies, if not all, require a fence around the pool and gates that lock.

A home in a poor location

Throughout the book you read the words, "location, location, location," something that you cannot always control and oftentimes cannot change. Location is important, however.

Properties that are close to work sites, shopping areas, public transportation, in a good school district, and in a great neighborhood often make good rentals. Stay away from busy streets or homes next door to a school or shopping center. Sure, these homes are usually priced lower, but the rent will also have to be lower. Usually, a home located way out in the country or up a long winding road doesn't always make the best rental, either. People don't like to hassle with a long drive or a narrow and long, winding road to get to and from their home.

Always consider the location when purchasing any type of property. The best tenants want to live in a good neighborhood, too.

Taking over occupied rental property

When you purchase a rental property, you may find that the property is already occupied with tenants. You need to know the steps to take to make this a smooth transition from the former landlord to you, the new landlord. The following is a list of items you need to sign and/or complete when taking over a property that is already occupied with a tenant:

- **Original rental agreement** Whenever possible, ask for the original rental agreements, along with any other changes or newer agreements that were signed after that.

- **Rental applications** Be sure to obtain copies of the rental application and the screening paperwork for each adult tenant who lives in the property.

- **Move-in inspection** Obtain copies of the original move-in condition report that was done prior to the tenants' moving in, plus any pictures that were taken.

- **Phone numbers**   Obtain their current home, business, and cellphone numbers along with an e-mail address if they have one. You need to know how to get ahold of your tenants.

- **Keys**   Be sure to obtain all keys to all doors, laundry rooms, pool gate, garage doors, back doors, and storage units.

- **Garage door/gate openers**   Sometimes, there are extra garage door or gate openers. Be sure to obtain these if they are available.

- **Rent increase letters**   Obtain copies of all rent-increase letters given to the tenant.

- **Correspondence and maintenance request**   It can be very helpful to have any correspondence and maintenance requests from the previous owner.

- **Payment history**   Usually, you can obtain a payment history from the current landlord or property manager so that you are aware of any tendencies to pay late or even bounce checks.

- **Notices served**   It is a good idea to have copies of any notices served on any tenants and any proof-of-service notices that are usually attached.

- **Estoppel certificates**   This is like an affidavit from the tenants as to how much rent they are paying, what the amount of the deposit they believe they paid when they moved in, and any other items they want to point out, for example, who owns the appliances or window coverings. You should have at least one per rental unit. Be sure to cross-check these with the lease agreements, what the current owner is stating the deposits are, who owns what appliances and window coverings, and so on.

- **Paint colors and brand used on the property**   Try to see whether you can find out the interior and exterior paint

colors and the brand. Sometimes, previous owners even
keep an extra supply on the property.

■ **Diagrams**   Try to obtain copies of any diagrams of the
property; oftentimes, the property manager or the landlord
has diagrams for emergencies of where shut-off valves are
located, as well as the light timers, water-timers, and large
appliances. On a larger property, the previous owner may
even have a parking diagram and a layout of the property.

■ **Security deposit**   Usually, you are given the total security
deposits given to the owner by the tenant, at the close of
escrow. Be sure to check the amounts with the legal papers,
such as the lease or estoppels you received from the current tenants, which state the amount of their deposit.

■ **Contracts**   Be sure to obtain copies of any contracts in
advance. Oftentimes, if there is a laundry equiment maintenance company in place on multiple-unit properties, the
contracts can be a bit tricky. They sometimes last for five
years, requiring notice in advance before you can cancel
them.

■ **Agreements**   Sometimes, you have an onsite manager and
you want to have copies and be aware of any agreements
in writing or even verbal with this person.

■ **Copies of bills**   Often, it helps to have copies of any
invoices that have been paid, especially for larger items or
things under warranty. Roof work and larger jobs generally
come with a warranty or guarantee. Copies of utility bills

  Bright Idea

Follow state and local laws in the proper handling of the tenant's security
deposit. Many state laws require the seller and/or purchaser of a rental property to advise the tenants in writing about the status of their security deposit.
Obtain the estoppel agreement from the tenants to avoid any problems.

help when you switch the common-area utilities into your
name.

▪ **Income and expense statement**   Usually, you receive this
statement during the escrow period but when you're still
considering making an offer, ask to see copies of the current and past six months of income and expenses. It's
better to obtain a full year. Take the time to review these
documents before you close escrow, and request information about anything in the cash flow statements that you
may think helpful to have or to review.

▪ **Business/special licenses**   Obtain copies of any type of
business or special license the property needs.

▪ **Tax bill**   Be sure to obtain a copy of all tax bills that pertain to the property. Look them over, as they give details as
to what special tax you may be responsible to pay or that
you will be paying with your property tax bill. Sometimes
the sanitation service is included in the tax bill as well.

▪ **Rent roll**   Obtain a copy of the most current rent roll. A
rent roll is a listing of all rental units, including the tenant's names, move-in dates, current and market rents, and
security deposit amounts. Also be sure to obtain a signed
statement from the seller that there are no verbal agreements, concessions, or side agreements with any tenants
regarding rent or security deposits. Be sure the rent roll
includes vacant units.

▪ **List of personal property included in the sale**   This may
include appliances, equipment, and supplies owned by the
current property owner. Don't run the risk of any disputes
regarding ownership of appliances and any other items.
Don't ever assume that something is included. Obtain it in
writing in advance.

▪ **Copy of current insurance policy**   It is important to
obtain a copy of the current owner's insurance policy in
advance, as you need to have it in place prior to the close

of escrow. Obtaining insurance in some areas can be a challenge, so start talking with your insurance agent right away. Your insurance agent may need to provide written proof of the policy to the escrow company prior to the close of escrow.

This is a long list of items to obtain prior to close of escrow. It is a good idea to give a detailed list to your Realtor in advance so he or she can give the current owner time to collect everything and make the necessary copies.

Closing on the loan and meeting your tenants

After you close escrow and you are the official new owner, there are a few things you should do. Call your tenants and follow up in writing, letting them know you are the new owner. You may have met some of the tenants during your initial walk-through of the property or during the inspection, but it is always nice to let them know officially — and of course you need to let them know where to mail their rent payments. A letter of introduction from the old owner introducing you is your best bet, so there isn't any question of where the rent should be paid and to whom.

Some owners like to meet with their tenants in person after they take over ownership. This will depend on the size of the property, the convenience of the property for you, and whether you are going to be managing the property yourself.

If you go to the property, bring a letter of introduction and the contact information they need to get in touch with you regarding anything to do with your rental property. Do another walk-through with your tenants at that time.

Expect all kinds of requests from the tenants. They may have been asking for new carpet or have maintenance problems that were never addressed before.

If they are on month-to-month agreements or have no written agreements, let them know you will be sending new rental agreements. Review the rent as to the market and let them know of your plans. Many times, tenants are nervous that the rent is going to go way up. Talk to them and let them know your plans. You should have done your research in the purchasing process and established what you think is the fair market value of your new property. Be careful; check out the local rent control laws, if any. And because tenants may become upset and confrontational you may want to do any rent increase in writing and through the mail.

If the tenants are on month-to-month agreements, you may even want to serve them a notice to vacate. Be sure to go by your state and local laws prior to serving them notice to move. In the same way, some of the tenants may give you notice to move. Don't take it personally; it may have nothing to do with you.

When sending out the first letter with the details of where tenants should pay the rent and how to call maintenance, you should include a tenant information form (see Appendix 4).

Hiring a real estate agent

One of the most important people you are going to need is a real estate professional. You need someone to be on the look-out for the right property for you to purchase and to represent you during the process.

You need to hire someone who is licensed as a real estate agent. This is a very important person in your process of acquiring rental property. There are usually many real estate agents in any given area; you need to know what to look for and how to hire the right one.

Realtor

A Realtor is member of the National Association of Realtors (NAR). They agree to conduct themselves according to a Realtor's Code of Ethics and are subject to the rules of the professional association. They must be licensed by the state and work under a license real estate broker. I recommend that you first look to hire a professional by hiring a Realtor. You can come right out and ask, "are you a Realtor, are you a member of NAR and the local board?" This is a great place to start.

Buyers and sellers are clearly better served when a real estate professional is engaged to assist in the sale or purchase of a property. In today's market, there are dozens of reasons why a Realtor can give you an edge, beginning with the information and experience necessary to arrive at

> 66 Always choose a Realtor. It is your assurance of getting the type of professional who is proud of his or her position — one who lives by and follows the strict National Association of Realtors (NAR) code of ethics. 99
>
> —Jack W., Realtor/Broker, GRI President, 2002 Marin Association of Realtors

an appropriate asking price to the knowledge of state laws and regulations for which both parties to the contract will be held liable.

Professional agents assist buyers in determining how much they can afford to spend, researching properties available on the market within their price range, and providing important disclosures about the property being shown. Like listing agents, subagents and buyer's agents also can assist prospective buyers in completing legal forms, reviewing the purchase and sale contract, and presenting an offer. Additionally, your agent may offer referrals for financing and legal representation, and usually will accompany you during the home inspection.

Your purchase of investment property is an enormous undertaking, filled with complex issues — both legal and financial. You should know that a Realtor is specially trained to attend to all aspects of each transaction, and his or her experience as professionals works for the buyer or seller he or she represents. Hiring a Realtor gives you a sense of security of knowing your real estate transaction is being ushered through the process by a professional who is trained to foresee potential problems and who will work hard to find solutions that satisfy you. Go to www.realtor.com, where you find a lot of helpful hints for both the buyer and the seller.

You should choose a real estate professional with as much care as you would a lawyer or doctor. Friends, neighbors, and co-workers are often good sources for referrals. Try to find out as much as possible about their home-buying or -selling experience. What kind of service did they receive? Would they choose this particular agent or real estate brokerage company again?

Agent, listing agent, and subagent

A subagent to a listing agent represents the owner of the property and is a dual agent. This is as opposed to a buyers' agent, representing the buyer only.

By talking to real estate agents who have experience buying and selling investment-type properties, you can obtain leads by reading the real estate ads in your local newspaper. Look to see who has rental property listings advertised for sale, even if that particular property doesn't interest you. Target local real estate companies in particular. Realtors who work your area are best equipped to answer questions about schools, businesses, taxes, and other issues of interest to prospective buyers. They will know about the best location, location, location.

Ask your Realtor for a referral to a professional property manager who can give you the information you need on rental values and what to look for in buying an investment property in that area. You discover the ins and outs of hiring a professional property management company in Chapter 17.

Most of all, make sure you feel comfortable with the Realtor you choose to work with. It all comes down to trust.

Just the facts

- There is a lot of work to be done before jumping into pur-chasing your first rental property.

- Buying investment property can be rewarding in many ways, quite often financially.

- Consult your advisors before making an offer.

- Thoroughly inspect the property.

- Turning your home into a rental takes a great deal of work and you must be prepared.

- Never leave valuables in your home when renting it out.

- Not all properties make great rentals.

- Prepare your checklist for taking over an occupied rental property.

- Make the current tenants in your new rental property feel at ease when you take over.

- Friends make good emergency contacts, but poor property managers.

- Hiring a professional Realtor to represent you as your real estate agent is the best way to go.

- Location, location, location is an very important factor.

- Plan for future costs.

GET THE SCOOP ON...
Shopping for financing ▪ Finding the loan that
fits you ▪ Fixed versus adjustable loans, plus
other types of loans ▪ The difference between
using a mortgage broker or going directly to a
bank ▪ Understanding the closing process and
knowing what to expect ▪ Working with the
closing agent ▪ Understanding costs that are
incurred during closing

Financing Rental Property

Chapter 4

U nderstanding the entire financial picture and
the escrow/closing process when preparing
to purchase your investment property is an
important part of your investment process. You need
to know your financial options, how to take title, and
what to expect from the time you apply for a loan
until the title is recorded, and you "go on record"
and officially own the property.

Before you start shopping for your first investment property or another investment property, take
the time to know where you are financially. Meet with
your accountant, and then meet with a mortgage broker or banker to find out what he or she is looking
for to qualify for a loan for an investment property.
Get pre-qualified so that you know where you stand
financially prior to looking at and finding a property
to purchase.

There are a lot of decisions to make after you find the property, make the offer, receive an accepted offer, and close the transaction. Take the time to know the process and what to expect before your clock is ticking and you are closing and have a limited amount of time. By doing your homework ahead of time, you can help eliminate some of the stress and get the best possible rate. If you don't shop around, you won't get the best loan.

Besides location of the property, the loan rate, terms, and conditions are the second most important things. A good loan can make the difference between success and failure in managing rental properties.

Not all lenders are alike. Some lenders like large apartment buildings and some like the smaller ones. In a competitive market, rates can vary in points and fees quite a bit. Most loans on investment property aren't the same as your traditional residential property or an owner-occupied loan. Your appraisal will also be more expensive, as well as the fixed costs and monthly expenses.

Sources of funding

There are many sources of money but really there are four main ones.

- Your local bank or savings and loan
- Mortgage broker
- Private-party lender (such as the current owner of the building your are purchasing)
- Hard money (see the "Hard money loan" section for details)

The Federal Housing Association (FHA) doesn't actually lend the money but are insurance industry lenders for the private mortgage bankers, banks, and savings and loans.

When you go to the money source, including the bank, you should know or have the type of building identified. The number of units makes a difference, along with the amount you want to spend and the amount you are qualified to spend.

Lenders want to be sure you'll have enough rental income to cover the mortgage payments, taxes, insurance, and maintenance. In some areas, you end up having to put down a larger down payment due to the price of real estate and the amount of income coming in. Lenders have strict guidelines that you need to know and follow. Not all of the guidelines are the same.

Residential loan (for one to four units)

There are many options that exist; more so if you are planning on living in the property or what the lenders call "owner occupied."

When the property is an owner-occupied property the lender usually requires 3 percent to 20 percent down. This can mean that you come up with the 20 percent or that you have the current owner carry back 10 percent as a second mortgage. It is important to check with the lender you are working with as to their lending policy regarding whether or not you can have a second loan. Some lenders absolutely don't allow a second loan. Don't be afraid to go to two or three lenders with the same loan packet. This way you have more options. If one lender says no, you can quite possibly get an approval from the second lender.

Check with your real estate property-management professional for a referral to a loan broker to help you understand and move through the process.

Sometimes, you may even be able to find a lender willing to do a 95 percent loan on an owner-occupied property. Putting down the minimum and having as much cash on hand as possible is always the best way to go. If something comes up with your building or if you have a chance to purchase the next investment property, having money on hand is important.

 Bright Idea

When putting together your financial packet and loan application, making two additional copies really doesn't take much more time or effort. This is time well spent. By having the extra copies, you can easily submit your loan application to more than one lender.

If you have a loan for more than 80 percent, you could be required to have private mortgage insurance, which is also known in the business as PMI. This insurance is protection for the lender against foreclosure. There are more added costs when you are required to have PMI, usually with a higher interest rate, and you could be charged higher points to cover the cost of the insurance.

A point is something the lender charges on top of other fees, and it is equivalent of 1 percent of your loan amount. So if a lender charges you 2 points on $100,000 loan amount, that would be $2,000. You still have all of the other costs associated with the loan such as title insurance costs, lender fees, appraisal fees. It can quickly add up to a lot of money.

Commercial loan

Non-owner-investment property or a property with five units or more have to go the commercial loan route. You will quickly realize that it is a different ball game. A lender approaches a non-owner-occupied property (property you don't plan to live in) differently than one you will be living in. The rates and fees and the amount of down payment typically are higher. It is usually beneficial to go to a small lender who does investment property lending in the community where you are buying your property.

The down payment on commercial loans can run on average between 25 to 35 percent of the total purchase price as compared to residential loans. A requirement like a large down payment can put most beginning investors out of the market. This is why quite commonly you purchase a single family home or smaller property when you first get started.

 Watch Out!

Don't hire just any appraiser, because not all appraisers are certified and approved by all lenders. You must be aware that each lender has approved appraisers. You must hire an appraiser who is approved by the lenders in your area. Large lending institutions even have their own in-house appraisers.

If you shop, you'll likely find several lenders offering 100 percent LTV (loan-to-value) loans, with varying interest rates and points on commercial and non-owner-occupied properties. However, commercial loans are always more difficult to qualify for and obtain than residential loans.

As with residential rental properties, qualifying for an investment property of five units or more is primarily based on the ability of the property itself to generate a good, solid cash flow that

> 66 I recommend going to a small lender and meeting with somebody at the bank that makes the decisions. It will give you the basic answers you need to make a better decision. 99
>
> —Jack D., mortgage expert

will in turn be repaying your loan. The building you choose to buy should have income that can cover your monthly mortgage payments, pay your regular expenses, and have some cash flow left over for you as the investor to put into an account as a reserve for your maintenance costs.

Most loans on investment property aren't 30-year fixed loans. They are most often variable and amortized over 30 years but due and payable in 10. Talk to a mortgage lender for additional details.

Private-party lending

It never hurts to ask the current owner (that is, the seller) whether he or she would be interested in carrying back the loan with a smaller down payment and a fair interest rate. Oftentimes, you can save a lot of money in lending fees and you do not have to come up with as much money for your down payment.

Hard-money loan

A hard-money loan is good short-term financing if you are in a bind. This is when a third party makes a loan on the real estate as if he or she were the lender. Most of the time, a hard-money loan

Know Your Banker

A banker is an important person to know and have on your side. A good relationship with a banker only makes your business and rental investing easier. In fact, having a good line of credit available and a good financial advisor you can consult before you need a loan will make all the difference in a transaction.

Start building your banking relationships early on with a few different banks and a good mortgage broker you feel you can work closely with. Don't wait until you need a banker to build that relationship. When you establish a relationship early on with your banker, he or she will know your financial history and have most of your records in hand if you establish with a bank you use on a regular basis.

Not all transaction are the same, so keep your banker aware of what your plans are after you have purchased your first investment property and are looking for the next one.

is used because the buyer can't get financing from a conventional lender or at least not enough to close the deal. Sometimes, a hard-money lender is used due to the purchaser having poor credit or because the property intended for purchase is in complete disrepair and is a true fixer-upper.

Keep in mind that all financing is just a tool to get into the property. Oftentimes, in only a few short years, your value goes up and you can refinance and possibly get even a better loan with plenty of time to shop for the best rate and the best loan.

Prepayment penalties

Most commercial and some residential loans have a pre-payment penalty if you want a lower rate. This doesn't mean you should not go with a loan that has a pre-payment penalty; just know what your penalties are and how long you must keep the loan to avoid the prepayment penalties. Just be clear about what you are getting into.

Understanding what happens during closing

Congratulations! Your offer has been accepted! Now what? Knowing the process and what to expect is important, and having an understanding of the process will help things run smoothly.

Your real estate agent usually walks you through the process and oftentimes will attend your signing of all the papers. In some states, you sit at the same table with the seller, and everything is signed at the same time. Some states use a third-party intermediary, sometimes called an escrow officer. In others, you work with a lawyer to make sure all the documents are legally drawn and recorded. For example, in North Carolina, only members of the bar can examine the property's title, prepare legal documents, and give legal advice. Non-lawyers' participation in closings is very limited.

The rest of the chapter tells you what to expect throughout the process after your offer has been accepted.

The functions of a closing

Buying and selling investment/rental property usually involves the transfer of large sums of money. It is imperative that the transfer of these funds and related documents from one party to another be handled in a neutral, secure, and knowledgeable manner. For the protection of buyer, seller, and lender, the closing process was developed.

Closing (or escrow) is a transaction where one party engages in the sale, transfer, or lease of real or personal property while another person delivers a written instrument, money, or other items of value to a neutral third person, called an escrow (closing) agent or escrow holder. This third person holds the money or items for disbursement upon the happening of a specified event or the performance of a specified condition.

Bright Idea

After your offer is accepted, you may select the closing agent, who may be an attorney and/or an escrow intermediary. It is a good idea to get a recommendation as to which company to use and which closing agent colleagues and friends recommend.

Simply stated, the escrow holder impartially carries out the written instructions given by the people buying and selling the property. This includes receiving funds and documents necessary to comply with those instructions, completing or obtaining the required forms, and handling the final delivery at all times to the proper parties upon the successful completion of the escrow.

When all of the instructions in the escrow have been carried out, the closing can take place. At this time, all outstanding funds are collected and fees/charge are paid. Payment of funds at the close of escrow should be in the form acceptable to the escrow, because out-of-town and personal checks can cause days of delay in processing the transaction.

Even though the closing process may be called something different in your area, the basic procedures are the same.

When your offer has been accepted, it is time to open escrow. Information you will need when opening escrow:

- Your name and address and company name, if you are running things as a business entity
- Listing realty company, if there is one
- Address of the property
- Parcel number
- Sellers' and buyers' full names
- Sales price
- Brief terms (for example, concurrent closing or exchange information)

- Approximate closing date
- New lender's name and address, along with a contact person
- Special information, if you have any
- Old loan information: lender's loan number and mailing address

The next thing that will happen is you will receive a preliminary report. Take the time to read it. Look for red flags such as:

- The plot map covers a different lot.
- The address is different.
- Easements are shown on the parcel that you were not aware of.
- There are loans or liens you were not aware of.

Follow up

Following up to get the closing completed in a timely manner is very important. Stay in close contact with your Realtor, if you're using one. Be sure to mark your calendar as to what dates you have to have items completed or even when you must increase your deposit.

For the buyer

As soon as you have received an accepted offer and your contingencies are removed, start working with an insurance agent to obtain proper insurance. Also expect to receive an explanation of all closing costs and your new loan terms in the mail. Here are a few other items to double- and triple-check.

- Homeowner's insurance (usually the insurance agent provides the policy details and proof of insurance)
- Explanation of closing costs
- Explanation of new loan terms
- Double-check all inspections performed on the property

For the seller

The seller is responsible for providing the following items. Be sure the seller takes care of these items in a timely manner to avoid unneeded stress during the transaction.

- Order payoff statements.

- Order and clear all work or negotiate who will take care of what items from the property condition reports, contractor's report, or any other property inspections performed on the property for sale.

- Stay on track for closing and as the date gets close, make arrangements to sign documents at the escrow/title company.

- Have everything in order so that there are no last-minute surprises.

Understanding closing costs

So, it is the big day. The day you sign your name on the dotted line several times, hand over the check, and prepare to take ownership of your new property and become a "landlord."

This is also the day that the seller will pay closing costs, which is usually accumulation of separate charges paid to different entities for the professional service associated with the buying and selling or real property. You also have closing costs, usually to the loan company, for insurance and other professional services.

It can be a day filled with much anxiety, stress, and uncertainty. By being prepared and knowing what to expect, however, you will eliminate most problems and a lot of the stress.

When your offer is accepted, don't be afraid to ask your Realtor whether he or she has some material you can read to get familiar with the process and what to expect. If it is not your first time purchasing, it is still a good idea to refamiliarize yourself with the process that is ahead of you to take ownership of your new property.

Normally the buyer can be expected to pay for:

- Escrow fees
- Homeowner's policy of title insurance
- Lender's title policy premiums (ALTA)
- Document preparation (if applicable)
- Notary fees
- Tax proration (from the date of acquisition)
- Recording charges for all documents in buyer(s) name(s)
- Homeowner's insurance premiums for the first year
- Beneficiary statement fee for assumption of the existing loan (if applicable)
- Assumption/change-of-records fee for takeover of existing loan
- All new loan charges (except those required by lender for seller to pay)
- Interest on the new loan from date of funding to 30 days prior to first payment date

When purchasing property, everything is negotiable. Your current market dictates who will be paying for the different costs within the closing. All of the terms are put in writing and are negotiated in the very beginning. In many cases, the following are some of the fees the seller may pay:

Normally the seller can be expect to pay:

- Real estate commission (if applicable)
- Document preparation fees

 Moneysaver

It feels good after you close to not have to make your first real payment on the mortgage for up to 45 days after the date of closing. It gives you some time to breathe and gather money for your first loan payment.

- Notary fees
- Any judgment, tax liens, and so on against the seller or the property that show up on title
- Homeowner's transfer fees
- Any unpaid homeowner's dues (where applicable)
- Any bonds or assessments
- Any and all delinquent taxes
- Documentary transfer tax (if applicable)
- Any loan fees required by buyer's lender
- City or county transfer tax (may be split with the buyer)
- Recording charges to clear all documents of record against seller
- Tax pro-ration (for any taxes unpaid at the time of transfer of title)
- Payoff all loans in seller's name (or existing loan balance being assumed by buyer)
- Interest accrued to lender being paid off, statement fees, reconveyance fees, and any prepayment penalties
- Security deposits (the seller will be debited all tenant security deposits, as well as any prepaid rent collected prior to closing)
- Any other items that were to be held back for repair within the contract

Keep in mind most fees are negotiable in advance and will be spelled out on the purchase agreement.

The role of the closing agent

The closing agent, sometimes referred to as an escrow officer, serves as a neutral party. An attorney may be able to serve as the neutral party, depending on the state and the laws. Either way, this person prepares all the paperwork and sees the transaction through until it has closed, disbursing all funds and giving a final accounting after the close of escrow. He or she also oversees the signing of all legal documents.

- Serves as the neutral "stakeholder" and the communications link to all parties in the transaction
- Prepares closing instructions
- Requests a preliminary title search to determine the present condition of title to the property
- Request a beneficiary's statement if debt or obligation is to be taken over by the buyer
- Complies with lender's requirement, specified in the escrow agreement
- Receives all purchase funds from the buyer
- Prepares and secures the deed or other related documents
- Prorates taxes, interest, insurance, and rents according to instructions
- Secures releases of all contingencies or other conditions as imposed on any particular closing
- Records deeds and any other documents as instructed
- Requests issuance of the title insurance policy
- Closes escrow when all the instructions of buyers and sellers have been carried out
- Disburses funds as authorized by instructions (in writing), including charges for the insurance, recording fees, real estate commission, and loan payoffs
- Prepares final statements for the parties accounting for the disposition of all funds (these are useful in the preparation of your tax returns)
- Sits with you while you are signing and explains and answers any questions you may have
- Calls you to let you know you have "gone on record." Congratulations you are the new owner of the property!

The closing agent may not be able to offer legal advice, negotiate the transaction, or offer investment or tax advice. He or she
is the neutral party and cannot offer advice.

Just the facts

- You have options when it comes to financing your property; be sure to take the time to shop your options.

- Your banker is your friend. Take the time to get to know
  the key people who are in the loan department at your
  bank.

- Understanding the entire process of applying for your
  loan is important.

- There are many different sources of money, but four main
  ones.

- A hard-money loan can be costly, but if it is the difference
  between purchasing the property or not, it may just be
  worth the extra cost.

- How you hold title helps minimize taxes and protects your
  assets.

- Your loan options change when you purchase a property
  of five units or more; it becomes a commercial loan.

- Some loans have prepayment penalties if you pay them off
  too early.

- Thoroughly investigate legal documents before you sign
  the loan.

- Understand what the closing agent does and what is
  expected of you ahead of time.

- Make a checklist of everything you will need when you
  close.

- All terms of who pays what are negotiated at the time of
  making your offer.

- Find out how closing is done in the state where you're
  buying your property.

Upgrading and Maintaining Your Investment

PART III

GET THE SCOOP ON...
Improving your property appeal ▪ Safety and
security ▪ Building a to-do list ▪ Securing your
vacant property ▪ Conditioning and preparing
the exterior and interior of your rental unit ▪
How to work with a limited budget ▪ Developing
curb appeal ▪ Creating a quality property
for a quality tenant

Preparing Your Property for Tenants

Chapter 5

When you rent your property, you want it to look clean and pristine to attract someone who will care about your rental. If your property is in excellent condition, you will attract an excellent tenant. As you're preparing the property for rent, prepare it as if you were moving in. Think about your first rental and the little things that made a difference to you. You also need to keep décor neutral. And don't over-improve your rental property. It is a fine balance between doing too much and doing too little that you must develop and that comes over time.

Where to begin

It is hard to know where to begin when you acquire a property or when your tenants have just moved out. If your tenants have just moved out, you need to begin with your move-out inspection to determine

Bright Idea

It is always a good idea to take pictures of the property right after your tenants have moved out. If there is ever a dispute, a judge will ask for photos to prove the condition or damage and justify the charges to your tenant's security deposit.

what damage, if any, the tenant has caused. You can find out more about that process in Chapter 10 and find a sample in Appendix 4.

After you have conducted your move-out inspection in writing and taken photos if necessary, begin getting your property in clean and pristine condition to market and attract your next great tenant.

Purchasing lockboxes for your properties

A lockbox is a box that sits on your front door or nearby that you can keep keys in. You open the lockbox with a code, usually a number code enabling you to send your contractors or cleaning company to the property without having to be there each time. The lockboxes make things quite convenient. Sometimes, landlords also give out the lockbox code to a prospective tenant to view vacant property. In addition, each time you go to the property you don't have to remember to bring keys. Changing the code on a lockbox is very easy. You can change it as often as you like and for each of your units or each turnover.

 Watch Out!

Make sure the tenants have turned in the keys and are completely out before you begin removing their belongings. A tenant is considered "out" when he or she returns the keys. Have something in your rental agreement that requires the tenants to return the keys to you or telephone you to confirm the tenant is completely out.

Many times, with your first rental property, you as the land-lord are the one doing the turnover work and getting the property ready. Be prepared.

Painting, cleaning, and replacing flooring

I suggest painting the interior of the property first. Tape off the doors and windows in preparation. After you paint the property, everything begins to look better. A fresh coat of paint can make all the difference in the overall appearance of the property. Or if you hire a professional painting company to paint the inside, you can be working on other parts of the property at the same time.

Remove any debris or junk that your previous tenants left in or around the property. Get out the list you made when you walked through the property prior to the tenant's moving out. Use the list to pick up everything you need at the hardware store, and you'll prevent multiple trips. Keep your list handy so that you can work from it and so that you don't forget something in preparing the property.

Hire a gardener (or take the time yourself) to clean up the outside, check your gutters, and do a cleanup of the appearance.

After the painting is done it is time to replace the floor coverings, if that is in your plan. This is something that should be prearranged, as you need to have the carpet picked out, ordered, and the installation date set up in advance.

If you have an area near the front door where you can put linoleum instead of carpet, it is usually a great idea. This way anyone walking in the front door, particularly in the winter, will not be walking right on to your brand-new carpet.

 Moneysaver

By choosing a high-quality carpet, you can assure that your carpet will last longer. Make sure to put a good-quality pad underneath the carpet. And never go with light colors. I choose a carpet color that I refer to as "coffee with cream." It is neutral but doesn't show stains.

Moneysaver

You can conserve a bit of energy by turning off the furnace, water heater, and air conditioning while the property is vacant. Generally, you do leave the power on, however, so you that you have lights available to show the property, plus water to do repairs, painting, and cleaning.

Take a good look at your window coverings. Most rental properties now have gone to blinds instead of drapes. Now there is a lot of competition out there, so be sure to shop for your blinds. I recommend faux wood or metal for all rooms except the bathroom — if you put blinds in the bathroom, use vinyl because of the constant presence of moisture. You can go to many home-improvement stores and have them cut blinds to fit while you wait.

I also highly recommend that you hire a professional cleaning company to come in and do a major cleaning. This includes window washing, inside and out. Having the property professionally cleaned eliminates arguments at the time of move out about whether or not the property was clean when the tenant moved in.

If you deliver a property to a tenant that's sparkling clean and in good working order, it will make life as a landlord so much easier. In addition, if you do happen to have a problem when your tenants move out, you can provide your written move-in inspection, photos showing the condition, and receipts showing all the work you had done prior to their moving in.

In all my years in property management, the largest problems that I see are in older properties that have not been cared for and maintained. During a turnover, in between tenants, is the best time to take care of maintenance.

When you read Chapter 6, you find things to do to keep up normal maintenance and how to hire your contractors.

Making a maintenance to-do list for yourself

The first thing I recommend is to walk through your new rental property and make a list of all the maintenance you would like to do. Your list should include:

- Exterior appeal
- Interior appeal
- Repairs
- Safety items
- Security concerns
- Upgrades
- Preventative maintenance

Begin from the minute you drive up to the property. The term "curb appeal" has been used for years to describe that first impression. You don't want to spend your time meeting prospective tenants at the property, and then see them gawk at the front and drive away. Give it a "Wow!" factor that will bring them into your property to see the entire package.

You want to pay special attention to property safety and liability hazards. You should survey your property, looking at any existing and potential hazards that could cause or contribute to a person being hurt on your rental property.

You need to look at:

- Child endangerment
- Trips and falls
- Fire safety

 Bright Idea

Go to the front of the property and take a good look at what you see when you first arrive. A poor first impression of the exterior of your rental property is hard to reverse, regardless of how great the inside looks.

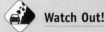

Watch Out!

You aren't responsible only if your tenants slip and fall but also if one of their friends or guests is injured on your property. If someone is injured, I guarantee he or she will be looking to you to take care of medical bills, loss of work, and so on.

- Burglary
- Building code and violations

You can have a check-off list or use the list in the following sections to review your rental property needs. For more on maintenance and repair, check out Chapter 6.

The exterior

A tenant's first impression starts the moment he or she drives up to (or even drives by) the property. You want to attract that quality tenant by taking care of the exterior and giving the impression that your rental property is well maintained.

- Walkways/pathways should be clear. It should be easy to get to and from the house's walkways/pathways as you enter the property.

- Any crack in the walkway or driveway that has lifted the paving higher than ½" is considered a trip hazard. *Hint:* Drag your toe against the crack — if it gets snagged, it's probably a trip hazard.

- Make sure shrubs or bushes don't block the entrance or the windows. If bushes grow above the level of the window sill, it allows a burglar to have cover while breaking the window and gaining access.

- Walk the yard to ensure there are no hidden holes.

- If you have any pipes sticking up from old sprinkler systems or other items, cut them off at ground level or box them in to prevent tripping.

- Walk the fences if you have them. You don't want a fence blowing or falling over and hitting someone or damaging the tenant's belongings. You are also open to liability if a dog gets through a hole in the fence that you are aware of and have not repaired.

- Look up. Are your gutters leaking onto the sidewalk or steps, making it slippery when the weather conditions are poor?

- Make sure the gutters and downspouts are securely attached so they will not fall in high winds.

- Check the roof. If the roof looks old, have a professional roofing company provide an evaluation.

- If there is a chimney, be sure there is a spark arrestor on the top and there are no cracks in the grouting that could lead to a fire inside the frame. The best thing to do is have a fireplace inspection by a qualified person. If the fireplace is unsafe, block it off or repair it.

- Do you provide adequate lighting as you enter the property and around the perimeters? You want to avoid someone tripping and falling on your property due to poor lighting.

- Have your decks and rails been checked for safety and support? Does your deck have a handrail if there are three or more steps?

- If you have a front door screen, make sure it is clean, hung properly, and in good condition. An automatic closer will help keep the door from hitting the person when they have an armload of groceries.

 Watch Out!

Always change all locks between tenants. This is a very inexpensive insurance policy. Also, if you have just purchased the property or a former tenant just moved out, make changing the locks your number-one priority and make no exceptions.

- Change all locks.

- Make sure you have deadbolt locks on all doors that lead to the inside. *Note:* Double-key deadbolts are against the law in some states. These are locks that have to have a key to open them from both the inside and the outside of the property. The problem is that during a fire, the person on the inside doesn't have time to find a key and put it in the lock in order to get the door open. Some people will say they leave a key in the lock all the time, but do you want to chance the one time that a key has dropped out or been taken out? Check your state and local laws concerning all deadbolt and locking mechanisms.

- Check the knobs to ensure they work correctly and that the door latches when it is closed.

- Think about installing peepholes in the front door. This is easy and not costly to do, and it gives your tenant a sense of security.

- If there is a doorbell, make sure it works.

- If you have an automatic garage door and an opener, have it safety-inspected by a professional who will check the door cable and the mechanism ensuring that the door operates properly. Also have this person check the actual garage door opener. Reprogram the control if your former tenant did not return the garage door opener.

The interior

Sure, you need to have the exterior looking good to attract the quality tenant to rent your property, but don't stop there. When you put the property on the market, be sure it looks great both inside and out.

- Smoke detectors, fire extinguishers, and carbon monoxide detectors are required in some states and recommended in others.

- If you have stairs, check the banisters and railings to be sure they are secure.

- Check the carpet for tears or rolls. These are trip hazards. Replace or stretch the carpet to repair. If you have stairs, be sure the carpet is attached.

- Look up again! Make sure those light covers are secure and replace any that are chipped around the holders. Also look for plastic light covers that have been misshapen by the heat of light bulbs. They are probably the wrong kind of bulbs for that fixture.

> 66 Work on training your eyes to look at each area of your property from the standpoint of 'Could this injure someone?' or 'Could this cause a fire?' or 'Does this make it easier for someone to break in?' 99
>
> —Sylvia H., investor and property manager

- While you are looking up, look to see if you see any obvious water stains on the ceiling.

- Open and close all drapes, blinds, shades, and so on to make sure they are solidly attached to the wall and operate properly.

- Remove any broken glass. Broken mirrors may look solid, but they could also fall at the worst time.

- Check the outlet covers. If you see a dark stain rising from the plug on the cover, it probably means there has been a short. Have an electrician check the outlets and repair them, if necessary.

- Replace light switch plates and receptacle covers.

- If you have a fireplace, have it safety-inspected and cleaned at least once every other year.

- Make sure all exterior doors lock and all windows open and lock.

- Make sure you have screens on the windows. The screens should be clean, unbroken, and secure, especially on the second floor.

- Look at the heat registers to see whether dark stains are above the register. This is probably soot or dust particles carried through the system and forced out through the register. Have the furnace or heating element checked. Changing the filters on the system will keep the furnace operating effectively and efficiently. You want to prevent a fire caused by faulty operation.

- Make sure the water heater is strapped properly and has gas flex lines, especially if you are in an area with earthquakes. Check the water temperature to make sure it is below your local area's recommendation. There are anti-scalding devices available that turn off the water at the shower head when it reaches 110°F.

- Look at the washing machine. Replace the rubber hoses for both the hot and cold water on your washing machine. They should be replaced with steel braid hoses.

In the kitchen

Some say the kitchen is one of the most important rooms in the home — well, the kitchen and the bathrooms — so make your kitchen clean and be sure it looks great.

- Check all faucets to be sure they aren't leaking and there is good water pressure.

- If your faucets are very old, replace them now so you won't have to replace them in an emergency situation, like on a Sunday.

- Check all your water supply lines and pipes under the sinks in the kitchen and bathrooms.

- Run your dishwasher through a complete cycle.

- Be sure the garbage disposal has the rubber cover in good shape to keep items from being thrown out of the disposer when it is running. Turn the disposal on to make sure it is working.

- Check the stove vent to make sure it is working and drawing out the smoke.

- Make sure you have the required GFI (ground-fault interrupt) outlets near the sink.

- Turn on the burners for the stove and turn on the oven to make sure they are all in working condition.

- Make sure your appliances are all properly installed and there is no problem with the hookup or gas line.

In the bathroom

The bathroom(s) are an important part of your rental. Take the extra step to be sure the bathroom is clean and safe.

- Replace the old toilets with new, low-flow toilets.

- Make sure your toilets aren't continuously running and that the toilet seat is not old and dirty looking. Put your hands on each side of the toilet tank and gently shake back and forth. You may be surprised how often you can prevent a leak around the base by simply tightening the bolts. Check the towel racks and toilet paper rack. Go ahead and put a new roll of toilet paper in each bathroom.

- Be sure there is a plug for each drain and that the faucets are marked for hot and cold, and that the hot water doesn't come out of the cold faucet!

- Caulk the bathtub. You need to remove old, mildewed caulking and replace it with clean, white caulk.

 Moneysaver

When replacing an older toilet with a new, low flow toilet, keep in mind many local water districts have a rebate program. In addition, you will be saving money on your monthly water bill.

Watch Out!

The prospect's first impression begins when he or she drives by the property. If it hasn't been maintained from the outside, prospects won't bother to call for an appointment to see the inside. You can have new carpets, paint, and appliances, but if the outside isn't maintained, it won't make a difference.

- Be sure the glass shower door is made of tempered glass. The older ones were not and can easily break if tenants fall against them.

- Ground fault interrupts (GFI) switches are a safety issue. You must have GFI outlets whenever the outlets are near water. See your local building code for the details, or call a licensed electrician as they know the codes.

- Check lighting fixtures, which are very inexpensive and can be replaced quite easily. *Hint:* Provide a package of 40-watt bulbs. Most people think 70-watt is better, but these burn too hot for many light fixtures.

- Make sure the mirror doesn't have cracks in it or rust around the edge. This is something your tenants must look at each day.

- Make sure the medicine cabinet is not rusty inside. You might be surprised at how little a new cabinet costs.

Just the facts

- Clean and pristine properties attract great tenants.

- You will attract a quality tenant if you take care of the front appearance of your property (curb appeal).

- Safety and security items on your list should always come first.

- The time to take care of your property's preventative maintenance is between tenants.

- Watch for trip hazards both inside and out.

- Keep good records (including photos) of what you have replaced or repaired.

- Plan for the failures; success takes care of itself.

- If you have the choice to repair or replace and have the ability and money to replace, always replace.

- Spend the money to take care of your properties, as this is one of the largest and best investments you have.

- Use lockboxes for easy assess on vacant properties.

- Provide your tenants with a safe and clean property. They will stay longer and be happier, treating your property like their home.

GET THE SCOOP ON...
Routine maintenance and repair ▪ Knowing how
to handle the most common problems ▪ Hiring
and training contractors of all kinds ▪ Teaching
your tenants to communicate maintenance
issues

Maintaining Your Property

Chapter 6

O wners often think that no news is good news. They believe they have the perfect tenants because rent is received on time, the tenants have lived there a long time, and the tenants never complain. Not true. You should be conducting a walk-through of the inside and outside of all your properties at least once a year. You can have the nicest tenants, but they may have not told you about any items in need of repair. There are many tenants who believe if they call the owner and let them know of repair or maintenance items they will, in turn, receive a rent increase. They feel if they say nothing and pay their rent on time you will not raise their rent.

So take action. Preventive maintenance should be a part of your regular routine in the care of your investment property.

If you live in the area and are managing the property yourself, drive by and check on the outside of your property at least once a quarter, preferably monthly. A lot can change in a month or two. But

89

Bright Idea

If you regularly use any contractors, ask them to let you know if they feel anything has changed in the care or routine of the property. Often they are the ones who will call you to let you know that the tenants have a new dog or that something is wrong.

keep in mind that your tenant also has the right of quiet enjoyment. Don't disturb the tenant when you drive by or get out of your car and investigate the rear yard.

Maintaining and repairing your property

When you own property, especially rental property, you will find there are many different needs for maintenance. You need to be aware of the different types of maintenance, have a plan in place, and develop a routine for these needs:

- Preparing the property when it is vacant
- Emergency maintenance
- Routine and preventive maintenance

In Chapter 5, I discuss how to prepare your property for rent while it is vacant — cosmetic and basic safety issues that make your rental more appealing to potential renters. You also want to do most of your routine and preventive maintenance work at that point so you will not have as many scheduling conflicts when a tenant is in residence. However, emergency maintenance has to happen whenever it's needed.

Emergency maintenance

Some things are out of your control. When you are a property owner, you have to expect and be prepared for emergency maintenance requests at all hours of the day or night. It never fails that an emergency on your property will happen on Friday at 4:45 p.m., especially on the Friday of a three-day weekend!

Bottom line: It is very common to have an emergency call of some type when you own rental property. You need to be sure you have instructed your tenants to call the proper authorities first if the emergency is life threatening or if safety is an issue.

Tenants tend to think the smallest things are emergencies. You have to educate your tenants about emergencies at the beginning of their tenancy. I talk more about that in Chapter 10 (shown in Appendix 4) when I discuss having a tenant's handbook and what to include. When a tenant calls you with what he or she thinks is an emergency, you have to first determine whether the nature of the problem is urgent. An emergency repair is something that cannot wait and must be done immediately in order to prevent further property damage, minimize the risk of endangering people, and/or restore an essential service to tenants. During the winter, you may get calls about burst pipes, roof leaks, or trees blowing down. Probably the most common emergencies are water heater problems, heaters not working, plumbing problems, and electrical problems.

When you get that emergency maintenance call from your tenant, advise the tenant which steps to take. Be prepared to stay on the phone and walk your tenant through what to do and how. This means you need to know what to do, where emergency shutoffs are located, and how to handle the call. You need to have a diagram that shows the location of your utility shut-off valves, where the clean-out for the sewer/septic line is located, the location of the furnace and water heater, and the location of all the circuit breakers. In some areas that experience freezing

 Moneysaver

Define "emergency" by asking the following questions and listening to the answers: Could you give me a better description? How bad it is right now? When did this start? How extensive is the damage? By asking the questions, you can determine how quickly to respond, which parts are needed, and which contractor to call.

temperatures, you will need to educate your tenants as to what to do in freezing temperatures to avoid the pipes freezing and bursting, which can lead to a real emergency.

After you've called a contractor, call the tenants back and let them know from whom to expect a call from and when. They are living the emergency and are probably in a stressful situation.

Determine as quickly as you can whether or not they will be required to obtain alternate housing. Know your insurance coverage and whether it will cover the tenants' housing and your lost rents during the time the property has to be vacated.

Routine and preventive maintenance

No one likes to hear about needed maintenance on the property because this usually means spending money. But there are times when choosing to make the appropriate expenditure means future dollars are saved and tenants choose to stay longer. Who wouldn't want to save money and increase the value of their investment?

It is often minor expenditures that save the most money, such as new doorstops, replacing filters, checking appliances, testing smoke detectors, adjusting doors, window latches, deadbolts, and more (see Chapter 5). Many of these items can prevent more expensive maintenance such as holes behind doors, clogged heaters and air conditioners, large appliance problems, dry rot, safety issues, and more. Of course, there are major items in a home such as the roof, the exterior condition of the building, carpeting, interior and exterior paint, and so on. When left to deteriorate, it almost always means you will have to spend more in the future.

You need to be familiar with your property and have a plan in place. By conducting routine inspections of the interior and exterior of your property, you will not have as many emergency problems. I often advise owners to plan their walk-through just prior to the expiration of the first year's lease. When you notify your tenants you will be coming out to do your property survey, let them know you are planning to come inside. If they are unable to be there and there are problems or anything they want you to see, ask them to leave a detailed note inside the property in an obvious place.

> 66 It is equally important to keep up with the same maintenance after the tenant occupies the property. No news is not always good news. Take a proactive approach to the maintenance and upkeep. 99
>
> —Jean S., investor

During your inspection, check basic items such as smoke detectors; caulking around the tub, toilet and sink; the overall condition of the property; fire extinguishers; and so on. Walk completely around the property looking for broken windows or anything that stands out, as well as any yard work or tree trimming necessary. You should plan to change the heater and air conditioning filters while you are there. Pay attention to details while you are there. You should identify and correct all safety issues, which may present potential liability.

You should have a simple file for each property where you keep a log of items you have checked and the things you do each time you are at there. Record the date, including the year, and the time. Don't rely on your memory. For larger properties, take the time to check all your common areas, the exterior lights, walkways, and laundry rooms. Make sure the common areas are free of cobwebs and debris. You can take care of most of these items yourself.

Use a detailed property survey checklist and take the time to complete it in its entirety (see Appendix 4 for a sample). Take it with you each time you review the needs of your property before a tenant moves in and at the annual property inspection.

The following is a list of maintenance tips that may help you protect your investment in your building and at the same time avoid possible problems with code violations and resident complaints.

Regularly check smoke detectors

Inoperable or improperly installed smoke detectors are a commonly found code violation. Smoke detectors are one of the most important life safety devices in your property. If you have an older property with battery-operated smoke detectors, these batteries need to be checked periodically by the tenant.

Every smoke detector includes instructions for use and diagrams to help you install them in the proper locations. If you have questions concerning the location of your smoke detectors, call your local housing inspector or contact your neighborhood fire station. Batteries are tested by pushing the test button on the detector. To find out if the smoke detector actually works, I recommend using one of the commercially available aerosol smoke detector-testing products.

Check for non-grounded electrical outlets

Older buildings built prior to the mid-1960s don't have fully grounded electrical systems. These buildings typically have older receptacle outlets with only two openings for plug attachments. Many modern appliances, electronics, and computers are equipped with grounded plugs. Tenants and property owners commonly replace older receptacles with newer u-ground type receptacles. This is a code violation and it is potentially dangerous to use a grounded receptacle on an ungrounded system.

You can use u-ground receptacles on your property if you either ground the outlet or provide GFI (ground fault interrupter) protection to the outlet. If you do not have ungrounded

---

 Bright Idea

Fire officials recommend that batteries be checked twice a year when clocks are changed for daylight savings time (April and October). Encourage tenants to check batteries and report any problems to you or your management as soon as possible.

outlets, repairing them is not a "handyman" repair; consult a licensed electrician. If you choose either one of these two methods for correcting your outlets, you may need to get an electrical permit and final inspection approval. Check with your city or county for more information.

Keep chimneys clean

Fires generally result from lack of cleaning or ventilation. This happens several ways. The most common is a blocked flue, which may be from debris falling into the chimney due to deteriorating material, or may even be a bird's nest blocking the ventilation. Fires often erupt from ignition of creosote accumulated on the walls of an unclean chimney.

Preventive maintenance is the key to maintaining a safe chimney. Here are some safety tips recommended by the Chimney Safety Institute of America: www.csia.org.

- Schedule annual inspections for all chimneys and use a qualified, certified chimney professional. This person should be able to not only clean the chimney and vents, but also inspect them for deterioration or weakness.

- Provide and install working carbon monoxide detectors in the property.

- Install a chimney cap if one is missing.

- Provide and install working smoke detectors.

- Have the chimney waterproofed.

- Have the chimney flashing inspected and maintained to prevent leakage.

- Following any violent events such as earthquake, flood, or lightning strike, have the chimney inspected for damage inside and out.

Peace of mind, reduced liability, and the safety of tenants are worth the expense to maintain a chimney.

Check the condition of balconies, stairways, decks, handrails, and guardrails

You have heard the old saying "an ounce of prevention is worth a pound of cure." It applies today, especially to balconies, decks, and stairways. These parts of your property are usually more exposed to weathering and water damage. Over time, water seeps into and under surface coverings and causes rot and deterioration to wood structural members. This process can be accelerated in some properties due to older construction methods that fail to divert moisture or hide moisture and damage behind stucco or siding.

Watch out for mold and mildew

Mold can be a serious problem, especially during the winter months. Exposure to mold can cause health risks for infants and children, the elderly, pregnant women, and people with allergies, asthma, and damaged immune systems. If your building has areas of mold growth, have an environmental inspection done to determine what type of mold is present and if it is surface or evasive. Make an appointment with a professional contractor who can determine where the moisture is coming from and how the problem can be corrected. Check your local phone directory for environmental inspectors and for contractors that provide such services. Code enforcement will expect property owners to locate and correct any sources of water or moisture infiltration in affected units. Replacement of damp or damaged materials is also required. Additional information on mold is available from your county health department. Some states are now requiring a mold disclosure be given to each new occupant (see Appendix 4).

Check your insurance policy to determine whether you are covered for mold damage. Don't put off fixing those pinhole water leaks. Mold only needs a day to start growing, and the resulting cleanup can be very expensive.

Tenants can help prevent mold in their units by taking the following steps:

- Keep the unit clean and dry.

- Use the exhaust fan or open the bathroom window after showering.

- Wipe down damp surfaces after showering.

- Wash bathrooms with mold-killing or mold-prevention cleaning products at least once a month.

- Use the kitchen exhaust fan to remove water vapor when cooking.

- Discard spoiled foods immediately.

- Empty garbage daily.

- Empty water pans below self-defrosting refrigerators frequently.

- Remove moldy stored items.

Remove trash, litter, debris, and inoperable vehicles

If your garbage bin is filled above the rim, the bin lid will not close securely. This can lead to rodents, flies, unpleasant odors, and trash falling or blowing out of the bin. Not only is this unhealthy, it also gives your property poor curb appeal for prospective tenants. If your bin is overfull two or more times every month, you have inadequate garbage service. Call your local garbage company.

Various collection options and price ranges are available to meet your needs. If your garbage bin is overflowing because a

---

 Bright Idea

Experts say that the best way to combat graffiti vandalism on your building is to paint over the graffiti "tags" as soon as possible. Taggers eventually get frustrated and find some other place to vandalize. And in some areas, it's a code violation to allow graffiti to remain on your property.

Moneysaver

Some cities have programs designed to help rental property and apartment building owners who are victims of graffiti vandalism. Free paint and other materials to cover or remove graffiti are sometimes made available through the program. To access this free service, call your local authorities.

tenant or unknown persons disposed of furniture, mattresses, or other large items in the bin, you can call your local company and ask for their bulk pick-up service. If this is not a multi-family residence, ask your garbage company for a brochure to provide your tenant with the appropriate procedures for bulk item pick-up or for obtaining additional bins. This should be your tenant's expense, not yours.

The general exterior picture that your building presents to the neighborhood is very important. An unsightly building can be a message to criminals, drug dealers, and other unauthorized persons that no one pays attention to what is going on. Trash, litter, and debris on your premises can be an invitation to criminal activity, graffiti, and illegal dumping. Inoperable vehicles use limited parking spaces and may create a nuisance, as well as provide places to conceal drugs. Excess storage on balconies is unsightly and can contribute to infestations of insects and rodents, and often promotes moisture damage to the supporting balcony structure. All of these items are also violations of many cities' blight ordinances and can result in the issuance of administrative citations and possible fines if not promptly corrected.

I like people to be able to drive by my property and not be able to recognize it as a rental unit. Pride of ownership ensures that tenants care about how they maintain their home.

Maintain a good relationship with your tenants

At this point you must be asking, "What is this item doing in a list of maintenance items?" Well, your tenants are at your property all the time. They are the first to know about that leak in the bathroom that could lead to serious water damage, and probably know about those tenants next door who may be dealing drugs.

A little work to keep up good channels of communication with your tenants can pay you big dividends. If your tenants feel comfortable informing you about maintenance problems and other issues, they can become active partners in the process of keeping your buildings safe, pleasant places to live.

Contractors are your best friends

Having good contractors with good skills who can take care of the problems efficiently and safely is half your battle of being a property owner. Good contractors (also called vendors) make your job easier as a landlord. Often, they take care of your problems and while they are there, are your eyes and ears as well.

There are many different types of contractors. Following is a list of some that you will get to know quite well over the years.

- **Maintenance person:** The person you can call for just about any minor problem. This is an important person to your success as a rental property owner, and is usually the best one to call and quickest to respond in an emergency.

- **Plumber:** Keep in mind there really are two types of plumbers. There is the plumber who repairs your faucets, running toilets, installs new plumbing fixtures and more. Then there is the plumber who comes to clear your drains and lines going to and coming from the street, when they are plugged up.

- **Electrician:** Always use a licensed electrician when it comes to electrical work.

- **Appliance repair person:** It is important to have a good, reliable appliance repairman. If the refrigerator stops working, there is not a lot of time to have it repaired or replaced. But when this person is at your property, ask that he or she call you before fixing an appliance. It may be cheaper to replace the appliance than fix it, especially if it is an older model that will continue to need maintenance.

- **Painter:** Make sure your painters know how important it is to properly dispose of unused paint. Make sure they don't dump paint in the garbage, rinse their brushes down your drains, or put products outside allowing paint to run onto the street. Expect a good job from your painters. A good painter can give you tips to keep from doing a full painting at every vacancy.

- **Floor covering installer:** You don't need to use the biggest company but be sure you are being provided the service and getting the quality you have paid for. Purchasing good-quality carpets and an upgraded pad is a good idea. An upgraded pad is key to making the carpets last longer. Don't use a carpet taken out of another building, even if it is a good deal — it's not likely to last.

- **Window covering maintenance person:** Usually you hire a professional company to take care of your window coverings. You may also consider having your handyman/ maintenance person use a home improvement warehouse place where they do the measuring, purchase the window coverings, and install.

- **Chimney sweep:** This is a good person to know to continue to service your fireplaces. I recommend you have your fireplace cleaned and safety-inspected at least once a year.

- **Glass company:** You can establish a good rapport with a local company. I recommend opening an account with them right away. Broken windows need to be addressed in a timely manner. Having an account in place and knowing they will take care of the repair will save you a lot of time and money. They may be able to handle screens as well.

- **Roofing company:** I usually have two or three companies I work with but one main company I always call first. When bad storms come, all the companies are hit hard with phone calls and emergencies. Everyone wants service first. Also, getting a roof inspection every five years could prevent some of those emergencies during a storm.

- **Gutter company:** Usually you can get a recommendation of a good, reliable company from your roofing company because they often work closely with gutter companies. Have those gutters cleaned yearly and leaks repaired immediately.

- **Gardener:** Most gardeners can care for your property on a regular basis. If your gardener stops by weekly or even monthly, he or she usually knows whether something has changed at your property, so let your gardener be your eyes and ears. However, your gardener can also be your greatest liability exposure, from chemicals on the lawn to a rock flying from the mower.

- **Tree company:** It is best to use a professional tree company for trees blown down during a storm. You can also use a tree company to trim trees in order to keep from having those downed branches and trees during storms.

- **Pool servicer:** If you have a pool, pay for a monthly pool service. Make sure the required signs are posted and the safety equipment properly installed around your pool.

- **Emergency service company:** It is a good idea to establish a rapport and open an account with an emergency service company in advance. When you have the emergency, you don't have time to shop around and are always in a hurry. Plan ahead. Ask other property owners for a recommendation. Your insurance company may already have designated companies they use and would be a good resource.

- **Cleaning company:** Unless you plan to do all the cleaning yourself, I recommend hiring someone. There are companies that specialize in move-in and move-out cleaning. They already have the products and the expertise. This is a good way to prove that the unit was clean when the tenant moved in. Additionally, if the tenant is not happy with the results, you can have your cleaner redo the areas overlooked.

The preceding is a list of most of the types of contractors you will work with over your years of owning rental property.

Prior to allowing any contractor to work on your property, you need to have proof of several very important items. I recommend you have a contractor information form with a list of items you need to receive prior to beginning any work.

When you hire a contractor, it is important to obtain the following items:

- Copy of an official document with his or her tax ID number and full name (for example, Social Security card, tax coupon, mailing label from an income tax return)

- Copy of his or her contractor's license and/or business license

- Two business cards

- Copy of a certificate of insurance and copy of the workers' compensation policy

- If the contractor is a sole proprietor, a letter of declaration on their letterhead stating there are no other employees and you will not be held responsible in the event of injury or accident; you still need to require general liability insurance

- Ask for at least two references from the contractors' clients

 Bright Idea

Ask your friends who own investment property for the names of contractors they've used and are happy with. Also consider shopping around for a local rental property owners' group, such as a local apartment association. Try the Web site of the National Apartment Association at www.naahq.org.

Watch Out!

Remember that when you pay a contractor over $600 during the year, you must submit a 1099-MISC (unless he or she has formed a corporation), a form that's available from the IRS. There may be other laws in your state concerning the reporting of income, so contact your accountant to discuss your individual situation.

Fair housing and your contractors

It is important to have something prepared that you can give to your contractors that will inform them of the importance of the fair housing laws. A prospect driving by your property where there is a "For Rent" sign out front may see your contractor and stop to ask questions regarding the availability and details. You need to instruct your contractors working on your property that they aren't to give out any details or answer any questions at any time, whether it is a current tenant or a prospective one. You may want to have a flyer available on the property that a contractor can give out that gives them more information and how to contact you.

Consider the following example: A family walked up to a vacancy and asked the gardener about availability. The gardener mentioned that they probably wouldn't want anything with stairs because it would be dangerous for the children. A discrimination charge was brought against the owner, not the gardener. This was a discriminatory remark and the gardener was working for the owner.

Discrimination can also be against tenants living in possession of the home. Any derogatory comments made by a contractor in regard to race, color, national origin, religion, sex, familial status (including children under the age of 18 living with parents or legal custodians, pregnant women, and people securing custody of children under the age of 18), and handicap (disability) can be considered discriminatory. These remarks can result in a fair housing suit against you, as the owner of the property. Note that some states have added to this list of items considered to be discriminatory.

Safety equals reduced liability

Providing safety for tenants is a common-sense approach to reducing liability for the property owner, as well as complying with building codes and laws. It is important that both the interior and exterior of a property provide a safe environment for a resident. See Chapter 5 for details.

Habitability standards

Many tenants and landlords get into disputes about whether a maintenance item makes the unit uninhabitable. Check with your local housing department to determine what state and local codes and statutes apply to your property. Basically, these codes are created to provide a safe and habitable home. They may include electrical, plumbing, access and egress (exit) standards, weather tightness, and many others. They are usually minimum standards.

The landlord who responds to maintenance needs, does preventive maintenance, and maintains the property in a safe and clean manner is, most probably, exceeding any local code requirements. Several local landlord/tenant non-profit organizations provide information regarding maintenance issues.

Responding to maintenance calls

Making sure to respond to your tenants' calls for maintenance will not only keep your tenants happy but will also protect your investment.

 Watch Out!

Some tenants ask excessive and unreasonable requests. Encourage all requests to be in writing, and then evaluate what is necessary. You need to be sure your contractors know to only take care of what is on the written maintenance request. If there is a change, they must contact you.

A maintenance call generally comes in from your tenants via the telephone. I truly believe you can educate your tenants to make it a routine to put their maintenance requests in writing (see Appendix 4 for a sample maintenance request form). You can provide blank maintenance request forms to your tenants at the time they initially sign the lease and at renewal time. I recommend you encourage all requests to be in writing, even via e-mail. Many people have e-mail these days and that is a great way to receive a written instant request in writing about work that may be needed at your property. You can also receive this form of notification while you are basking in the sun in Hawaii.

You need to obtain details from the tenant and determine the best way to repair the problem at the property. On your written maintenance work order, there are places for important details. Find out information such as whether your contractor has permission to enter or whether there are any pets to be concerned with. For example, if there is a plumbing problem, be sure to find out where, not just in "the bathroom" but which bathroom and which faucet/drain. Plumbers get paid by the hour, and more details make the service call more efficient, helping your bottom line.

I encourage you not to get in the habit of allowing your tenants to make repairs themselves. Most tenants lack the skills to properly make the needed repairs and what started out as a small problem may just turn into a large one. The initial reaction of an owner is to allow the tenant to make repairs, especially if you think you are saving money. Believe me, it is not worth it. If a tenant gets hurt while making a repair on your property it will cost you a lot more than the initial repair.

Remember to always keep the tenant informed. If they know you are working on the problem or have to wait on a part, it is less likely you will receive an angry phone call or a letter because your tenant thinks you don't care and aren't doing anything. Some repairs may require multiple phone calls to find a contractor that is able to help. Don't get discouraged. Just keep a log of all you do.

A word about building codes. Most people are confused about building codes. The Uniform Building Code (UBC) was created in 1997 and is generally accepted as the standard for all states. However, that changed in 2003 when the ICC created the International Building Code (IBC). Some states, such as Utah, have already incorporated the new IBC standard into their state building codes. States pass laws to make the UBC or ICC more stringent to cover their particular needs. Of course, many counties want to improve on that and the cities have their special needs as well. So, at every level of government, a few more codes are added. Ask the local building department or a professional contractor what the code is for whatever maintenance you are doing. The advice is usually free — just be sure to get the person's name and the advice in writing, if possible. Remember that the code is there for a reason. It isn't just to make your life more difficult — it is to save a life!

Just the facts

- Routine inspections of your property are extremely important.
- Preventive maintenance will save you money.
- It is important to get all required information from all people who you hire to perform any work on your rental property.
- Insist on receiving your basic maintenance requests in writing.
- Responding promptly to your tenant's reasonable maintenance calls will keep your tenant happy.
- Having reliable, responsive, and honest contractors will make your life easier as a rental property owner.
- You, the owner, are responsible for the actions of the people you hire to work on your property.

Renting Out Your Property

GET THE SCOOP ON...
Types of discrimination ▪ Advertising mistakes
that can lead to a fair-housing complaint ▪
Companion and service animals ▪ Sexual harassment ▪ Housing rights of tenants with disabilities ▪ Avoiding common fair-housing complaints
▪ Setting standards and selecting tenants the
fair-housing way

PART IV

Avoiding Fair-Housing Complaints

This is an extremely important chapter and one you may want to read more than once. You must completely understand fair housing before ever renting and managing your own investment proper- ties. This chapter helps keep you out of trouble within the day-to-day operations of your new business. You need to truly understand all forms of discrimination and avoid them.

It is crucial when renting a property that you avoid discrimination at all costs. There are many pit- falls, so it requires good policies, procedures, and practices, as well as a very good understanding of the fair housing laws on all levels. You want to under- stand and know your local, state, and federal fair housing laws to prevent unwanted fair housing com- plaints. In addition to your procedures, be sure to document everything you say and do, especially when you decline an applicant for good cause.

Chapter 7

Understanding the law

Since 1968, the Fair Housing Act has made it illegal to discriminate against a would-be tenant or homeowner. Now, federal agencies and housing advocates have stepped up enforcement. Since 1990, $180 *million* has been paid out in fair-housing complaints. This chapter gives you, your staff, or anyone who may work for you all the information needed about fair-housing compliance, so that you can avoid litigation. You need to make sure you never discriminate at any time.

Avoid housing discrimination by knowing and understanding the laws. According to the 1988 Fair Housing Act, you cannot refuse to rent to someone because of:

- Race
- Religion
- Color
- National origin or ancestry
- Sex
- Familial status (including children under the age of 18 living with parents or legal guardians, pregnant women, and anyone with custody of children under 18. There is an exemption to this law for housing for older persons)
- A mental or physical disability

In addition, most state and local laws prohibit discrimination based on a person's age, marital status, sexual orientation, source of income, military status, and so on.

On the other hand, landlords are allowed to select tenants based on criteria that are valid business reasons. These include a required minimum income and positive references from previous landlords, as long as these standards are applied equally to all applicants and tenants.

The Fair Housing Act covers most housing. In some circumstances, the act exempts owner-occupied buildings with no more than four units, single-family housing sold or rented without the use of a broker, and housing operated by organizations and private clubs that limit occupancy to members. To find out more information, go to www.hud.gov and click on Fair Housing. There, you find publications you can download and forums to join. The site also contains links to every state so that you can locate an office in your area and look at highlights of what the Department of Housing and Urban Development (HUD) is doing in your state. To locate additional fair-housing information for the state in which your property is located, search the Web under "fair housing," plus the name of your state.

Discriminating on the basis of any of the just-mentioned protected classes is illegal. This is a federal law, which applies to everyone in the country. Keep in mind many states and local governments have passed their own legislation that may also apply to your rental property. Discrimination is a major issue and has serious legal consequences for the owner who is uninformed and discriminates, even if it is unintentional. Complainants don't have to prove intent, so ignorance of the law is no excuse.

The Fair Housing Act and amendments prohibit landlords from taking any of the following actions based on race, religion, or any other protected category:

- Advertising or making any statement that indicates a preference based on group characteristics, such as skin color

- Falsely denying that a rental unit is available

- Setting more restrictive standards, such as higher income, for certain tenants

- Refusing to accommodate the needs of disabled tenants, such as allowing a guide dog, a hearing dog, or service dog

- Setting different terms for some tenants, such as adopting an inconsistent policy of responding to late rent payments

- Not responding to maintenance requests for certain tenants

- Terminating tenancy for a discriminatory reason

Watch Out!

The consequences of ignoring the laws and discriminating against tenants (or potential tenants), even if you do this unintentionally, are severe. Claiming ignorance is never an option, so read up on the laws, take classes, and so on. The penalties are large if you're found guilty of discrimination. Many award settlements can exceed $100,000.

For additional examples, see the "Fair housing, then and now" section. You can be discriminating and not even realize it, just by being too nice. For example, you can be discriminating if you make an exception to your standards because a person is down and out and you feel sorry for him or her. You really want to help this person, so you make an exception to your normal policy for qualifying a tenant and allow them to move in without going through your normal qualification procedures like you always do for anyone else. Yes, discrimination comes in all forms, even when you are trying to help someone.

In a recent ten-year period, fair-housing discrimination cases investigated by HUD alone resulted in awards over $42 million. People always think, "It won't happen to me!" That is simply not true. If you know the laws, have your policies and procedures in writing, and document everything, you should be able to prove you have not discriminated. But you must have good records and know what you can and cannot do. Know how to avoid a complaint against you, your on-site manager, an employee, or even an independent contractor you have hired to work on your building (see Chapter 6). You, the owner, are ultimately responsible for the actions of anyone working for you. Discrimination has serious legal consequences for the uninformed.

Fair housing, then and now

Fair housing actually began in the United States in 1776, with the Declaration of Independence, which states, "all men are created equal." Unfortunately, despite this solid foundation, discrimination persisted. Subsequently, it led to the enactment of many federal laws that directly affect rental housing. Some of these are the Civil Rights Act of 1866, the Civil Rights Act of 1964, Fair Housing Act of 1988, and the 1990 Americans with Disabilities Act.

Based on race, color, national origin, religion, sex, familial status, or handicap, a landlord cannot:

- Refuse to rent
- Refuse to negotiate for housing
- Make housing unavailable
- Falsely deny a dwelling is available
- Set different terms, conditions, or privileges in the rental dwelling
- Refuse to rent to disabled persons
- Refuse to rent to disabled persons with assistance animals
- Tell prospective tenants that because they have children, they can only rent a downstairs unit

It is also illegal to:

- Threaten, coerce, intimidate, or interfere with anyone exercising a fair-housing right or assisting others who exercise such rights
- Advertise, or make any statement indicating a limitation, or preference, based on race, color, national origin, religion, sex, familial status, or handicap
- For profit, persuade owners to sell or rent because of the presence of a person or persons of color or foreign nationality in the neighborhood (which is referred to as blockbusting)

The Fair Housing Act also specifically makes it unlawful to refuse to permit, at the expense of the handicapped person, reasonable modifications to existing premises occupied or to be occupied by such a person if such modifications are necessary to afford such person full enjoyment of the premises. With respect to rental housing, the Fair Housing Act provides that a landlord may, where reasonable, give permission for a modification on the renter's agreeing to restore the interior of the premises to the condition that existed before the modification, reasonable wear and tear excepted. The act also makes it unlawful to refuse to make reasonable accommodations in rules, policies, practices, or services to afford a handicapped person equal opportunity to use and enjoy a dwelling.

Keep in mind that there are private, non-profit organizations nationwide whose mission is to ensure equal housing opportunity. These organizations counsel and investigate claims of housing discrimination and assist clients through the enforcement process. One of their primary investigative techniques is "testing." Using paired, trained "testers," one of whom represents the complaining party and the other a control tester, fair housing groups can determine whether all applicants are being treated equally. Testers are often hard to detect, but if you're doing your job correctly, you won't show evidence of differential treatment. My suggestion is that you get to know the local fair-housing organization in your area. They often have helpful literature on fair housing do's and don'ts and can offer helpful advice on creating non-discriminatory policies. Be encouraged to call them whenever you have a fair-housing question.

Additionally, there are some state and local fair-housing laws. For example, the Unruh and Rumford Acts in California prohibit discrimination based on a person's marital status, age, or sexual orientation.

It may first appear that property managers and owners must rent to anyone, but the law doesn't convey this meaning. Landlords can select tenants using criteria based on valid business reasons, such a requiring good credit, minimum income, and good rental references from previous property managers and owners. The key is that these standards must apply equally to all applicants and tenants.

Fair housing guidelines for advertising

You already know your advertising must not contain anything indicating a limitation or preference based on a protected class as defined under both federal and state fair-housing laws. However, there seems to remain a bit of confusion in the industry as to whether you can use certain words or phrasing to describe residences in your portfolio.

A 1995 internal HUD memorandum addresses this issue. The secretary's report is still relied upon today by investigators and enforcement personnel, and is a good guideline for housing providers. It doesn't allow discrimination in advertising for a rental unit on the following basis:

- **Race, color, national origin**   Real estate advertisements should state no discriminatory preference or limitation on account of race, color, or national origin; advertisements that are racially neutral will not create liability. Thus, use of phrases such as "master bedroom," "rare find," or "desirable neighborhood" should be okay.

- **Religion**   Advertisements that use the legal name of an entity that contains a religious reference (for example, Rose Lawn Catholic Home), or those which contain a religious symbol (such as a cross), standing alone, may indicate a religious preference. However, if such an advertisement includes a disclaimer (such as the statement "This home doesn't discriminate on the basis of race, color, religion, national origin, sex, handicap, or familial status") it will not violate the act.

 Bright Idea

The general rule is, "Describe the property, not the prospective residents." If you aren't sure whether your ad is in violation, have it reviewed by your attorney or call your local fair-housing office. Or, for the latest fair-housing news, go to www.hud.gov.

- **Sex**   Advertising for a single-family dwelling or separate unit in a multi-family dwelling should contain no explicit preference, limitation, or discrimination based on sex. Use of the term "master bedroom" doesn't constitute a violation of either the sex or race discrimination provisions. Terms such has "mother-in-law suite" and "bachelor apartment" are commonly used as physical descriptions of housing units and don't violate the act.

- **Handicap**   Real estate advertisements should not contain explicit exclusions, limitations, or other indications of discrimination based on handicap (for example, "no wheelchairs"). Advertisements containing descriptions of properties (great view, fourth-floor walk-up, walk-in closets), services or facilities (jogging trails), or accessibility features (wheelchair ramp) are lawful.

- **Familial status**   Advertisements may not state an explicit preference, limitation, or discrimination based on familial status. Advertisements may not contain limitations on the number or ages of children or state a preference for adults, couple or singles.

Fair-housing guidelines during interviews

Often, landlords or property managers ask, "How can I be sure I'm treating all rental prospects equally?" The initial interview with prospective residents sets the stage for the rental relationship. Your responses and behavior at this critical stage of the relationship are the first indication the prospect has of your professionalism, and will either make or break the rental transaction. Many fair-housing complaints are filed at this stage of the relationship. Why does this happen?

One of the errors most often made by landlords or property managers is to assume they know the potential tenant's needs. For example, a person in a wheelchair enters your office. You may immediately assume that the prospect is not interested in renting anything but a single-level home. This is not necessarily the case and could be a dangerous assumption. Another example would be to assume someone of a particular ethnic background would prefer renting in a neighborhood where there is a high concentration of that particular ethnicity.

The surest way to avoid these errors is to have a predetermined list of questions you ask each and every prospect prior to showing a property. The benefits of this approach are two-fold. First, you avoid the possibility of making inaccurate assumptions that could result in a claim of discrimination. Second, you save valuable time for both yourself and your prospect. After conducting a standard interview, you are well-equipped to determine whether any properties in your inventory will suite the prospect's needs.

You will find that during this interview process, the prospect will provide you with a great deal of information, expanding on the answers to the questions you ask, as follows:

My name is Melissa. What is your name?

May I have your telephone numbers?

How soon are you planning to move?

Do you have pets?

How many bedrooms and bathrooms do you need?

Do you require a garage?

What area of town are you interested in?

How many people will be occupying the property?

What is your rental price range?

Are you employed locally?

 Watch Out!

Keep all of your notes from the very first contact through all of the process. If you ever have a fair-housing claim filed against you, you will be required to produce your notes on that applicant and maybe even some others. Remember to record the date and time on all documentation.

Do you need a fenced yard?

What other requirements in a rental property do you have?

Pay attention, listen, and take notes. At this early stage of the process, you will often be able to determine whether or not the prospect is able to qualify financially to rent from you. It is an efficient and fair way to handle all rental prospects. It also eliminates the "no shows" for scheduled rental viewings, which can be not only frustrating but also a complete waste of your time.

Fair housing guidelines when showing your property and taking applications

Property showings must be available to all interested parties. I answer questions when prospective tenants call regarding my vacancies, and these answers sometimes discourage them from wanting to see the property. However, the answers derive from the business requirements previously listed: the size of the property, the location, the list of amenities, or other non-discriminatory issues. The caller makes the determination and decision on whether to go see the property, based on individual needs.

Offering different terms and conditions to different parties is one of the major offenses many landlords commit. My company communicates the same terms and conditions for renting the property to all perspective applicants. If the terms change, everyone receives the same information.

The rental application supports fair housing, and I issue the same documents and requirements to all perspective tenants. Upon receipt of each application, the processing procedure is the same for everyone. Acceptance or denial is always the result of valid business requirements.

It is not always an easy task to avoid discrimination. The majority of today's tenants are aware of the fair housing laws and the procedures to file complaints. There are many organizations available to assist them. However, I work diligently to avoid unfair practices and to prevent unwanted lawsuits or claims.

Bright Idea

When drafting any rule for your property, consider its purpose. Is the rule intended to preserve, protect, and enhance your property value? Does it apply to all renters? Does it address a specific problem, providing a specific solution that's rational and fair? Above all, does it employ common sense?

Determining occupancy restrictions

Many property managers restrict the number of people who can live in a home. The justifications for occupancy standards are numerous, and on the surface the policy may appear to be fair. However, numerous fair-housing complaints have been filed as a result of occupancy restrictions, which had the effect of discriminating against families with children.

Different states have different laws covering occupancy standards, which is known as the state or local uniform housing codes. The California guideline (not law) is two people per bedroom plus one. Common sense and reason have to be used. If you have a 1,250 sq. ft. 4-bedroom home, nine people sounds excessive. However, five people in a 1,250 sq ft 2-bedroom 2-bath home with a den may be reasonable.

The Federal Fair Housing Act doesn't prohibit state and local entities from adopting restrictions on the number of people who occupy a dwelling. The act allows "reasonable" government restrictions on occupancy, as long as they apply to all occupants and don't discriminate on the basis of race, color, religion, national origin, sex, familial status, or handicap. HUD, the federal agency charged with administering the Fair Housing Act, has never adopted occupancy standards, and there is nothing in the act that indicates intent to develop such standards. This has been a source of concern for housing providers for many years. Many of us have urged HUD to develop guidelines, which would, in the absence of state and local regulations, dictate a maximum occupancy level.

Watch Out!

If you decide to adopt an occupancy standard, make sure that it is reasonable and is evenly enforced with all renters. Never specify how many adults and how many children are allowed. Always refer to the total number of people.

Some property managers use the standard of two people per bedroom, plus one extra person per household. The National Association of Residential Property Managers (NARPM) wrote a position paper adopting this standard as a fair and reasonable occupancy standard. Keep in mind, however, if the dwelling is exceptionally large or would easily accommodate additional persons, this policy could easily be challenged if a complaint of child discrimination were filed and investigated.

Avoiding steering

Steering is a form of discrimination. Steering is when you attempt to guide an applicant toward living where you think he or she should or may want to live, based on group identity. Steering is illegal and absolutely not allowed.

A common thing that owners do is to try to direct, suggest, or steer a prospective tenant who has a family to a particular location. Although you may think you're doing the right thing, this is illegal and a common complaint received by fair housing.

Steering can be subtle, accidental, or very direct. You must be careful not to make suggestions or comments that someone may misinterpret. Always show all units available and let prospects decide where they would like to be.

Avoiding linguistic profiling

You may have recently heard the term "linguistic profiling" as it relates to housing discrimination. It is making news across the country, and there is new research to substantiate its existence.

Do you draw conclusions about someone's race, sex, age, sexual orientation, or other traits by the sound of his or her voice? New research points to the fact that, by an overwhelming majority, people do exactly that.

What does this mean to the world of rental property? It demonstrates even further the necessity to establish and abide by consistent and fair practices when handling rental inquiries. Not only do you need to be sure you return all calls promptly, but you should be sure you're treating all callers in the same manner. Many people use a script or needs-assessment form when discussing available rentals with potential tenants. Use of these standardized forms and methods provides assurance that all callers receive the same information in the same way.

But perhaps the three most valuable procedures are these:

- **Return every voice message call.** No matter what! There should be no excuse not to return a call from someone who was interested enough in your property that they called you. Not only is failing to return calls rude and bad business, it is now potentially dangerous. Instruct your staff that every message will be responded to promptly and pleasantly, and that they should make a record of it.

- **Always conclude with an invitation.** Be sure that at the end of any conversation that an invitation is extended to the prospect. Again, no matter what! The conversation could be misconstrued as discriminatory is some way, through no fault of the leasing agent, and the fastest way to correct that misrepresentation is to invite the prospect to visit. "Even though we don't have any two bedroom apartments now, you are still welcome to visit us . . . may I set up an appointment?" or "Would you still like to visit us even though we don't have tennis courts? If so, let's make an appointment. . . ." Something like this can be an insurance policy for you as the landlord. If the prospect declines the invitation, this should be noted accordingly.

- **If you have staff or an on-site manager, test that person.** From time to time, check to be sure that your employees

are following the just-mentioned procedure. Have different people leave messages, asking to be called back. Have
them call and ask about an amenity you don't have and
see how your on-site manager handles this. If calls are
returned and invitations are issued, reward your manager.
If you find a problem, work with your manager or find
someone who will not put you at risk. *Bottom line:* Treat
everyone equally.

Avoiding unintentional discriminatory practices

When drafting policies and procedures, it is important to recognize how others may perceive your policies. Does a policy appear
to discourage occupancy by one or more protected classes under
the Fair Housing Act? The majority of discrimination claims filed
today are the result of unintentional discriminatory practices
and/or statements. Discrimination is no longer strictly a case of
blatant expression of racial bigotry. More often than not, the
accused is not even aware that their actions were perceived as
discriminatory. You, your property manager, any on-site manager, or other employee are all at risk for a fair-housing claim.

I urge you to take a good, hard look at rental policies and
procedures, which should be in writing and be updated often.
Put your policies to the test. Play devil's advocate for a moment
and examine your policies under the following criteria:

- Could the policy be perceived as discriminating against a
  protected class under the Fair Housing Act?
- If so, is there a clear business justification for the policy?
- Is there no less-discriminatory alternative?
- Are you being fair to all parties involved?

Use of the pool

A rule I often see in multi-family properties (apartments and
condominiums) concerns the use of the common swimming

pool. There are many variations of the rule, but it serves to limit the use of the pool by children during certain hours of the day. Example: "Adults only between 8:00 p.m. and 10:00 p.m." What is the purpose of this rule? Property managers have explained that the rule allows peaceful enjoyment of the pool by those who want to swim, rather than play. Dedicated swimmers know that they can work out between those hours without the interruption of pool toys and roughhousing. Those who wish to play in the pool have many hours to do so each day. This rule seems to have a clear business justification, doesn't it? After all, everyone residing in the community has a right to enjoy the facilities. Is there a problem with this rule?

Let's examine the rule under the criteria just mentioned. Could the rule be perceived to discriminate against a protected class? The answer is yes! It appears to discriminate against families with children. I've already established the business justification for the rule — allowing peaceful enjoyment of the facilities for all residents. Is there a less-discriminatory alternative? Yes! Rather than saying "adults only" between 8:00 p.m. and 10:00 p.m., you could say, "Lap swimming only" between those hours. This simple change in language removes the discriminatory nature of the rule and accomplishes the business goal of allowing peaceful enjoyment of the pool that is fair to all people.

Renting to roommates

Some owners or property mangers have a policy whereby married couples need only submit a joint application to rent while unmarried persons must each apply separately. Is there anything wrong with this policy? You apply the criteria again: Does the policy

 Watch Out!

Be sure to always offer an application to each and every person who comes to view your available unit. Take care when you start ask questions, as it is really easy to ask a discriminatory question when you're just trying to be friendly.

appear to discriminate against any protected class? Unless your state lists "marital status" as a protected class, the answer is probably not. However, is it possible that a same-sex couple could perceive this policy as limiting housing opportunities to them because of their relationship? Is there a clear business justification for an application policy favoring married people? Very questionable. Is there a less discriminatory alternative? Yes. You can require a separate application from potential residents over 18 years of age, regardless of their marital status.

With this simple change in policy, you accomplish a great deal. Not only do you treat all applicants the same, regardless of their marital status, but also you gain additional background information of your adult residents. When it comes time to enforce the terms of the rental agreement, the more information, the better!

Laws that protect tenants with disabilities

The federal Fair Housing Act prohibits discrimination against people who:

- Have a physical or mental disability that substantially limits one or more major life activities (could be hearing, eyesight, physical disease, mental illness, mental retardation, and so on)

- Have a history or record of a disability

- Are regarded by others as though they have such a disability

Discriminatory questions and actions

Landlords aren't allowed to ask whether or not the applicant or tenant has a disability or illness, or ask to see medical records. Even if the disability is obvious (for example, the applicant uses a wheelchair or wears a hearing aid), it is nevertheless illegal to inquire about the severity of the disability. In short, you cannot treat a tenant with a disability differently than you treat other tenants.

For example, if there are two units for rent — one on the ground floor and one three stories up — you must show both units to the applicant who uses a wheelchair, however reasonable you think it would be for the person to consider only the ground-floor unit. That is not your choice or decision to make for the applicant.

Modifications

Landlords must allow disabled tenants to make reasonable modifications to their living unit or common areas at the tenant's expense, if needed for the person to comfortably and safely live in the unit. Disabled tenants have the right to modify their living space to the extent necessary to make the space safe and comfortable, as long as the modifications will not make the unit unacceptable to the next tenant (e.g., widening an entrance) and if they agree to undo the modification when they move out. A tenant cannot be required to undo modifications to common areas. However something like raising the cabinets to the original level upon move out would be a reasonable requirement.

Examples of modifications undertaken by a disabled tenant include:

- Installing a ramp to allow wheelchair access
- Installing special handles and rails in the bathrooms and inside the tub and shower enclosures
- Lowering countertops for a tenant using a wheelchair
- Modifying locks so that someone in a wheelchair can either remotely open and close the doors or the locks are placed in a lower part of the door.
- Installing or modifying special appliances to accommodate a blind tenant
- Installing special faucets or door handles for persons with limited hand use

All modifications must be reasonable and require prior approval before your tenant may make any changes. You are allowed to require the tenant to obtain the proper permits and pay an additional deposit as a guarantee that the unit will be restored to the condition in which it was found.

You can require proof of a disablility, which would be a certification letter from the disabled tenant's doctor, but this proof doesn't need to specify or explain the disability.

When a pet isn't a pet

Ordinarily, property owners have the right to refuse animals. However, there is a specific circumstance when an animal cannot be denied and is not considered a "pet." When a disabled person with an assistance animal applies to rent a property, a landlord cannot refuse to rent to the prospective tenant because of the animal.

Under federal, state, and local fair-housing laws, individuals with disabilities may ask their housing provider to make reasonable accommodations in the "no pets" policy to allow for their use of a companion/assistance animal.

What defines a service animal?

A service animal is one individually trained to do work or perform tasks for the benefit of a person with a disability. A service animal can be any breed or size. It may wear specialized equipment such as a backpack, harness, special collar, or leash, but this is not a legal requirement.

How do you determine whether it truly is a service animal?

Housing providers may ask an applicant or tenant to provide documentation from a qualified professional that the individual has a disability and requires a service animal as an accommodation.

Housing providers may not ask an applicant or tenant to provide:

- Any details about the applicant's/tenant's disability
- Medical records
- Proof of training (such as a training certificate)

Service animals are normally trained to assist the disabled person with individual needs relative to that person's disability. While some animals receive certification papers, others don't. It is legitimate for a person with a disability to train his/her own service animal. There is currently no national standard with which to evaluate the training or performance of any type of service animal, including guide dogs. You may not require the disabled tenant to provide proof of the service animal's training.

What about additional deposits for the service animal?

A service animal is not a pet and you cannot lawfully require any additional deposits. What can be done if there is damage by the service animal? The tenant is responsible for the actions of his/her animal and can be held accountable for any damage to your property. Additionally, the tenant must comply with any of your established policies such as cleanliness and maintenance of the unit as well as leash requirements and noise guidelines. In most cases, however, assistance animals are usually well-behaved.

You cannot refuse to rent to disabled tenants and their service animals, but as the property manager, you require them to process through your usual screening practices.

Remember, a property owner doesn't have to rent to a poorly qualified tenant, disabled or not.

 Bright Idea

Fair-housing classes are provided by HUD, local apartment associations, and private fair-housing organizations. There are also publications that you can subscribe to, such as the *Fair Housing Advocate* (at www.fairhousing. com). Stay up to date as laws change.

Fair housing and sexual harassment

Fair housing and sexual harassment? Do they really have anything to do with one another? Absolutely, and the courts continue to expand on the connection.

Housing law recognizes two types of sexual harassment claims:

- A conditioned tenancy or quid pro quo claim, which in non-legalese means making a sexual demand on a resident in order for that resident to get needed maintenance on the apartment, to get a rent concession, or to avoid an eviction.

- A hostile environment claim, which can give rise to claims concerning the psychological well-being of a resident who can demonstrate such a situation.

Furthermore, fair-housing law has been broadly applied to define sexual harassment as a violation of the Fair Housing Act prohibition against sex discrimination and, of course, the FHA provides for significant financial punishment and penalties for violations. So in theory, sexual harassment within the context of the landlord/tenant relationship can be financially costly to you.

Some fair-housing lawyers have worked to charge landlords with criminal battery, as well as for violations of the sexual predator laws. In fact, one landlord was successfully convicted of the latter.

Don't ever abuse the power you have over residents.

Sexual harassment doesn't stop with the owner, but in fact extends to anyone the owner hires, including anyone performing maintenance on the rental property. You need to have a clear, written policy with all of your contractors about sexual harassment.

Also consider a policy encouraging and allowing employees or maintenance professionals the opportunity to leave a unit at any time they believe the situation is inappropriate. If a resident is making comments or gestures, or touches an employee, or if the environment itself is threatening (a hardcore pornography video being played, as a real-life example), no one should have to remain and deal with that.

- In return, the maintenance employee should be required to immediately notify management of the scenario and advise management that he or she has left the unit and why.

- Respond to the input from your maintenance professionals that they are uncomfortable with a particular resident, and either send someone else to complete work orders or send someone to accompany your employees.

- Insist that no maintenance professional will ever be in an occupied unit unless there is a written work order (emergencies excepted — fire and flood!). If a resident entices your employee into the unit and the employee doesn't respond as hoped for, that resident is likely to contact management and accuse the employee of wrongdoing. Without a written work order, your employee could be in a dangerous situation.

- Make it clear to residents and maintenance professionals alike that unless there is an emergency (fire or flood), no maintenance professional will be alone in the unit with someone's minor child. To require otherwise offers the potential to have your employee's professional and personal life ruined.

 Watch Out!

If the fear of losing vast sums of money is not a motivating factor to avoid sexual harassment, what about jail time? One current idea is to charge landlords under laws related to prostitution. How? With the argument that requiring sex for rent or other benefits is in effect coercion into prostitution.

Bright Idea

Consider having your application and policy and procedures done in other languages that are dominant in your area. In California, having an application and letting the applicants know what is expected in Spanish really helps. In other areas, other languages may make sense.

A wise landlord will consider these ideas and develop a written policy to incorporate them. Why? Well, actually, there are three reasons. First, it is the right thing to do. Second, if the first reason doesn't motivate you, then how about this: Your failure to protect your employees from sexual harassment (or worse, to expect them to take it) can result in your being sued by your own employees! And finally, industry surveys consistently show that your number-one resident retention tool is your professional maintenance staff. And isn't it just good business to protect your assets?

Conducting your rental business with good, fair-housing policies is a must. Take the time to know the laws, have written policies and procedures, and always treat everyone fairly and equally.

What to do if a discrimination complaint is filed against you

If a discrimination complaint is ever filed against you, be sure to do the following:

- Respond immediately.
- Gather together the pertinent paperwork and present your case.
- Consider agreeing to helpful suggested remedies, such as fair-housing training for all staff.
- Insist on neutrality on the part of the enforcement representative.

Just the facts

- Fair housing violations are extremely serious and can be costly.

- There are many different forms of discrimination: Local, state, and federal laws vary.

- There are specific fair-housing requirements for advertising — avoid discriminatory wording.

- Be careful when setting occupancy standards.

- Steering a tenant to a particular apartment or neighborhood is illegal.

- Tenants with disabilities have the right to make the unit accessible and useable with your prior approval and are required to return the property to the same condition it was in prior to move-in.

- You must allow a tenant to have a service or companion pet.

- You may not ask a tenant or applicant the nature of the disability.

- Many landlords discriminate unintentionally, which is not protection from the law.

Marketing Your Rental Property

Chapter 8

Determining the rental price for your investment property is an important step before you begin marketing your property and signing a new tenant. After reading Chapter 5, you know that before marketing your vacancies, you must have the property in pristine condition to attract a quality tenant. You have to do your homework and research the rental market to determine the current value prior to advertising. Before you can begin marketing your available rental, you also need to set your asking price and have your applications and lease paperwork ready. You need to know the appropriate security deposit to request and the entire move-in cost and what other expenses the tenant may incur, such as utilities or parking. When you begin to market the property for rent, have your marketing file as well as your written policies and procedures easily accessible.

After you determine the price for your up-and-coming rental, you need to have a marketing plan.

You want prospects to call and view the entire property inside and out. Hold their interest by selling the features of your property. Take it a step further and have them fill out and return the rental application promptly and completely. By having the property in excellent condition, being organized and prepared with your paperwork, and pricing your rental competitively, you will be on your way to having a quality tenant.

Determining the appropriate rental price

Setting your rental price is an important decision and what you decide depends on your situation. If you have taken over a rental property with tenants in place, you may not need to market a rental right away. However, you should know the rental value when you purchase the property. You may choose to raise your tenants' rent appropriate to the market.

If you price the property too high, it will sit vacant and you will have a loss of income that you will never be able to recapture. Usually, you need to price your rental according to the current market. Tenants who are willing to pay an above-market rent for a property usually have bad credit or have been forced to move. Of course, if your market has more demand than supply, even with a high rent, you probably will receive several applications as bidding wars occur.

Find out what comparable units in the area rent for by checking sources where other landlords advertise. A comparable property is a property that is similar to your rental property. They may be located right in the same neighborhood or they

 Watch Out!

Some states or counties have laws that determine just how much notice you must give to raise the rents, as well as how much you can raise a tenant's rent within a certain time limit. Make sure you check your local laws.

may be similar but located across town or in a nearby city. Also watch the advertisements for a week or two. You may find that the properties aren't renting at the higher price and only disappear from the ads when their rental rate has been reduced to the appropriate level. Drive around the area. Do you see banners saying, "move-in special," "special rates now," "ask about our incentives"? If so, this tells you that supply is higher than demand and you will need to be at the lower end of the market to rent your property quickly.

Plan to raise current tenants based on their length of time at the property, condition of the unit or the property, and the current rental agreement. When purchasing a property with a tenant already in residence, be sure to read the rental agreement prior to proposing any rent increases.

Ways to determine your market rent

Not sure how to price your rental? Try the following tips:

- Pick up the local newspaper in the area of the available rental. Go through the section where you find properties for rent. Highlight the ones that sound similar to yours and make a few calls to get the location and drive by.

- Search the Internet for available rentals by entering the city and the type of rental.

- Call a local property management company and offer to pay them for an hour or two of consultation. Have the rental agent or property manager meet you at your available rental. The key is to offer to pay for the service. See Chapter 16 for more on hiring a property management company.

- Go to a few local property management Web sites and look up their available rentals. They usually provide addresses, current rents, and even photos of the comparable properties. If you just purchased the property, there will be some rental comparables in your appraisal report.

Moneysaver

Don't overprice your rental. Overpricing a rental causes frustration and loss of income you can never recover. Remember, your goal is to fill the rental unit and rent to a quality tenant who will pay on time and take care of your property. Pricing the rental correctly saves you time and money.

- Call on properties nearby from the "FOR RENT" signs placed in front of the units. Ask the person who answers how much he or she is asking for the rental. When calling, you have two choices: You can ask the questions as if you were the prospective tenant, or you can introduce yourself and let them know you own a property nearby and you are conducting a market analysis. I recommend being honest, as you usually can get additional information and sometimes more information than you expected.

When setting your asking price, do your homework to find the market rent, and then stay at the lower end of the market. This will be one of the incentives that will draw a prospect to your property rather than the similar one for more money. Having your rental price just under the other comparable ones will save you time, money, and hassles while finding a tenant promptly. Of course, you should consider particular aspects of your own market as well as your financial needs when determining the final price to ask.

Looking at an example

Consider the following example: You've done your homework and the rental range for your unit appears to run between $500 and $525. Of course, you want to maximize your investment over the next 12 months, so you decide to advertise at the higher amount and wait for the person willing to pay that much — because your unit is in pristine condition. However, it takes you an extra four weeks to find a tenant.

12 months @ $500/month is $6,000 for the year.

11 months @ $525/month is $5,775 for the year.

You also have additional advertising costs and more show-ings and phone calls to get it rented. How much is your time worth? Do you think it will be easier to raise the rent next year from $500 per month or from $525 per month? Look at the long-term return on your investment.

Offering a discount or move-in bonus

If your market is really soft and you are having trouble renting your property, consider some type of move-in bonus or dis-count. Some people offer a discount off of the last month of a lease, but this may not be an incentive if you are looking for a long-term tenant. Check the local newspaper when you are researching your market price and see what the others are doing and what type of incentives are being offered. Keep in mind that the tenants are aware of the competition in a soft rental market. They may call you and ask you to match what the property down the street is offering.

Rental markets, like everything else, are subject to change. There will be strong markets where you no sooner get the sign up or the advertisement in the paper and you have a qualified prospect turning in an application. Then, other times, you may have tried everything possible to rent your property and a significant amount of time has gone by and you still have not rented the unit. Don't be afraid to lower your rent — do it quickly and be aggressive. Avoid chasing the market down and going weeks without a tenant. Getting a qual-ity tenant quickly sometimes means being extremely competitive

> **❝** Prepare your property for a good tenant, and they will come. By pric-ing your rental fairly and competitively you will get a quality tenant who in turn takes care of your investment staying long term. **❞**
>
> —Jack D., investor

with your asking rent. Remember your property should be in excellent condition and priced to rent right away to a qualified long-term tenant who will care for your investment.

You want to create an appropriate advertisement and marketing plan to get in front of people who desire the amenities you offer, who want to live in your area, and, of course, who can afford the rent you are asking. This is your business and it takes time to market your property to the greatest extent possible. Only you can determine the correct balance between time needed for a full-blown marketing campaign and dollars lost on a vacancy. It's your choice.

Preparing yourself to market your property

You need to be prepared and organized prior to placing the property on the market for rent. You will save yourself time and money, but most importantly, you will avoid the headaches that come when you have not taken the time to have your systems and procedures in writing well in advance. When you are making appointments, let the prospective tenant know what you will be expecting up front and in detail. If you have a Web site for your rental property, you will be able to allow prospective tenants to view the photos of your property. You will also be able to provide the option to download your application and your lease policies in advance. Technology today can truly assist you in managing and renting your rentals. By having a Web site, you will attract tenants who are also up to date with today's technology.

Here are some questions to ask yourself before you begin marketing your property:

- Who do you want to reach?
- What is your select market?
- What kind of market are you in currently?
- Are there more rentals than prospective tenants, or vice versa?

- How much money and time are you willing to spend on your marketing for a new tenant?
- Where can and should you market to reach your intended audience?
- When is the best time to advertise? Weekends only? Continuously, ten days in a row?

Finding effective places to market your property

Right now there are dozens of potential renters out there who are looking for just the right place, a place just like yours. You should be able to advertise and draw them in to view your property. A good advertising and marketing program lets you pinpoint and attract just the kind of tenant you want for your property. You need to know how to identify, understand, and find your ideal tenant. Think about what you consider to be your ideal tenant and what you value in a tenant. Consider at this time whether you are going to allow pets, whether your property is suitable for pets, and what type of pets you will consider. Some landlords believe accepting pets gives you a longer-term tenant, while others have had so much damage from tenants with pets that they have sworn never to accept an applicant with pets again.

Note: Companion or help animals aren't considered pets and you cannot use this as a reason to turn down the applicant. See Chapter 7.

You need to decide where the best, most-effective places are to market your property. The following sections give you several options.

Remember: Effective marketing involves differentiating your property from other properties that are listed for rent. In a tight rental market, advertising may not be as critical, but when renters have many places to choose from, you need to be creative and competitive. Think about that special attraction for your property that tenants are looking for. Effective and catchy

Bright Idea

Take the time to go down to your local sign store and have a professional sign made up with the basic teaser information: "FOR RENT" should really stand out as well as a contact phone number. Keep in simple enough, however, that you can reuse the sign.

marketing will increase your number of calls and showings, which increases your chance of attracting the ideal tenant for your property The more clearly you state the property's special or unique features, the greater the odds of attracting quality applicants.

Place a sign on your property

Start by placing a "FOR RENT" sign on your property. You need to be sure the sign is professional looking. What do you think of when you see an 8½" x 11", red-and-white sign stapled to a telephone pole? Pay the extra money to get a sign you can actually stick in the ground. You can easily put one together with vinyl letters on a hard plastic 3' x 4' Plexiglas or hard plastic board, put a screw through it and attach to a pole. This sign is going to attract more qualified renters and sets the tone of professionalism. Your sign reflects that you care about your property.

A sign works well because prospective tenants who want to live in the area drive by. Make sure your rental sign is in good condition, as the sign is yet another reflection of you, the landlord. The phone number needs to be clear and easy to read from the street. If you have a sign with extra space, include a few details on the sign, such as number of bedrooms and bathrooms, and the asking price. Make sure everything written is legible. You should always have signs available and ready to place on your property. This is a very inexpensive way to fill a vacancy.

The advantage of a sign is the person calling already knows the location and the area and has seen the exterior of your rental. This is again where the curb appeal of your property comes in. Sign placement is also very important. Place the sign where it is clearly visible from the street. If you are placing it in front of your property, it is nice to have a double-sided sign. If your window faces the street, place a sign in that window. After you have placed the sign, drive by and see how it looks. Make sure you can see the sign clearly from both directions.

If you have a multiple-unit building, your local sign company can also make a banner for you that can be hung on the outside of the building. If you have multiple vacancies, don't leave the sign up indefinitely. Try taking it down for a week or two, and then putting it back up. This will give the impression you just had new vacancies come up.

Many owners choose not to put up a sign while their current tenants are still living there because many people driving by will go right up to the door and ask for more details. If you put up a sign where your tenants are still living in the unit, be sure to put up a "Don't disturb occupant" sign. You can also minimize the disturbance to the tenant by putting up a box with flyers in it next to the sign.

You can utilize the time of a good current tenant by offering him or her an incentive to show the unit, especially if you don't live nearby. Make sure to consider your current tenant carefully and how that person will represent your property. Give them a handout with the features and fair-housing guidelines. I've found that some tenants are great, but they also want to gossip about the owner or the neighborhood.

If at all possible, show the unit yourself. You are the expert and the one who wants to sell your unit. Obviously, if you have a

 Watch Out!

By placing a sign on a vacant property you give a message that the property is vacant. Put up a "DON'T DISTURB OCCUPANT" sign as a precaution to avoid any vandalism. When describing the property on the phone, I always say, "Please don't disturb the tenant."

tenant leaving under difficult circumstances or if the tenant doesn't have good housekeeping skills, you need to wait until the tenant has moved out prior to showing the unit.

Newspaper advertising

By far the most common form of renting your property is advertising in your local newspaper. However, the trend in the last three years has been toward the Internet. This is especially true in areas where people are relocating from other parts of the country (or world) or around universities.

Choosing which newspaper

You need to decide which paper is the most effective one to place your ad to get the results you need to rent your unit. In many areas you have more than one paper to choose from to advertise your property. Usually, you have at least one larger paper that has a large classified section, plus at least one smaller,

---

Providing Information 24/7

Callers who can't get through to you won't keep calling back. Have a voice mail system or answering machine with a friendly but professional message providing the move-in details and features of your available property. Make sure the message gives the total move-in costs and informs the caller whether yours is a non-smoking property and whether pets are allowed. You may even provide the address and welcome a drive by, but ask prospects not to go onto the property or disturb the occupant. Let the caller know when the property will be available to view and how to go about making an appointment. In addition, tell the caller what the move-in date is and that you have a Web site or other place to view digital photos and obtain an application.

privately owned paper. The smaller paper is usually read by people in the area and can be effective and the least costly. It really depends on the type of rental and your specific area. Sometimes advertising in the large city paper costs a lot, but it covers a wide area.

Be sure to review whichever paper you choose and check out your competition. See which ads catch your eye and think about why.

Keep in mind that many newspapers now have online newspapers so that anyone searching will also pull up the newspaper online as well as reading it in the actual paper they pick up at the newspaper stand.

Writing an effective ad

When placing your ad, list the key features. Start by describing the property from the inside to the outside, listing the features that matter. Let prospects know what makes your place unique and better than the others. List items that not all units have, such as a view, a fireplace, a garage, new appliances, and list the condition. Is it newer, does it have upgrades, large bonus rooms, and so on?

Place yourself in the tenant's position. What would you want to know before calling to get details? What would entice you to call? The hardest part of placing your classified ad is figuring out what is important to the reader. Put in the benefit and value of the property.

- **Location**   You will find most newspapers list the ads by location. It is a good idea to mention the neighborhood or area that someone reading it may be familiar with. Some locations aren't for everyone or offer some particular benefit like being close to shopping, buses, or schools.

- **Size**   This is the next important criteria in your ad. You should list the number of bedrooms and bathrooms, as well as any bonus rooms, offices, family rooms, sun porches.

Bright idea

Describe the location first, using a catchy word or two to draw in your reader, and then describe from the inside out. List the features, especially those that separate it from other rental properties. End with the price, lease term, and the contact number.

Mention the size of a room or rooms if the bedrooms are large or if there is a large living room or kitchen. Also, it is important to mention whether any part of the property has been newly remodeled. Square footage may be important if that description is needed to support the rental price being above market for the number of bedrooms and baths.

- **Amenities**   Next, mention the special features of the property such as fireplace, pool, spa, appliances, laundry, garage, yard, deck, patio. It is important to talk about the view and the setting. Use descriptive words such as "quiet, private." Consider the time of year. Air conditioning is important when temperatures soar above 80°F, but not when the furnace is needed. If gardening is provided, this may be very attractive to the person who travels a lot and/or currently doesn't have yard-maintenance equipment.

- **Monthly rent and terms desired**   Include whether a lease is required. Communicate whether pets are allowed. Mention move-in bonuses.

- **Utilities**   It is important to mention any utilities included, especially if all utilities are (or aren't) included in the rent.

- **Cleanliness**   If the rental is newly painted or has new carpet, or something has been upgraded, mention that in your ad. I sometimes state, "Clean and ready for immediate move in."

- **Contact information**   The last thing in the ad is usually a telephone number where you can be reached or where the reader can obtain additional information. I highly recommend you have a answering machine or voice mail system. Your outgoing message is so important. I also feel this is the time to give the drive-by address and mention any pre-arranged showing times or open houses.

Looking at a typical ad

A typical ad may look like this:

> SF—apt 2 bdrm 1 ba w/incredible views frplc, newly remod kit, sm deck, gar. Avail. 6/1. Lse. No pet/smoke $1,700. 379-9038

Or, like this:

> SF/APT, 2/1 w/views, FP remod kit, DK, gar. Avbl 6/1, lse, N/P/S. $1,700. 379-9038.

Don't be afraid of a short ad. Keep in mind most newspapers will assist you if you tell them you want the ad as short as possible and you want to them to abbreviate wherever possible. Some papers even provide you a list of common abbreviations. Here are the most common ones:

- Apartment: apt
- Townhouse: th
- Bedroom: bdrm
- Bathroom: Ba
- Fireplace: f/p
- Dishwasher: d/w
- Large: lg
- Small: sml
- Room: rm
- Laundry: lndy
- Washer and dryer: w/d
- Garage: gar or 2cr or 1cr
- Air conditioning: a/c

- Yard: yrd

- Renovated: Reno'd

- Move-in bonus: M/I bonus

- No pets or smoking: No pet/smk or N/P/S

Check the ads in your local newspaper to find out what abbreviations are commonly used. Your newspaper can help you reduce the ad to get in the important features.

How big to make your ad

Your ad will usually be placed in the classified rental section under the available category, based on the type of property and/or area. In this case, bigger is not better. Placing a small ad that will attract your reader is important. Prospective tenants tend to look for smaller ads in certain areas with quick-and-easy details to read. Therefore, your ad needs to be short, yet packed with the valuable and basic information.

How often and when to run your ad in the paper

Most newspapers give a discount based on the commitment of running your ad for a specific number of days. I feel the best time to run an ad is the end of the week. You can begin the ad on a Friday and run it for ten straight days. This gives you their ten-day rate and hits two weekends.

Find out whether you can change your ad without charge. After the first weekend, if you didn't get any calls, consider changing the price or changing the verbiage to get more interest. Taking your ad out for a couple of days, and then placing it again with different information may also spark interest.

 Watch Out!

It is important to check your ad the day you expect it to come out in the newspaper. Be sure the information is correct, especially the price and phone number. Don't expect the ad to be correct, and call the paper immediately if you find an error.

I find the busiest days and most active days for rental calls and rental showings is toward the end of the month, with the last weekend before the first of the month being a very good time to advertise and rent your property. Remember, good tenants give 30 days' written notice to their current landlords. They look around toward the end of the month with plans to find a place and give notice to their current landlords on or around the first of the month when they pay their rent.

Advertise in rental publications

There are many local, weekly, and monthly rental publications that are widely used by prospects looking for a rental. The most widely circulated rental publications are *For Rent* and *Apartment Guide*. Rental guides are primarily designed for larger rental housing communities. If you have a large building with several vacancies, this may be the route to go. Keep in mind that advertising in these publications can be quite costly and may not be your first choice.

If you do decide to run an ad in a magazine, I recommend that you keep it small. Refer the prospects to a Web site or a rental hotline where they can get up-to-date information about what you have available at the time they make the call. There is also a lead time before the ad will be published, sometimes up to 10 days. Be sure to find out the cancellation policy if you rent the property.

Use a Web site or online ad

As more and more people have become Internet savvy and have learned to search for what they need on the Internet, it is important for you as a landlord to have an Internet presence. It would be great to have a Web site or to list your property for rent on a local or national Web site. You should have a detailed description and digital photos of the property and the unit.

There are many Internet providers that offer Web sites at little cost. You may find an online service where you can list your

Bright Idea

Take the time to create a simple Web site. After spending the initial money to get it started, it won't cost you much to maintain, yet it will provide many leads. The Internet is the way to have a presence for tenants to find you and learn about your available property.

vacancy with photos. Search on your computer or go to Yahoo! or Google sites, type in "online ad housing rentals," and include the area or city.

Many of the rental publications offer online advertising as well. Many local newspapers now have all their advertising online as well as in the printed page. Some will charge an additional fee for this advertising but many are including it in their ad costs. To find out which Web sites are most effective, go to the Web and search for rental homes with the name of the city your property is located in. You may find that there are local places to advertise that you were not aware of before.

Put up flyers

Think about posting flyers in your laundry room and around your neighborhood, with details about your upcoming unit. In some cases, it makes sense to have a nice flyer with a photo or two on it, along with the address and showing information. Flyers are great for college towns, where you can post the flyer in a central location. You need to have a plan, though, because distributing the flyers could take a lot of time. At a minimum, handing the flyer to the other tenants or neighbors is effective.

Try community bulletin boards

Some areas have an electronic community bulletin board, such as Craig's List (www.craigslist.org). If not, consider using a physical bulletin board, where you can post your flyer. Sometimes, even your local post office has a place to post flyers. Local grocery stores and restaurants may have a bulletin board you can use. If your property is in an area that has a homeowners association, ask about posting the flyer in its newsletter or on the complex bulletin board. This is not as effective as some of the other methods, but it only takes one person to walk in and call from your posting of the flyer.

Your local chamber of commerce may be a good resource. Many people moving into an area drop by the chamber to pick up information about the area. Ask if you can put your flyers in their information stand.

Contact a local employer or relocation department

Large employers nearby are a great source for rental prospects and usually have a break room or a person you can contact to possibly post a flyer. Making contact early on is important. Many employers have a rental-assistance or housing-referral office or relocation person. Most rentals are located close enough to a few large companies. Many employers find it is essential to assist in affordable-housing resources nearby their offices.

If your rental is a large single-family home, using a relocation company can be quite beneficial. You can search for relocation companies in your local Yellow Pages or on the Internet.

Use your current tenants or other word of mouth

If you have a building with more than one unit and you receive a notice to vacate, utilize your current tenants to help you fill your vacancy. Offer them some type of incentive. You could offer lower rent for a month, movie passes, free carpet cleaning, a gift certificate for a local restaurant, or some type of upgrade

---

 Watch Out!

Never place your flyer in anyone's U.S. mailbox. This is illegal and absolutely not allowed. In addition, be careful where you put the flyers and how you secure them, so that they do not blow out into the street or neighborhood with the wind.

Moneysaver

You may find that you know someone or have a current tenant who happens to work for a large employer where you can post your flyer. Sometimes, having a name or a contact within a large company can save you a bundle in marketing costs. Utilize your contacts when trying to rent a property.

in their unit if their friends rent a unit. If your tenant is involved in helping you find a tenant, this could be a win-win situation. You will fill your vacancy and have a current tenant who is happy with their new neighbor. Think about the tenant who is referring the prospect, though — do you want more of the same type of tenant in that property?

Hiring a property management or rental company

Some management companies (discussed in detail in Chapter 17) handle only the renting of your property. They refer to the service as a one-time rental service or a lease-only or lease-up service. When you hire the rental company, you will also get a professional opinion about the condition of the property and the price they think the property should rent for. If you are using a professional company to do your renting only, make sure your agreement states that you get to meet the prospective tenants prior to approval of the application and before they sign a rental agreement if you live in the area. Don't let this get in the way of closing a deal to get the property rented.

Hiring a local property manager to lease your property is preferable when you don't live in the area of the property. Some companies will take care of the move out of the old tenant, advertising, showing, and moving in the new tenant. Balance their fees against your time and money spent traveling to the property and doing the research and showings yourself. Interview several companies before choosing one.

Bright Idea

In hiring a professional company, choose one that handles rentals in your immediate area and that has a great deal of experience. Look for a company with professional accreditation and rental agent or property manager with designations. And be sure you feel comfortable with the person or people who will be managing your property.

In addition, there are local real estate and relocation companies that assist tenants in locating rental units. Realtors may feel that if they assist the prospect in finding a rental home, perhaps down the line they will have an opportunity to sell them a home. (See Chapter 3 for additional information on Realtors.) Another advantage of hiring a real estate office or a property management company is that they will handle the necessary screening and lease paperwork. Real estate companies, rental agents, and property management companies are usually up to date on the current laws and market conditions.

In addition, many property managers or Realtors are members of a multiple listing service (MLS) and can list the rental in this system. This reaches all the members within that MLS system and usually doesn't cost you any more than what you have offered to pay the rental company. They usually split the commission 50/50, very much like they do in the sales market. Be sure you know who is going to pay the advertising, which rental agreement is going to be used, and who will be doing the move-in inspection with the tenant.

Advertising and fair housing

When you place an ad, set up a Web site, put up a sign, or record your message, be aware that you are responsible to know and to abide by the fair-housing laws (see Chapter 7). There are many words you may not use in your ad when you are searching for that qualified tenant. Here are some examples:

Sample Alternative Wording

Discriminatory Phrases	Alternative Words
Adult home	Quiet area
Executive home	Designer touches
	Dramatic Home
Perfect for couple	Starter home
	Cozy home
Perfect for young professional	Commuter's dream
	Sophisticated
	Elegant
	Ambiance
	Made for entertaining
	Wired for home office
Family home	Affordable
	Large home
Great for kids	Close to schools/parks
	Large back yard
	Roomy home
Perfect for singles	Cozy studio
	(List square footage)
Employed	Responsible
	Confirmable income

Note: This is not a complete list.

Whenever in doubt, check with your local or state fair housing office. Advertisers must determine whether the proposed advertisement indicates any preference, limitation, or discrimination based on race, color, religion, sex, handicap, familial status, or national origin, or an intention to make any such preference, limitation, or discrimination.

It is easy to innocently and unknowingly make a subtle statement in marketing your vacancy that violates federal and state fair-housing laws. These laws apply to all, whether you are an owner or a professional in the business of renting properties. Any form of advertising is subject to these laws, and all owners and agents are required to know and abide by the local, state, and federal housing laws. It is your responsibility to know the fair-housing laws and makes sure you don't at any time violate them. There are many places to obtain the up-to-date information for fair housing. Not only can you find it on the Internet but you can also call your local, state, or federal fair housing office. The U.S. Department of Housing and Urban Development (HUD) has developed pamphlets to help you understand the law. Its Web site at www.hud.gov/fairhousing is a wealth of information.

Adhering to the Fair Housing Act as well as local fair housing laws is paramount. If you aren't sure whether your advertisement is in violation of federal and local fair-housing laws, have your ad reviewed by an attorney. Any discrimination in rental housing advertising is illegal and can result in major penalties.

You find a lot of details in Chapter 7 regarding fair housing. In addition, I highly recommend you take a workshop on fair housing so that you know how to stay out of trouble while advertising your rental.

Just the facts

- Your financial requirement for the positive cash flow of your property doesn't determine your rental price. The current market does.

- By pricing your property according to the current market you will attract the tenant you want.

- There are many ways to research your asking price. Take the time and do the homework.

- If you are getting little or no activity showing your rental, either the price is too high or you need to reevaluate the condition.

- A good ad and marketing campaign will attract a quality tenant.

- There are many resources to market your property — use them.

- Fair-housing laws apply to your advertising.

- View your available unit through the eyes of a prospective tenant.

- It doesn't hurt to get a professional opinion. Hire someone in the business to consult with you on your price and condition.

GET THE SCOOP ON...
Qualifying your applicants ▪ Showing your
property ▪ The application process made easy ▪
Section 8 tenants ▪ Turning down an applicant

Finding the Best Tenants

Chapter 9

After spending valuable time finding the right property in the right location and marketing your property to potential tenants, the hard work really begins. Now you have to show the property, screen the applicants, and find the best-qualified tenant to live in your rental property. This chapter shows you how to prepare yourself for the rigors of finding a tenant, establish criteria for selecting tenants, showing the property, qualifying (or disqualifying) applicants, and working with clients who use federal or local housing subsidies.

Establish your tenant selection criteria in advance

Before meeting with any potential tenants, sit down and decide what criteria you're going to use to choose the best tenant. Without clear guidelines about your perfect tenant, you have only your instinct to rely on when you meet him or her. And although your gut feel about a potential tenant is not something to

155

ignore completely, if you rely only on your feelings about a potential tenant to make your decision about renting to him or her, you not only risk renting to someone who can't afford your rental unit, you also risk letting your own biases interfere with your decision, and that may be grounds for a discrimination lawsuit (see Chapter 7).

Instead, set up hard-and-fast criteria to help you select the perfect tenant. And be sure to let potential tenants know that you use a fair system to judge them, for example, by including the following on your application: "It is our policy to rent our units in compliance with the federal, state, and local fair-housing laws." If you are uncertain of fair housing laws, you can find the guidelines at www.hud.gov/offices/fheo/FHLaws/index.cfm. Your state and local fair-housing offices may also have Web sites available or are listed in the government section of your local telephone book.

Use concrete criteria, such as the following, for all potential applicants:

- **Verifiable identification:** Require a photo ID with each application and make a photocopy of the ID. Getting this information assists you in the future if you need a description of your adult occupants. Require identification for co-signers as well.

- **Sufficient income-to-rent ratio:** Try to find applicants for whom gross monthly income is three times the amount of the monthly rent. You can verify income from copies of the applicant's prior month's pay stubs, which you ask her to provide with the application. Ask self-employed

---

 Watch Out!

When collecting a photo ID, make sure it is a government-issue ID, such as a military ID, state driver's license, or government-issued passport. Also be sure the ID is current and has not expired.

applicants to provide their most-recent tax return and three months' worth of bank statements. Don't consider applicants with unverifiable income.

- **Excellent credit rating:** In order to show that an applicant demonstrates financial responsibility, obtain a credit report on all applicants and co-signers over the age of 18 and emancipated minors. Don't accept credit reports supplied by the applicant; obtain the report yourself (see the "Obtain a credit report" section later in this chapter). Discharged bankruptcies are usually also acceptable.

- **Sterling references:** Look for applicants who can provide you with names and telephone numbers in order to verify all income sources, as well as the applicant's current and previous residences.

- **Reliable rental history:** You want applicants who have successfully rented another property and have paid the rent on time. In lieu of this, consider requiring a co-signer.

- **Excellent employment history:** Unless your applicant is independently wealthy, you want a tenant who takes his or her job seriously.

Prescreening begins with the first phone call

The screening process begins with the first telephone call. You want to obtain preliminary information about the applicant and also provide information about your rental. In order to successfully rent your properties, you need to find qualified

 Watch Out!

Keep a list of your prospects, their contact information, and the time and location of your showings. You may also want to record this information on a calendar or day planner. For your personal safety, share this information with another person so that he or she is aware of your location.

tenants through your selection process, and this means making a fair evaluation of applicants according to the law while trying to find a financially qualified tenant who is stable, quiet, and responsible.

Put your questions in writing and ask the same questions of all prospects each time you have a vacancy. Begin by asking some prequalifying questions on the telephone prior to showing the property. (See Appendix 4 for prescreening telephone questions.) As you speak to each prospect, remember to be friendly but professional.

Direct the prospect to drive by the property to get a feel for the neighborhood. Take the time necessary to provide clear and concise directions so that your property is easy to locate. After driving by, ask her to call you to make a personal appointment to view the interior of the property.

> **66** The first impression is the most crucial. I try to be very friendly while answering a potential tenant's questions, thus creating a good owner/landlord image. **99**
>
> —Natalie M., real estate investor

As you're prequalifying, you're also selling. While the prospect is on the phone, ask questions like, "What are you looking for?" and "What is important to you?" and "How long have you been looking and in what area?" Discuss special features of the property while you are chatting.

Show applicants the property

One of the most time-consuming components of owning and managing your property is the time you spend showing the rental. By making it an efficient process, though, you can minimize your time and maximize your profits.

Set up a date and time you and the prospective tenant are planning to meet at the property. You may want to call to confirm the appointment, depending on how far in advance the appointment is. Even if the tenant has driven by, again provide clear and concise directions to the property. If you have several different prospects who want to view the property, schedule the appointments at least 20 to 30 minutes apart, allowing sufficient time with each individual applicant.

Another option is to hold an open house. For example, allow anyone to stop by the property on Sunday from noon to 3:00.

Many times, a person viewing a property will not decide to rent it at that moment. She may want to come back with a friend, a family member, or a potential roommate. Perhaps she wants to view other rentals before making a commitment. If this is the case, be sure she brings everything she needs to the second showing, so that she can make a decision.

Showing a vacant property

If your property is vacant, arrive a few minutes early. Turn on the lights and open the blinds in order to make your prospect feel welcome. If you're showing your rental in the winter, arrive in time to make sure the rooms feel comfortably warm. And during hot summer months, try to cool rooms down. You don't want to show a rental property and have everyone feel uncomfortable and anxious to leave.

As you show the property, point out its positive features. Open up the closets and kitchen cupboards to show the available storage space. Also talk to the prospect and listen to what she is saying. If the prospective tenant is really interested, she will begin to talk through just how she may lay out some of her furniture. Listen and give feedback.

 Bright Idea

Try to obtain the prospect's cellphone number so that if you or the prospect are delayed, you can still make contact. Provide your cellphone number as well. Stress to the prospect that you would appreciate a call if he or she won't be able to view the property or will arrive later than planned.

Watch Out!

When showing your available rental, carry a cellphone and make sure it is turned on, so that you can call in an emergency. Always leave your purse and your personal belongings in the trunk of your car. Be cautious and trust your instincts.

If someone asks whether this is a "safe neighborhood," direct them to police reports or neighbors, but don't give a false impression. You don't want to be held liable if you say it's safe and something happens.

Showing an occupied property

When your current tenants give notice, provide them with your rental-showing policy, which you provide in writing when the tenant first occupies the property (see Chapter 10). Let them know when they can expect the property to be shown and find out whether a babysitter, large dog, or other occupant will be on the premises when you plan to show it. Be sure to abide by your local, state, and federal laws when showing property; you may want to review those laws regularly to remain up to date.

Respect your current tenant's time and space, because he or she is still a paying tenant prior to vacating the property. Always call at least 24 hours in advance (at home or at work, depending on the tenant's wishes) and inform him or her about a showing. If you don't speak to your tenant live, leave messages both at home and at work. Provide the date and time of the showing, and assure your tenant that you will be there personally.

 Moneysaver

By marketing and showing your property during the last 30 days of your current tenant's occupancy, you minimize the length of time your property is vacant, with no income coming in. If you wait until the property is empty, you're already losing money.

Watch Out!

Before putting in your passkey and opening the door to enter, ring the door bell and knock loudly prior to entering the rental. Call out, "Property manager" or "Hello, is anyone here?" before entering.

The rental application

Continue to show the property until you have a complete and signed application, a signed rental agreement, and part of a holding deposit. Only then can you guarantee that your prospective tenant is renting the property. Your application, as well as what you expect from the applicant, should always be in writing.

Offer your application to anyone who views your available rental. Require one completed application for each adult (18 years or older) who plans to live in the property. This applies to any applicant, whether married, related in some other way, or unrelated.

Your application should be clean and legible, with written instructions and expectations. (See Appendix 4 for a sample application.) Be sure your application complies with local, state, and federal laws.

Keep your application simple as well. Include as much information as you need, but don't make it so long that it takes hours to complete. Shoot for an application that takes 20 minutes to complete, but be sure the application has all the details you need to make your decision. Don't ask any questions that might be used in a discriminatory manner, such as, "What nationality are you?" as opposed to, "Are you a U.S. citizen?"

As a rental-property owner, the period of your greatest exposure to discrimination claims occurs when you are showing prospects the property and processing the application. For this reason, offer each and every person who views your available property an application.

Bright Idea

Have copies of your applications at each showing, along with your procedures for renting. Make sure each document has your name and telephone number on it so that prospects know how to reach you and where to return the completed application.

When collecting the application and necessary paperwork, always collect an application processing fee and a hold deposit, if allowed in your locality. The processing fee covers your cost for running a credit report and going through your processing procedures. The processing fee is not returned if the applicant backs out or you find that she doesn't qualify. The holding deposit, a portion of the regular deposit fee and a guarantee that the property will be held for the potential tenant until she is qualified, tells you that the applicant is serious about renting the property.

Items you want on your application form

Complete a prospective tenant verification/screening form for each applicant (see Appendix 4). Using this form keeps you out of trouble with the federal government's fair housing laws, because it forces you to ask the same questions of all applicants.

Be sure to include the following items on your tenant application:

- The address of the rental property
- Requested move-in date
- How the potential tenant heard about your property
- Full legal name
- Current address
- Landlord's or agent's name and phone number
- Current rent/house payment
- Date of occupancy
- Reason for leaving

- Previous address
- Social Security number
- Driver's license number
- Phone numbers: home and cell
- General information
- Other occupants and their relationship to the applicant
- Animals, how many and the type
- Make, year, model, and color of the applicant's car, along with the license plate number
- Present occupation, position held, and phone number
- Address of the business
- Supervisor
- Hire date and length of employment
- If self-employed, the name of the company and detailed information about the work done
- Monthly gross income
- Previous employer, if employed less than two years
- Bank name address and telephone
- Account numbers for checking and/or savings
- Credit reference, including account information and address of the company
- Amount owed on credit cards
- Names of personal references, including the relationship and how long the two have known each other
- Emergency contact information for future reference

 Watch Out!

You must complete the same screening process on each applicant across the board. Consistency is the key to your screening activity. If you're consistent, you cannot be accused of discriminating against certain applicants.

Additional questions may include the following:

- Do you plan to run a business in the residence? If yes, what type: _____

- Do you own any liquid-filled furniture, such as a waterbed? If yes, describe: _____

- Do you have a housing voucher? If yes, name of issuing agency and amount: _____

- Have you ever filed a petition of bankruptcy?

- Have you ever been evicted from any tenancy or had an eviction notice served to you?

- Have you ever been convicted of a misdemeanor or felony other than traffic or parking violation?

- Are you a current illegal abuser or addict of a controlled substance?

- Have you ever been convicted of the illegal manufacture or distribution of a controlled substance?

If the answer to any of these questions is yes, ask for a detailed explanation.

Because you need to know which marketing source is working best for you, ask the question, "How did you hear about this property?" on your written rental application. Provide a checklist of choices for the applicant to inform you as to how she heard about your available rental.

The fine print on your application

End your application with the following type of statement: "Applicant represents that all the statements are true and correct and hereby authorizes verification of the following items including, but not limited to, the obtaining of a credit report and agrees to furnish additional credit references upon request."

You need to include a few important statements within your application, such as the following:

- "This application is for qualification purposes only and doesn't in any way guarantee the applicant that he/she will be offered this property."

- "Processing costs are non-refundable."

- "Applicant understands that the owner can and will accept more than one application on this rental property and that the owner has the sole discretion to select the best-qualified tenant."

- "Any application with missing information, including signature, will be returned."

Screen applications to find the best tenant

The following sections give you some tips on how to find great tenants — the ones you wish could stay forever.

Obtain a credit report

The first thing to do after reviewing the application is obtain a credit report. If the applicant doesn't pay her bills on time, you know they she not pay the rent on time.

You can obtain credit reports online or by telephoning the companies directly and paying a fee. The following three major credit bureaus provide credit reports:

- **Experian:** www.experian.com

- **Equifax:** www.equifax.com

- **Trans Union:** www.tuc.com

 Watch Out!

Be sure the application has a signature, thus allowing you to run a credit report. Ask for signatures on all applications for anyone 18 years or older. Take a moment to be certain the application is complete and that you have everything you need prior to the applicant's leaving the property or your office.

Most credit reports are simple to read and easy to interpret, especially if you opt to obtain a FICO score. A FICO score is the dominant method a lender uses to assess how deserving you are of their credit, such as a mortgage, car loan, or home-equity loan. Named after Fair Isaac Corporation, the firm that developed the scoring model used by the three major credit bureaus, the FICO score is calculated using a computer model that compares the information in your credit report to what is on the credit report of thousands of customers.

Take the time to understand the credit report you're using. If you are unsure about the information or don't understand what is presented, phone a customer service representative at the credit bureau(s). Never assume anything

> **66** Screen well. Don't deviate from your screening process, or you will pay for it in the long run. **99**
>
> —Mike G., real estate investor

FICO scores range from 300 to 900. Generally, the higher the score, the lower the credit risk, although there is no "good" or "bad" score range. If you decide to use the FICO score method, you need to decide what score is acceptable for your property, and then be consistent with each application. Keep in mind that scores fluctuate depending on credit activity, and using FICO scores is only one way to look at the applicant's credit.

Keep in mind that a credit report alone doesn't reflect the qualities necessary to be a good tenant or a good neighbor. Don't rely strictly on the credit report and forget the rest of the screening process. Undesirable tenants can have great credit, and vice versa. You need to do your homework to find the perfect, qualified applicant.

You may also want to consider using a professional screening company. Do an Internet search for tenant screening service, and several companies will appear for you to research and choose from.

Bright Idea

Continue to show the available rental while processing the application and awaiting the additional information you need. Also continue to market your property until a lease is signed and a deposit is holding the property. Don't assume a person's application will result in a rented property until you have that information in hand.

Contact the applicant's current and previous landlords and ask the questions you have on your verification/screening form (see Appendix 4). When you first contact the landlord, explain why you are calling, and be sure to listen carefully to his or her reaction. Ask the question, pause, and listen to the answer, recording the landlord's response.

Ask whether the landlord would consider renting to the applicant again and inquire about the amount of rent the tenant is (or was) paying. Also find out whether the tenant has pets, has ever been served a notice, and gave 30-days notice of intent to move. You may also ask whether the landlord is any relation to the applicant.

Verify current employment

Although you want to ask for copies of the two latest paycheck stubs for a potential tenant, it is still a good idea to contact the current employer directly. Ask with whom you are speaking, his or her title, and whether he or she is any relation to the applicant. Inquire as to how long the potential tenant has been with the employer and what her current position is. You also want to obtain verification of monthly income.

Also check to see whether the credit report reflects the applicant's current occupation, but keep in mind that this information can sometimes be inaccurate.

Verify personal references

Some people don't believe personal references are important, but I believe they are critical. When asking for the personal

Watch Out!

When it comes time to sign the lease, have the co-signer read the lease, but not sign it. Instead the co-signer signs a separate co-signer agreement. See Appendix 4 for an example. Always give a copy of the lease and the co-signer agreement to the co-signer.

reference, find out how long the reference has known the person and what the relationship is. And make the calls. Don't assume that, just because you have the names, your work is done. Call the references and chat for a while about the applicant.

Call co-signers

You may have a great applicant who has no credit or bad credit. In this case, you may elect to have a co-signer; for example, if you rent to a student, the parents may co-sign. Offer a separate application to the co-signer and follow the same screening procedures. It is advised that the co-signer live locally or at least in the same state.

Recognize the danger signs in tenant applications

Qualifying a tenant can sometimes seem effortless, but other times, it's extremely difficult. Some applications seem like pure gold, while others may frustrate you. So, when processing an application, remain cognizant of certain danger signs. Here are some signs to watch for.

- The applicant must be in the property today. He or she just found out they have to move. Huh?

- The applicant refuses to fill out part of the application, saying you don't need financial information because she has always owned her home and had her own rentals.

- The applicant's father or mother is separating from a spouse and will be living in the property with the applicant; only the mother or father has adequate income or good credit.

- When cross-referencing the application, you see that the employer or landlord is also a personal reference and/or has the same family name and phone number.

- The application can't remember where she lived or her landlord's name or telephone number, although she lived there within the last year.

> **66** When I review an application, I stick to the facts on paper. If there's a problem, I make exceptions to my procedures one at a time as long as I still feel secure within my own guidelines. **99**
>
> —Christine G., property manager

- She is 40 or more years old and has lived at home all her life with her parents.

- Her bad credit is someone else's fault (of course!).

- She has three family pets but is going to get rid of them. (Isn't it strange how those animals seem to find their way home?)

- Her employer answers the phone, "Hello." The company listed is a multi-million dollar company, and the last two paycheck stubs are handwritten.

- The address on the credit report doesn't match any of the addresses provided on the application or her driver's license.

- The application says she has no pets, but when you call the previous landlord, he or she says the dog has never been a problem.

- When you call her landlord and ask your reference questions, you hear long pauses or a hesitation before answering.

Watch Out!

Inquire about any discrepancies in the applicants' applications. Be sure to ask for an explanation if you find conflicting information on the application. Just remember: If something looks too good to be true, it probably is.

Of course, some of the preceding warning signs could be manageable, but you can't afford to ignore the signs. Check them out and cross-reference everything on that application. A suspicious nature now can save you valuable time and money in the future.

Section 8 — murky waters

The Section 8 program was established in 1974 by the U.S. Department of Housing and Urban Development (HUD) to assist very low income families, the elderly, and the disabled in renting descent, safe, and sanitary housing. This program allows low-income residents to receive monthly vouchers for rent payments from HUD and are most often administered through a local housing authority.

In most cases, when processing the applications of those who qualify for Section 8 assistance, you are allowed to use your own application and addenda. It is not against the federal law to turn a Section 8 applicant away simply because she wishes to pay rent using this assistance. This is because if you accept a Section 8 participant, you must agree to follow certain rules and procedures and execute an agreement stipulating that with HUD. The rules

Watch Out!

Screening Section 8 applicants can be difficult, because they may not be working (or at least not full time), may have little or no credit, and may not have a verifiable rental history. In any event, be sure to check your local, city, and county laws before refusing to accept Section 8 vouchers.

of the contract often limit the security deposit amount an owner or manager can require and sometimes also restricts an owner/manager's ability to evict.

Non-Section 8 Programs

Section 8 housing is a program overseen by HUD, but because of the many needs of local communities, other programs have started being run by states, counties, and cities. Some cities make funds available to owners who want to fix up their rental properties. These funds are available at a reduced interest rate, but usually are accompanied by a requirement that the owner provide one or more of the units at below market value (sometimes called BMR). A few communities also make funds available through redevelopment grants, although these are sometimes reserved for owners who actually live in the residences and make below a certain wage. In addition, some areas have been designated as high-risk and need rehabilitation or clean-up from drugs and crime.

In addition, state funds have been made available for rehabilitating or building units for disabled or people at risk of becoming homeless. Again, the funds are made available in return for providing housing at a reduced rate.

Most of the programs run at the state or local levels have specific guidelines for you to follow. Should you take advantage of one of these programs or look into purchasing an investment property that is under one of these programs, be sure to understand all the limitations. Normally, there are income and/or other requirements for potential tenants to meet before they are approved to apply. Sometimes, additional lease clauses are required. Most of these programs follow the HUD Section 8 guidelines for the number of occupants and the amount of rent that can be charged.

So, in most cases, you have a choice about whether to accept or decline a Section 8 applicant. At this time, however, a few states ban discrimination based on the source of rent payments received. If you live in one of those states, you are required to accept a Section 8 application for review.

Section 8 guidelines usually stipulate the maximum amount that an applicant can spend on rent, as determined by the local housing authority. If you review the application and find it acceptable after going through your screening process, you then meet with an agent from the housing authority for a move-in inspection prior to the tenant's moving in. After you go through the process and your property is approved, the first rent payment takes a few weeks. After the initial payment, however, the rent arrive in the first few days of each month like clockwork. Once a year, an inspector from the local housing authority conducts a walk-through prior to the end of the one-year lease term.

Turning down a potential tenant

Sometimes, you will find it necessary to turn down an applicant. Some of the reasons may include the following:

- **Incomplete application:** If you find that the rental application is missing some information, call the applicant and give details as to what is missing. If, after calling, you still don't receive the missing information, use a form letter checklist on which you mark the required information (see Appendix 4). If after several attempts, you still don't receive the information you need, you may want to turn down the applicant.

- **Lack of references:** If the application fails to list references and the tenant cannot provide you with names and phone numbers to call for verification, you have a good reason to turn down the application.

- **Conflicting information:** The information on the application should match up with what you are finding as you go through the screening process.

- **Insufficient income:** Generally, you want applicants to be paid three times the amount of the monthly rent by an employer. If this isn't the case, you may want to deny the application. If the applicant is self-employed, ask to see proof of income (such as a tax return) for the last two years.

- **Negative feedback:** Getting negative feedback from her current or previous landlord is a clear warning signal to you.

- **Poor credit and other negatives:** Poor credit combined with other negatives received while processing the application can be enough to deep-six the application.

- **Deposit troubles:** A tenant should be able to pay the move-in money with a cashier's check or money order, shortly before move in. He or she should also be willing to pay a slightly higher deposit if he or she has a pet or poor credit.

- **Undisclosed pet:** You find this out during your call to the current landlord. If you don't allow pets, deny the application of anyone with pets.

- **Not ready to move:** If the applicant cannot move in for 30 days or more and is not willing to pay rent any sooner, rent to someone who is ready to move in immediately.

- **Tax troubles:** If the applicant is self-employed and doesn't report annual income entirely on his or her tax return (and the stated income is not enough to qualify), you're dealing with a dishonest person.

If you decline the applicant, you are required to inform her in writing with a reason why she has not been accepted. This is a federal requirement — you must decline the applicant in writing. Refer to the Federal Fair Credit Reporting Act at www. ftc.gov/os/statutes/fcra.htm. You can also do an Internet search on "federal fair housing credit reporting"; you'll be directed to several public sites that explain the application of the law. In addition, if you decline the application, return the holding deposit to the applicant in a timely manner.

Keep all applications on file for three years. Keep one file with paperwork on the applicants who become your tenants. For those you reject, attach detailed notes to the applications, explaining why you did not rent to them or that they had decided not to rent your property. Always put the full date (including the year) on your notes. Keep all your paperwork organized and make good notes on your processing forms, paying close attention to details. (See Chapter 11 for more on managing paperwork.)

Just the facts

- Make sure your property will attract a quality tenant by providing a clean and quality property.

- Be friendly and professional when you answer the rental calls.

- Make sure you have everything in writing.

- Be sure to offer each person who views your property an application.

- Always collect an application and run a credit report for any occupant 18 years or older.

- Be sure to complete your screening process all the way through, sticking to your policy.

- Don't take the property off the market until you have qualified the applicant and they have signed the rental agreement.

Chapter 10

GET THE SCOOP ON...
Obtaining rental forms ▪ What to include in the rental agreement ▪ Differentiating between a lease and a month-to-month agreement ▪ Including legal clauses and disclosures ▪ Protecting yourself by using addendas ▪ Managing roommate agreements ▪ Knowing when you need a co-signer agreement ▪ Determining whether to allow pets ▪ Finding out about federal, state, and local laws and required forms and disclosures ▪ Collecting security deposits ▪ Calculating and collecting move-in funds ▪ Doing a move-in evaluation ▪ Understanding the Service Members Civil Relief Act

Working Out Details with Your Tenants

O ne of the most important things you can do is to have everything — or at least as much as possible — in writing. Most importantly, your rental agreement and any additional terms should be in writing. It must be signed in advance, prior to anyone moving in, by everyone on the lease to make it 100 percent complete.

The rental agreement spells out in writing just what is expected of both parties. With a strong rental agreement, you will have a much easier time dealing with your tenants. When you educate tenants on what is expected up front, you prevent misunderstandings that can later cause hard feelings — and even a trip to small claims court.

Most states do have a law that states you must have a written lease agreement for a period of one year or less. Even if your state doesn't, written leases are highly recommended because they define everyone's responsibilities and obligations. A written lease provides clarification and brings out discussion, if they don't agree with any of your terms, before move-in.

Finding a good lease

You should choose a lease that is professional and has been used for some time. Don't simply go to the Internet and download a free lease agreement and expect that it has everything you need to cover yourself and the tenant. I have been using the same lease agreement for over 22 years and it has been modified and updated over this time. (Of course when laws change, the lease has to be amended.) However, after you have an agreement that has been reviewed by your attorney, the changes are simple.

Ending a Lease Early

Leases are beneficial when dealing with problem tenants, nuisances, and all legal matters. The negative side of having a lease is that if you have a tenant who is just plain obnoxious or annoying, there is nothing you can do but wait until that lease expires. However, if your tenant is violating the lease or not paying the rent, send letters and document everything. In the same way, if other tenants are complaining, ask those tenants to send you something in writing for your files. (Let them know that any letter they send to you will be kept completely confidential.) You need to document everything to build a case for an eviction. Even with letters and documentation, however, it can still be difficult in some states to evict tenants.

Keep in mind that if you are using a professional lease from a forms company, part of what that company does is to keep up with current laws and continually make changes. I use a company called Professional Publishing (www.profpub.com), and I pay for the ability to use the forms online. You can either download a program with all of the forms included or order a single transaction packet for leases or residential sales. You can also complete forms online by using www.TrueFormsonline.com. The company allows you to fill in the blanks, has ongoing updates, and keeps up with the current requirements. You can also obtain rental forms from several other companies. Go to the Internet and search on "rental forms."

The difference between a lease and a rental agreement

There is a difference between a lease and a rental agreement. A rental agreement is the basic agreement between you and your new tenants. A rental agreement can have all the same agreements and obligations contained in a lease. However, a rental agreement doesn't bind the tenants to a specific time period the way a lease does. Rental agreements are generally month-to-month agreements as opposed to a lease, which is a fixed term. In some situations, it may be better to use a rental agreement and have the tenants on a month-to-month residency. This is especially true if you don't know your plans for the property in the short term.

Perhaps you are considering selling your home. In some instances, like if there is a chance a buyer may want to occupy the

 Watch Out!

If a tenant has a lease and not a month-to-month agreement, you cannot raise the rent or make changes to the terms during the lease term. You must wait until the lease term expires. If you plan to raise the rent or make changes, give notice prior to the lease expiration according to the laws in your area.

property, you would want to consider a month-to-month agreement. Similarly, if it is the holiday season and not a great time to rent in your area, you may keep them on a month-to-month until you are in a better market and can raise the rent. Sometimes, you would just have a six-month lease instead so it will expire in the summer rather than in the holiday season so if they move out it will be easier to rent again. This doesn't mean you raise the rent or want the tenants to move at the end of the lease. However, I would let the tenants know that after the six-month lease has expired, you will be planning to provide them an additional one-year lease extension if both parties agree.

> 66 I like to keep all my tenants on a month-to-month agreement so that they don't feel locked in. If they want a lease, though, I give them a lease. I try to be flexible. 99
>
> —Patty F., investor

After you approve your new tenants, it is important to have them come in right away to sign the rental agreement and pay a holding deposit or increase the deposit they may have given to you. This will eliminate the risk that they may change their mind. After the tenants sign the agreement, they are committed to move in or pay the rent until someone else is found. Sometimes there may be weeks between the time the applicants look at the property, you screen and approve them, and the time they move in. It is extremely important to follow through and have them sign, pay, and agree to the terms of your written rental agreement

 Moneysaver

By having your new tenant sign the rental agreement and pay a substantial amount of deposit in advance, you can save money and headaches if he changes his mind and decides not to move in after all. By having a signed agreement, you have a commitment.

and addenda within a few of days of their approval. There is nothing worse than taking the property off the market thinking the property is rented, allowing time to go by, and then receiving a phone call saying that your new future tenants have changed their minds and will not be taking the property. You have now lost valuable marketing time and you could lose income if you aren't able to rent the property to someone else right away.

Drawing up a written agreement

A key factor in renting property is your written agreement. What some refer to as a "standard" lease or rental agreement can be found in stationery stores, office supply stores, the real estate section of any bookstore, and sometimes even through the local Board of Realtors. You can search online for forms that have usually been tried and tested. Of course, you can always go to a lawyer and have one drawn up for you, but that will not be inexpensive. After you have looked at several agreements to find the one that fits your property and that you feel comfortable using, you will see after reviewing them they all mainly deal with the same issues and potential problems. Be clear and concise.

The important thing is that you have a lawyer review your legal agreements, especially if they aren't the standard agreements put together by a professional. There are different requirements in different states and sometimes even in the local areas.

Keep in mind that preprinted agreements contain the minimum information required by law. In almost every circumstance, you will need addenda (see the "Addenda" section later in this chapter).

 Bright Idea

Some professional property management companies provide a service in which you find the qualified applicant, but the management company processes the applicant, going through the complete screening and drawing up all the necessary paperwork so that you're in compliance with all current federal, state, and local laws and regulations for a one-time fee.

Bright Idea

Purchase a stamp that you can use to mark where you want the tenants to initial on the agreement. You can find these at a stationery store, and they are small and inexpensive. Stamp the places you expect them to initial and high-light where you want them to sign in advance.

Agreements should be in plain language as tenants can claim they did not understand what they were signing. In particular, people get confused when you refer to the "lessor," so at the beginning, use "landlord" and "tenant." In the same way, if there is an important point or item in your agreement you want to be sure the tenants read and understand, ask them to initial those items.

If your tenants don't speak the language the lease is written in, ask them to bring an interpreter with them when they come in to sign. Always have the interpreter provide his or her name and phone number in the event there are questions in the future.

Determine what names go on the lease agreement

It is important to have a policy as to what names go on the agreement and who is required to sign. I require all adult occupants (defined as over the age of 18 in most states) to sign the agreement. It is good to know who all will be in the property, including children. Require all adult occupants to fill out an application and to sign the agreement paperwork — even ones who don't have a job or any other income. Check with your attorney to make sure what is required in your state.

Make sure the agreement clearly states that each tenant is jointly responsible. Each signatory will be responsible for timely payment of rent and all other provisions of the entire agreement. It is a good idea to ask for the rent to be paid by one person instead of accepting different checks. This helps if you have to evict for non-payment of rent.

LandlordSource.com: Products for the Landlord

If you're going to own rental property, you need the right documents for your tenants to sign. I use a great source for tenant documents: LandlordSource.com. This company is a great place to find forms for leases, maintenance instructions, addendas, check-in sheets, and more. These forms come in Microsoft Word and RTF formats, which means you can customize them with any wordprocessing software. Visit the Web site at www.landlordsource.com.

If is important for legal purposes to use the tenants full legal names but you can ask the tenants how they wish to be addressed. Some tenants want correspondence addressed to their legal names and some shorten their name or have nicknames or maiden names. You may want to use professional titles for someone like a physician or dentist.

Make sure to spell all names correctly, checking and double checking for spelling errors, both to keep tenants happy and to make sure documents are legal. Don't cross out your mistakes on the written agreements, do it right the first time.

Choose a lease term

A residential agreement is either a month-to-month rental agreement or a term lease for a specific time period. The most common lease periods are six months and one year; however, it could be for any time period, including two years or beyond. I always recommend not going over one year if possible. I like to have control over the choice to renew a lease with my tenants based on my walk-through of the property, the interaction during the term of the lease, the market condition, and my long-term plans.

All agreements need to be clear and state the amount of the rent, security deposit, and the total move-in cost. Make sure to require a written notice to vacate when the lease is over or even if the tenants are on a month-to-month agreement.

The agreement should identify the property by the legal street address, the city, county, and state. The lease term, if not a month-to-month, should include the start date and end date and the terms for renewal. Always include the monthly rent and the total amount of rent to be collected during the lease term along with where and how the tenants can pay their rent.

Consider a co-signer agreement

Oftentimes, you would like to rent to someone who doesn't qualify based on your standards of qualification. Perhaps this person has never rented before and has no references, a new job, and/or bad credit due to a life situation, but everything else looks good. In this case, you can use a co-signer agreement in which someone who is local is willing to sign as a co-signer, knowing that he or she will be responsible if the tenant defaults in any way, including non-payment of rent or damage to your rental property that the security deposit will not cover.

The key is that you meet the co-signer and that he or she is local. However, this may not be possible if you have property around a university or military base, and you may still decide to proceed. You want to have the co-signer complete an application and provide you with the same information and items you required for the actual applicants. You need to run a credit report and go through the entire screening process as you did with the applicants. Make sure the co-signer has read the rental agreement, agrees to all the terms, and understands that he will

 Watch Out!

Don't let the co-signer sign the actual rental agreement and addenda. You should have the co-signer sign only the co-signer agreement. Make sure the co-signer completes the entire rental application and that you obtain a copy of the co-signer's photo I.D.

be held responsible during the entire term of the occupant's tenancy, including any extension to the rental agreement.

Spell out late charges and bounced-check charges

Spell out clearly when the rent is considered late and what the penalties will be. Let tenants know that the rent is due on the first and is late after midnight of the fifth day, if that is what you choose to do. Some people have the rent due on the first and late on the second. It is up to you as to how you want to set that up. Also, if tenants bounce a check, not only is there a bounced-check charge but also it makes their rent late. Usually, you have a late charge in your rental agreement along with a bounced-check charge. I always let tenants know when they complain about the amount of the late fee or the bounced check that it won't matter if they are never late. Just don't be late. Be reasonable, because if you have to go to court, you want the judge to view your lease as fair and your late charges and bounced-check charges as reasonable.

> 66 Late fees aren't cheap and they're there to motivate my tenants to pay on time. If they pay on time and don't bounce the check, the late fees don't really exist. 99
>
> —Patty F., investor

Always spell out exactly how many occupants you allow in the rental based on the rental applications you received. Be careful to refer to them as the number of people, not the number of adults and the number of children allowed in your rental property. This could be a viewed as a violation of fair housing or discrimination based on the number of children living in the property (see Chapter 7).

Explain what utilities are (or aren't) included

Spell out what is included in the rent. Sometimes, in a large building, the water and garbage is included in the rent. Sometimes in

Moneysaver

Give your tenants a list of all the important phone numbers. Especially the utility companies that they need to call to put in their name. You need to let your new tenants know they need to call immediately and put the utilities they are paying for in their name.

a single-family home, the pool service or gardener is included. Put those items in writing. Very rarely do I still see the cable for the television included, but some owners do include the water if they want to make sure the lawn is kept watered. Be sure tenants know when and whether snow removal will occur and who pays.

Most owners have the utilities put in their name between tenants for unit turnover and showings. So if the new tenants don't change the utilities over to their names, you may end up paying some of their bills. Then you have the hassle of calling them and writing a letter to get reimbursed. To avoid this, contact the utility companies as soon as your tenant has the keys and let them know to take the bills out of your name. I would go over all this with your tenants while they are signing and let them know you have taken the utilities out of your name and that it is very important they call right away. If you really want to be thorough and not have to worry about it, you could go ahead and make the calls right there while your tenant is sitting with you doing the signing. You can cancel the utilities and hand the phone to your tenant to change them into his or her name right there on the spot.

Provide for pets

Many rental properties don't allow pets and don't allow pets to be brought on the premises without the owner's consent. However, if you are in a really soft market or if you have a nice large yard and want to allow a dog or even a cat, you need to state what type of pet and how many you are allowing in your rental agreement. You need to have a separate agreement that describes the pet and gives the condition for having a pet. (See the pet addendum in Appendix 4).

Remember that birds, fish, miniature goats, and snakes are all considered pets. Decide ahead of time just which pets you are willing to allow. Check with your insurance company to see whether any kind of pets would violate your insurance. Some companies will not pay liability for certain breeds of aggressive dogs.

> 66 Some of my best tenants have had pets. I find that tenants with pets tend to stay longer than other tenants. Just be sure an increased security deposit covers any potential damage. 99
>
> —Will F., investor

Other rules and regulations to include

In the event that the rental property is a portion of a building containing more than one unit or has shared common areas, you need to have the tenant sign that he or she agrees to abide by all applicable rules, whether they are adopted before or after the date of the agreement. State that this may include rules with respect to noise, odors, disposal of refuse, animals, parking, and use of common areas. Let tenants know that they will be responsible for any penalties, including attorney fees that may be imposed by homeowner's association for violations by either the tenants or the tenants' guests. As a part of your rental agreement, have a copy of the association rules and regulations for your new tenants to read and sign. (See a sample in Appendix 4.)

Ordinances and statutes

You need to state in your agreement that tenants will comply with all statues, ordinances, and requirements of all municipal, state and federal authorities now in force, or which may later be in force, regarding the use of your rental property. Put in writing that the tenants will not use the premises for any unlawful purpose including, but not limited to, using, storing, or selling prohibited drugs. If the premises is located in a rent control area, the tenant should contact the rent and arbitration board for his or her legal rights.

Assignment and subletting

You should get in writing that the tenants agree not to assign the agreement or sublet any portion of the rental property without prior written consent of the owner.

This is important to spell out. You may even want to have your tenant initial this paragraph after reading it.

Maintenance, repairs, or alterations

A good agreement contains repair-notification requirements and provisions requiring the tenants to obtain permission before installing fixtures or making improvements. It usually states the tenants are required to maintain the rental in clean and sanitary condition and will immediately notify the owner of any damage to the rental or its contents or any inoperable equipment or appliances. Put in your lease that tenants will not paint, paper, or otherwise redecorate or make alterations to the property without the written consent of the owner. If there is a gardener, state what he or she will do, and what day the gardener will be on the premises.

Don't let tenants do repairs themselves. Sometimes, you will have tenants who are painters or workers in other trades who want to trade their work for a portion of the rent. The problem is that you constantly have to be checking to make sure the work is done correctly. So tell them that the rent stays the same, but that

 Watch Out!

It is a good idea to have in your agreement that the owner's insurance doesn't cover the tenant's personal property. You may encourage your tenant to look into obtaining renter's insurance. Tenants often think the owners insurance covers their belongings if anything should go wrong. Not true.

when some specific repairs come up, they should notify you, and you can work out something — in writing — for each situation.

Inventory

Be sure to list any equipment or personal property that you are leaving on the property. Have the tenants sign the inventory checklist concurrently with the lease. List the number of keys given to the tenants and what they go to, and how many garage door openers they are given as well.

Entry and inspection

Put in your agreement that the owner and the owner's agent have the right to enter the premises at the following times:

- In case of emergency

- To make necessary or agreed-upon repairs, decorations, alterations improvements; supply necessary or agreed services; show the premises to the prospective or actual purchasers, lenders, tenants, workers, or contractors

- When tenant has abandoned or surrendered the premises. A good rule to follow is to give at least 24 hours prior written notice to tenant, including the date and approximate time and purpose of entry. Be sure to follow the laws in your county and state for notice to enter. Some states don't have laws covering entry. Other states have very specific laws stating the type of entry and when it can be done.

Remember that the tenant has a right to quiet enjoyment, so refrain from making the agreement so broad that you are going to be entering every week or every month.

Always leave a business card or a note that you were in the property if you entered when no one was there. Be careful of entering if only a minor is present in the unit.

Indemnification

Include the following wording: "Owner will not be liable for any damage or injury to tenant or any other person, or to any property, occurring on the premises, or in common areas, unless such damage is the legal result of the negligence or willful misconduct of the owner or his or her agents or employees." This is commonly called a hold harmless clause. If the agreement you are using doesn't have one, your attorney probably already has a canned version you could use. Or, look at other agreements and pull one out of there.

Physical possession

Always address what happens if you can't deliver possession right on time; that is, stating that "if the owner is unable to deliver possession of the premises at the commencement date set forth above, the owner will not be liable for any damage caused, nor will this agreement be void or voidable, but the tenant will not be liable for any rent until possession is delivered. Tenant may terminate this agreement if possession is not delivered within _____ days of the commencement of the date stated above." Three to five days is a reasonable number to put in the blank for the number of days.

Default clause

You should have a default clause in there to address the "what if," such as the tenant failing to pay rent when rent is due or to perform any provision of the agreement after not less than three days written notice of such default given in the manner required by law. Use wording like, "The owners, at their option, may terminate all rights of the tenant, unless tenant, within said time, cures such default." Make sure you follow your laws regarding these types of notices — always.

Security deposit

Let the tenants know in the agreement that the deposit will be used to cover any damages they, their pets, or their guests may cause, as well as any late fees or unpaid charges. In some states, you can also deduct for cleaning, changing the locks, and preparing the unit for rent. Tenants should be informed that they cannot use their security deposit as last month's rent.

You need to check with your local ordinances regarding paying interest on the security deposit. Some areas require you to pay interest on a tenant's security deposit. You also need to check with laws in your state to find out how much time you have before you must return the deposit and an accounting of the money if you deducted any amounts. California requires owners to return the deposit within 21 days of the tenant's moving out, and to attach copies of all invoices for any charges. In Mississippi, you can charge for cleaning, damages, and unpaid charges and have 45 days to return the deposit. State laws vary a lot.

Holding over

This is an important clause that should be in your lease; it doesn't have to go in a rental agreement, though, that doesn't state a term. My lease states, "Any holding over after the expiration of this agreement, with the consent of the owner, will be a month-to-month tenancy at a monthly rent of $_____ payable in advance and otherwise subject to the term of this agreement, as applicable, until either party terminates the tenancy by giving the other party written notice by law." I put in the blank "to be determined." I have seen some landlords fill in an automatic increase so that everyone knows what the rent will be after the first year.

Time

Time is of the essence in any agreement, and words to this effect are usually on the agreement, letting all parties know that the clock is ticking. Time is important because if the signed lease agreement doesn't come back within a day or two, you could end up not renting the property for several weeks.

Attorney's fees

Some rental agreement address attorney's fees; the agreement I am currently using states that the prevailing party will be entitled to receive from the other party a reasonable attorney fee, expert witness fees, and the cost to be determined by the court or arbitrator. Some states will not allow you to require a tenant to pay for your attorney's fees.

Fair housing

Always address fair housing in your agreement. You read in Chapter 7 how important it is to know your state and federal fair-housing laws and to abide by them. The lease I use states that the "Owner and Tenant understand that the state and federal housing laws prohibit discrimination in the sale, rental, appraisal, financing or advertising of housing on the basis of race, color, religion, sex, sexual orientation, marital status, national origin, ancestry, familial status, source of income, age, mental or physical disability." Again, find out what your state requires for fair housing.

Megan's Law

In some states, you must have in writing that a person has the right to go to the local authorities to find out whether there is a registered sex offender within the area in which they will be renting. You as the landlord/owner don't need to do this, nor would I recommend you do this. In California what you put in your lease would read something like this:

Notice: The California Department of Justice, Sheriff's Departments, Police Departments serving jurisdictions of 200,000 or more and many other local law enforcement authorities maintain for public access a data base of the location of persons required to register pursuant to paragraph (1) of the subdivision (a) of Section 290.4 of the Penal Code. The database is updated on a quarterly basis and a source of information about the presence of the individuals in any neighborhood. The Department of Justice also maintains a Sex Offender Identification Line through which inquiries about individuals may be made. This is a 900 telephone service. Callers must have specific information about the individuals they are checking. Information regarding neighborhoods is not available through the '900' telephone service."

Disclosures required by law

The federal government, most states, and some local authorities have disclosures that must be made by law to all tenants. They could be on mold, water quality, munitions, farming, mediation, rent control, and so on. You can go to the Internet, enter a search for "residential rental disclosures." The larger municipalities will have a section on their Web sites for landlords or tenants that provide the information needed to be disclosed on the agreement.

Addenda

Some forms are required by the federal government, the state in which your rental property is located, and sometimes in your local area, too. Be sure to check with your attorney as to what must be included in order to be in compliance with all regulatory organizations. You want to be sure you are always in compliance. The following sections get you started.

Lead-based disclosure

Giving out the booklet and having tenants sign the lead-based paint disclosure form is a federal requirement. It is very important to know if the property was built before 1978. If it was, you must give your tenants the federal booklet and have all of them initial and sign the disclosure agreement. (See the form in Appendix 4.) Just having one person sign doesn't protect you. The EPA (Environmental Protection Agency) regulates this law and provides a booklet called *Protect Your Family From Lead in Your Home.* Just go to the EPA Web site, www.epa.gov to order or to download free.

Notice regarding hazardous material

This is something that you may consider as an addendum. This states that various materials utilized in the construction of improvements to the property may contain materials that have been or may in the future be determined to be toxic, hazardous, or undesirable.

Mold notification addendum

Mold has become a huge area of liability for owners. You need to be proactive in making sure you have no mold in your rental; professional companies specialize in testing for mold. It is a good idea to have an addendum addressing mold (see the sample in Appendix 4).

Roommate addendum

You should have a detailed roommate addendum that clearly spells out that the tenants are jointly liable. (See an addendum in Appendix 4.)

Pet addendum

This is important. If you are going to allow pets at your rental property you need to have a pet addendum. You need to have a description of the type of pet. Sometimes your tenant will have an older dog that is calm and you think will not cause any problems. Perhaps that pet goes to "doggy heaven" and they go out and get a puppy. This is a real problem, as puppies can do a great deal of damage not only in the house, but also in the yard.

If you are in a soft market, allowing pets may just get you a tenant faster, but be prepared with your written addendum. Make sure you get an additional deposit, but don't call it a pet deposit. Simply add it to the total of the security deposit. For example: If the deposit would normally be one and half times the rent without a pet, you may consider taking two times the rent for deposit if the applicants have a pet. During your reference check,

---

 Bright Idea

Take a photo of the pet at the time of move-in and put it in your files in case you go to the property and there is a different pet there. By taking the photo, you may deter the tenants from getting another animal without telling you.

ask the current and previous landlords whether the applicants had a pet, if there were any problems during their tenancy or any damage when they moved out, or that the owner may have noticed while at the property.

If the tenants have a dog, require your new tenants to obtain renter's insurance. The renter's insurance policy generally will cover if the dog bites someone or does damage. There are several types of dogs that you should not allow on your property. You can usually get a list of these aggressive breeds from your insurance company.

Some property owners require a copy of the registration papers and list of shots for the animal to ensure that it is healthy.

Authorization for automatic payment from bank account

This is a form (see Appendix 4) that allows the rent to be paid automatically on the due date specified. Tenants complete the form and enclose a copy of a voided check. Each month, the rent is automatically put into your rental property account. This makes it so much easier for both you and your tenants, which is why many people are collecting rent this way now. Of course, the tenants must have the funds in their account for this to work. (Usually, the bank will make two attempts, and then notify you that the funds were not available.) You would need to contact your tenants immediately and go through the process for non-payment if you do not receive the rent on time.

Keep in mind that it is extremely important to have everything in writing, especially for automatic payments.

 Watch Out!

If the tenant's rent check was returned in error, the bank will usually cover the fee and provide the owner or property manager with a letter of proof. If there is no proof, the tenant is responsible for the bounced-check fee and the late fee.

Other addenda

Consider additional addenda, including the following:

- Deductions to the security deposit, listed in detail

- Smoke detectors in working condition; it is the tenant's responsibility to maintain the smoke detectors and replace the batteries. Smoke detectors must be working at all times.

- Renter's insurance — require it!

- Utility changeover, making sure that tenants change all utilities over to their names effective the first date of their tenancy; I recommend that you provide your tenants with a list of all of the phone numbers for all of the utility companies and the garbage company if they are required to pay garbage.

- Vehicle care, including where to park and whether tenants can work on their cars in your parking lot or on your rental property grounds; state that all cars must be operable at all times and the registration must be current. I also don't allow my tenants to wash their cars at my rental properties.

- Notice to vacate and/or breaking a lease

- Move-out procedure

You can see samples in Appendix 4, but always have your attorney review any forms or additional terms and conditions prior to using them.

Meeting your tenant for the signing of all documents

After you have approved your tenant and called the tenants to agree on their move-in date, set a date to meet for reviewing and signing the agreement. This should happen relatively quickly (within a couple of days). Usually, when you take the applications and processing fee, you also take a holding deposit. This

Watch Out!

Never give the keys to the tenants to move in prior to collecting all signature from all tenants on the agreements and collecting all the move-in money in a cashier's check or money order. Remember: Keys equal control.

indicates that the applicants are serious and want the rental, providing everything checks out. After you call the applicants and tell them they have been approved, set up your date within just a day or two and cash their holding deposit. Let the applicants know that when they come in to sign, you will need an additional holding deposit that will go toward their security deposit and their total move-in costs. At the meeting, be prepared with all the copies necessary for them to sign. Have a copy for each person if you aren't in a business office or a place to make copies. Make sure you mark the original and have marked each place on each copy where you need an initial and or a signature. Be sure you retain the original.

The ideal situation is to have all parties there at one time to sign the documents so that you can explain everything once and ensure that everyone is on the same page. It rarely happens that way, but it is worth a try. Sometimes, you may have to e-mail or fax the agreement to someone, especially if he or she is relocating from a different area.

It is very important to makes sure you take the time to review each page of all of the documents, especially your rental agreement. By having the tenants initial in certain places after you have reviewed the items, it helps show that you went over the items and that the tenants read and they agreed at that time.

The security deposit

You need to know how and when to collect a security deposit, as this is an important step in managing your rental property. Don't accept partial security deposits when new tenants are moving in. When it is time for your tenants to move in and you

Watch Out!

The funds for the rent due at the time of move in and the full security deposit should always be collected in a cashier's check or money order. Don't accept a personal check when the tenants are paying the balance due prior to receiving the keys and moving in.

are ready to give them the keys, you should have the first month's rent and the security deposit in full. Set this standard at the beginning and stick to it.

Never accept a personal or a post-dated check, and keep to your policies even if the tenant has a long sob story. Don't make an exception, because it will only get you in trouble. And don't allow the tenants to make payments on their security deposit. It is very difficult to evict a tenant who did not pay the security deposit in full. Your security deposit is a guarantee. You should collect a large deposit according to your laws and what the market will bear. My standard is to collect one and half times the rent for the security deposit, *standard* being the key word. When there are any variances to our standards, I look to my state's legal limit for the security deposit I may collect for an unfurnished rental. Variances that would require two times the rent would be:

- Tenant has a pet.
- Tenant that has a waterbed.
- The application needs a co-signer.
- Tenant doesn't quite qualify financially but is very close.
- Tenant has no landlord references and has never rented before.
- The tenant has poor credit but everything else checks out perfectly.
- Tenant has a prior discharged bankruptcy but all else is in place.
- Tenant is new to this country.

Watch Out!

In most states, a non-refundable deposit is illegal. Instead, inform tenants during the lease signing that the security deposit belongs to them. Your goal is not to keep the money, but to receive the property back in the same condition in which they received it.

A security deposit should be referred to as just that. Don't complicate things by breaking it down by cleaning deposit, pet deposit, key deposit, and last month's rent. Keep it all in the same category and label all "security deposit." The legal limits of what you can collect refer to the entire security deposit, no matter what you call it.

Increasing the deposit

You may find yourself buying a property with tenants already in place. Chances are, they may have lived in the property for years and have a very small security deposit. You may also have a tenant living in your current rental property who has been there for quite some time. This may mean that you need to be sure to keep up with the security deposit amounts over the years.

As the new owner of the property, you may consider setting up a payment plan to collect the amount of the deposit you want, within your standards and the law. Be sure you also follow your signed rental agreement.

Paying interest on the security deposit

Several states and local ordinances have specifics, detailed requirements regarding what you can and must do with a security deposit after it is collected. Be sure you know the laws and requirements in advance so you know how to handle the deposit.

There is no law that says you can't pay interest on the security deposit. On the high-end rents, this can be a substantial amount of money. Offering to pay interest can be a positive way of beginning your landlord/tenant relationship. It may also give you the competitive edge over other landlords and available units.

Last month's rent

For many years, the standard for move-in was to collect the first and last month's rent, plus a few hundred dollars as a deposit. Over the years, owners and property managers have moved away from this. Tenants often gave notice and because they had the last month's rent paid, they left the place in horrible condition. The small amount of security deposit remaining would not come close to covering the cost of the damages and cleaning the property when the tenants moved out. Instead, make sure your rental agreement clearly states, "The security deposit is not to be used as last month's rent."

Special circumstances for the military

The Soldiers' and Sailors' Relief Act of 1940 gives certain rights to military personnel in regard to their lease commitments.

There is a lot more than just rental provisions in the Soldiers' and Sailors Relief Act of 1940, but here are some basics that apply to rentals:

- A tenant does have the right to terminate a lease upon receiving orders, but normally is required to give a 30-day notice.

- A tenant and/or his dependents cannot be evicted during this time, unless it can be proven that military service doesn't affect their ability to pay rent and if the rent doesn't exceed $1,200.

- Additionally, there must be a court order to evict a tenant, and a stay can be granted to the tenant. Normal eviction proceedings don't prevail under these circumstances.

- This doesn't excuse the tenants from paying rent, but can give them relief if there is difficulty paying.

- This act applies to both reservists and active military and can be applied after the lease is negotiated and after orders are received.

In addition, in 2003, President Bush signed into law the Service Members' Civil Relief Act, which amended the Soldiers' and Sailors' Civil Relief Act of 1940:

- The type of member covered was expanded to include some non-military citizens.

- The minimum amount of rent was increased to $2,400 per month.

- The landlord now cannot subject the property to distress during this time.

- Protection now extends to dependents as well.

- Penalties were increased for not adhering to the law.

The best course of action is to support your tenants and work with them to resolve the situation to everyone's satisfaction. Work out a payment plan, if needed, and cancel the lease only when necessary. Only by working together can landlords and tenants make the best of a difficult situation. You can obtain more information on the Soldiers' and Sailors' Relief Act of 1940 by searching the Web for "soldiers and sailors relief act." Doing a similar search, you can find information about the Service Members' Civil Relief Act.

Calculating and collecting move-in funds

After you decide on the move-in date, you need to calculate the total amount due prior to the tenant's receiving the keys and moving in. If the tenant is moving in on the first day of the month, it is quite simple: You collect the entire rent in advance for that month, plus the security deposit, less any holding deposit you may have collected in advance.

If the tenant moves in during the month, prorate the rent. Take the total rent, divide it by the number of days in the month to obtain the daily rental amount, and then multiply this by the number of days he or she will be in the property for that month.

Facts about Carbon Monoxide

Carbon monoxide (CO) poisoning is often called "the silent killer" because it is a colorless and odorless gas. It comes from incomplete burning of carbon-containing solid, liquid, and gaseous fuels.

Often, it cannot be detected until it is too late. Early symptoms can be nausea, headache, dizziness, and flulike symptoms. However, most of the time, it is not detected at all and death occurs without any noticeable warning. It is one of the leading causes of accidental death in the United States and is one that can be prevented.

Carbon monoxide can stem from faulty fireplaces, water heaters, gas appliances, space heaters, charcoal burning devices inside buildings, running car engines enclosed in a garage, and more.

One way to expose this deadly gas is to install a battery-operated carbon monoxide detector that meets the requirements of the current UL standard 2034 or the requirements of the IAS 6-96 standard and emits an alarm. These plug into an outlet and are relatively inexpensive. When the battery beeps, the occupant should *not* ignore it.

However, relying on a CO detector is not the solution. Instead, take preventive measures. Make sure the gas dryers and other gas appliances are well ventilated to the outside, check fireplaces for proper operation, advise residents against using charcoal devices or camping equipment inside a property or leaving their car running inside a garage, and notify the gas company if you or the tenants detect any indication of a gas smell.

Many states require carbon monoxide detectors for new construction, and there are a few municipalities in some states requiring them in rental properties. As CO-related accidental deaths occur in rental housing, more legislation is expected. Meanwhile, the bottom line is prevention.

For example: If the rent will be $1,000 per month and the tenant is moving in on the 10th of March, count the 10th and count the number of days in March the tenant is responsible for the rent. In this case, there are 22 days of rent, so take $1,000 divided by 31 days in the month of March, which is $32.26 per day. Multiply this by 22 days. The prorated rent would be $709.67. Charge the tenants the prorated rent and collect the balance of the security deposit in full, prior to giving them the keys to move in.

A word about prorating rent. Some states define all monthly charges to be prorated on a 30-day basis. In the example above, the daily rent is $33.33 and the prorated rent would be $733.33.

Keep in mind that whomever holds the keys has the control! As long as you have not given the new tenants the keys, you are still in complete control. Make sure you have all the move-in money in a cashier's check or money order, and that you have all the signatures you need before giving tenants keys or garage door openers to move in.

Creating a move-in evaluation

You and the tenants should fill out a written move-in evaluation prior to the tenants' moving in. I do the move-in evaluation as the very last thing prior to meeting the tenants and collecting the entire move-in monies in exchange for the keys. When doing the evaluation, make sure to write down all details of the condition of the property and be sure everything is in working order. Check the appliances, turn on all lights, make sure there are working light bulbs, make sure everything is clean, verify that all locks have been changed, be sure the property is ready to move in. Taking pictures is a good idea, and some people even take a video.

I then give the tenants a copy of the move-in condition report along with a blank one and tell them to send back any additions or changes they find within 30 days of their move-in. Otherwise, the move-in evaluation I gave them is the official record that I use at the time they move out.

Having a written move-in inspection completed in detail along with photos comes in handy if there are any problems when the tenants move out.

Tenant welcome handbook

I have a great handbook that I give to all my tenants as a part of their move-in package that reviews and goes over lots of my policies. It includes:

- Contact information
- Maintenance guidelines
- Care and use information
- Utilities and service directory
- Local police and fire department phone numbers

You can review the one I use in Appendix 4 and have something similar you give to your tenants upon the exchange of the keys.

Just the facts

- A rental agreement and addenda should always be in writing.
- Don't write your own lease; use a form.
- Purchase your rental agreements and lease through a provider that keeps up with the laws.
- Have your attorney review your lease and addenda.
- Any adult over 18 most be on the rental agreement and sign and agree to all terms as well.
- You can choose to have your tenants sign a lease or keep them month to month.
- Use a month-to-month agreement when you're unsure of you plans for the future of your rental property.
- Have the agreement signed within a couple of days of approving the application.

- Absolutely don't let the tenants move items in early unless they pay the deposit and rent and have signed everything.

- Understand the Service Members' Civil Relief Act and the Soldiers' and Sailors' Civil Relief Act before renting to someone who works for or is a member of any of the armed forces.

- Be fair when charging late fees and bounced-check charges, but be sure these fees are spelled out in your written rental agreement.

- If you allow a pet, include a pet addendum and ask for an extra amount for the security deposit.

- After the co-signer reads the entire rental agreement, he or she should sign only the co-signer agreement.

- Lead-based paint disclosure is always required on residential properties built prior to 1978.

- Always collect a cashier's check or money order for the final move-in money prior to providing the keys to the tenants.

- Always perform written move-in inspections and consider taking pictures.

Managing Tenants

GET THE SCOOP ON...

Setting up and organizing your files ▪ Keeping the books manually ▪ Record-keeping for multiple properties ▪ Using a computer to maintain your records ▪ Looking at the available accounting software ▪ Collecting rent without receiving a check ▪ Bill paying made simple ▪ Documenting, documenting, documenting ▪ Helpful reports to run ▪ Interviewing and hiring an accountant ▪ Meeting with your accountant

Keeping the Books — with or without Technology

Chapter 11

Accurate record-keeping is a very important part of your success in managing your investment property. There are many different ways one can do this, from the most old-fashioned to state of the art. While a simple system suits many people, taking advantage of technology can be extremely efficient and can save you a great deal of time.

In the bookkeeping process and for tax reasons, keep accurate records of your income and expenses. You have rent coming in, accountability for the security deposits, and perhaps garage income if you have the ability to rent garages separately. On the other hand, you have many expenses you must account for: mortgage payment, insurance, property taxes, and common utilities. You also have repairs and unexpected expenses to account for.

Most rental property owners begin small and own a single-family home, a townhome, or a condominium. At this level, the accounting and record-keeping is very simple and often done manually. As you expand and purchase more properties and manage more units, you will need to look into better systems. Without a doubt, as you grow, using a computer saves you time and money.

The Internal Revenue Service (IRS) requires that you keep all documentation for your income and expenses. Keep detailed records, so that if you are ever audited or challenged on your income and expenses, you will have documented proof. The last thing you want is to be audited and have no written record of your income and expenses as backup. Remember, the burden of proof for your tax records lies with you.

There really is a great deal of paperwork in owning rental property. Many property owners don't mind the people part of the business and marketing and showing the rentals, but few enjoy the accounting part. However, the financial side is a crucial element of owning rental property.

You can't be expected to be good at everything. Some people are best at showing the properties and being in contact with people, while a few are best at the record-keeping. If you have a partner or someone else to help, you may find you each can offer different skills.

Understand how much bookkeeping is required

Make an appointment with your accountant either before you purchase the property or soon after the transaction is complete, so that you are certain what is expected of you from a tax perspective and an accounting point of view. I meet with my accountant at least once during the year, plus right after I have found a property to purchase and have closed escrow. There

Bright Idea

Maintain separate files for each rental property you own. Keep track of the income and expenses separately, and keep the records very clear. If you hire a property management company, ask for everything to be separated per property.

never seems to be enough time to meet before you purchase the property or during escrow, but I do make it a point to meet with my accountant after closing so that I can know what is expected. I can then plan for what the IRS will want or need while reviewing how my finances look on paper.

Maintaining your files the old-fashioned way

There are many different ways to maintain your files for your rental properties. At first, you can use a simple system, but as you build your portfolio, you may want to change your system to a higher-tech one (see the following section). For now, I recommend that you visit your local office supply store and purchase a few simple things, such as the following:

- A file box that will hold a few files, your records and bills, along with all your paperwork pertaining to that property. You will have your original paperwork from the purchase along with any items you received at the close of escrow. If you own a small property with one to five units, purchase a portable box that you can bring with you so that at any given time you have the records you need while at the property. You may even consider purchasing a box that has the ability to lock. If you want to keep it really simple, you can begin with the accordion-type file with dividers. As you purchase additional property, however, move up to a file box and/or a filing cabinet. I recommend a fireproof box for tax documents, lease agreements, and move-in inspections.

- A box of letter-sized one-third-cut file folders. Get multiple colors; one for leases, one for expenses, one for the purchase documents, and so on. Use the same color organization for each property. This will help you find documents later.

- A set of labels to clearly label each file.

In the beginning, less is definitely more and keeping it simple is the right idea. Set up just a few files at first, and as you get going, add files. Begin with the following files and other office supplies:

- **Ownership papers file,** which is for all the paperwork associated with owning your property.

- **Mortgage and taxes,** a separate file for items like the mortgage, taxes, and homeowner's association (if you have one). Note that homeowner's associations come into the picture if you own a condominium, townhome, or planned unit development (PUD). In this case, you may need to refer to the CC&Rs (conditions, covenants, and restrictions) to be sure who needs to pay for a problem in the unit, so keep a copy here.

- **Property reports file,** such as your contractor's inspection report, termite report, soil report, city and/or county report.

- **Insurance file,** where you keep your insurance papers, along with paid invoices.

- **Bank statements file,** so that when your bank statements arrive, you can easily reconcile your checking account, and then file it away.

- **Duplicate deposit slips and a stamp,** so that you can keep track of the details for each deposit. When you open your bank account, order a "For deposit only" stamp to make depositing your rent checks easier. Even if you only have one or two units, why not make each month's deposit easier?

Watch Out!

If you own more than one rental property, be sure to keep your property files separated, particularly any income and expenses. When it comes time to sell the building, you'll be grateful that you've kept separate tax records for each property. Also be sure to keep your personal income and expenses separated as well.

- **Credit card receipts file,** in which you place any receipts you charged on a card or on a line of credit. Then, when the statement arrives, you can easily attach the receipts to the paid invoice and double-check for any errors that may occur.

- **To-be-paid file,** so you know all of the outstanding bills are located.

- **Paid-bills file,** with paid bills; be sure to write or stamp "paid" on each and include the date (and perhaps even the check number).

- **Large repairs/capital expenses,** including a new roof, new driveway, new decks. These are expenses that probably have to be depreciated (ask your accountant for additional information).

- **A file for each apartment,** in which you file the lease, application, screening information, move-in documents, telephone numbers, rent-increase letters, notices served and the proof of service, and any correspondence to and from you and your tenants.

- **General file,** if you own a larger building (more than five units); keep a file with letters, house rules, and anything you do or send to all tenants.

- **Key tags,** but not with the address attached to the key. Instead, the key tag could be color coded, or you can create your own code. The important thing is that you will have a key to enter the property in the event of an emergency.

- **Travel expense record book,** in order to track your mileage and other travel expenses associated with the purchase and management of your rental property.

Remember to keep your personal income and expenses completely separate. When you open a separate checking account, order a different style or color from your personal checks. I recommend that you order the larger-style checks and include the name of the business, the name of the building, or at minimum the property address. If you are using a computer to print your checks, these larger checks are very convenient. If you are doing things manually, order checks in duplicate so that when you are away from your home office and write a check, you will remember to update your records. Always keep those documents and your receipts with your check records.

If you plan to charge expenses for your property, obtain a separate credit card that you dedicate to the building. If you prefer not to add an additional credit card, keep a separate envelope with your credit card purchases. Write the property address and what you purchased on your copy of the charge if it is not already evident. Keep these receipts in the envelope that is clearly marked for that property. Each month, when your credit card invoices arrive, match the receipts with that statement.

If you own several properties, it is important to keep records separate, so that you know where each building stands with negative or positive cash flow. Also when it comes time to sell, you want to have your records in detailed order for a smooth and easier transaction.

You can check with your accountant to see whether he or she has forms that you can use or can recommend for a manual system. Also try your local office supply store and check out all the different forms it offers.

Moneysaver

Set up everything as easily as possible, whether you are keeping records manually or using a computer. Spending cash? Be sure to keep track of it. You may file the receipts in an envelope and once a month reimburse yourself. You can lose track of cash easily and forget this.

Computerized accounting systems

In this day and age, many people own computers. Computers make your life so much easier in property management, and the good news is you can still keep even a computerized system fairly simple. As you acquire more properties, you will find that a computerized accounting system is the way to go.

If you only own one property and want to keep your book-keeping simple, check with your bank to see whether it offers an easy, online accounting system or shop online for a simplified computerized system that is similar to the manual system; you enter data just like you write a check manually. Contact Peachtree Business Products located in Atlanta, Georgia, either by phone at (877) 495-9904 or at www.peachtree.com. Peachtree has a simple accounting system that is based on the pegboard system that accountants recommend to clients. When used alone, it offers a simple cash-basis system for smaller clients whose needs are simple and whose knowledge of accounting and of computers is not extensive. You can also contact SAFEGUARD Business Systems at 1-800-909-3611 or www.gosafeguard.com. There are many software packages on the market. You may decide to use Quick Books or Quicken, but I strongly recommend that you first research software that is specifically for property management, particularly if you own several properties or more than one unit.

More complex rental management software accounting packages include a general ledger, accounts receivable, accounts payable, check writing, budgeting, and the ability to run financial reports at any time and for any time period. In addition, you will find there are many details in the software that will help you maintain your records for both your tenants and your properties. There is usually a way to track a lease expiration, maintenance requests, reminder notes, utility billing, and all contact information for your tenants and your contractors. The more you want the software to do, the more it is going to cost, but consider the value of your time. Spending more up front may save you hours of manual recording throughout the year.

> ❝ When evaluating and shopping for different software packages, compare a few and ask for references from some of the users. Test the trial version as well. ❞
>
> —Julie D., bookkeeper

The reports you can generate can help you track your monthly maintenance costs, your monthly mortgage expenses, your insurance costs, utility costs, and so on. At the end of the year, it is easy to run a year-end financial statement that reflects all income and expenses for each property, which is very helpful for your year-end appointment with your accountant.

If you want to determine your vacancy factor, return on investment, or maintenance requests, you will be spending more for your system. This level of detail is not necessary at first, but it will become more important as the number of your investment properties grow. For managing these complex functions, consider contacting the following companies:

Logicbuilt, Inc.
Phone: 800-GO-LOGIC
E-mail: sales@logicbuilt.com
Web site: www.LogicBuilt.com

London Computer Systems, Inc.
Phone: 800-669-0871, 513-583-1482
E-mail: sales@rentmanager.com
Web site: www.rentmanager.com

PROMAS Landlord Software Center
Phone: 888-591-5179
E-mail: sales@promas.com
Web site: www.promas.com
Note: This is the software I am using and I am very happy!

Property Automation Software Corporation
Phone: 800-964-2792
E-mail: tpsales@propertyautomation.com
Web site: www.propertyautomation.com

Winning Edge Software, Inc.
Phone: 888-344-3343, 509-852-8000
E-mail: sales@pmedge.com
Web site: www.PMEdge.com

Yardi Systems
Phone: 805-699-2040
E-mail: sales@yardi.com
Web site: www.yardi.com

You now have six companies to research and determine which may work for your needs. The amount of properties you own and your technology skills will be the deciding factor. Don't forget to call some of the users who may own rental property similar to the type you are thinking of purchasing.

Use demonstration disks or a trial version to see how you like the way you can navigate through the system. Check out the accounting package, the reports you can run, and how easy and simple it is to use. Again, work with your accountant, as you want the reports to be easy for him to use.

 Bright Idea

If you're using a professional management company, review your reports on a monthly basis. This gives you a good understanding and some control of your investment. Ask questions! Make sure you understand what you are looking at. Don't wait until the end of the year to review your reports.

Your computerized system can also help you control your expenses and know the maintenance history at any given time, as long as you are inputting the information.

Utilizing automatic funds transfers

Technology can be very effective and assist you in managing rental property efficiently. More and more, you may see rent collection without ever seeing a rent check. The same goes for the bills you pay, which you can also do without ever writing a check.

Collecting rent without receiving cash or a check

The latest way of collecting rent without ever receiving a check is electronic funds transfer (EFT), also referred to ACH (automated clearing house). This allows the funds to be transferred from your tenants' checking or savings account to your investment account. Your tenant can schedule the rent transfer on a specific day and before the due date. Keep in mind this process may take one to two business days to complete.

You must be certain that the details of the electronic transfer are in the rental agreement or addendum. You must have a form prepared that has been approved or provided by your bank (see Appendix 4 for a sample) and you must have a voided check from your tenants' account.

You will find that some tenants would like to use online payments. There are a few companies that will accept payment directly over the Internet and transfer that money ʹo your account. Search the Internet for "pay rent online." The payment could be by eCheck, credit card, or ACH. Of course there is a cost, but the benefit is that it takes you completely out of the loop.

Paying your bills automatically

Not only can you collect rent without a rent check, you can pay almost all of your bills the same way. The best part is that when

Watch Out!

If you are going to use the automatic systems, be sure to record the charge each month to obtain an accurate balance. It is very important that you double-check the amount of the automatic payment.

you set up your bills to be automatically deducted from your rental property account, in many cases, you can choose what date you want the amount to be debited from your account. This enables you to receive your rents first. For example: If your rent checks arrive on the 1st and are late by the 5th and your mortgage is due on the 1st and late on the 16th, you can have your mortgage paid automatically on the 15th and you will never be late. Paying your bills online or as an automatic debit saves you not only time in having to write all those checks, but it saves you the cost of postage as well. It allows you to go on a trip without being concerned that you are going to miss those payments.

Hiring an accountant

A very important part of owning property is the accounting part of the equation. Accounting is the procedure that lets you know how things are running, and you need to know whether your investment is running in positive or negative numbers. A good accountant will be able to tell you not only that but also what you need to do to increase your profits. If there are losses, your accountant will make sure to point them out. The information he or she provides you allows you to refocus your direction, if need be. This is why I recommend two appointments: one during the year, and one early on in the year when you begin ownership. Later on, you and your accountant will adjust the appointments according to need.

You need to be sure to hire someone who can handle the accounting for you professionally. Your accountant will perform an audit of your records to make sure you are allocating things correctly.

Remember: Accountants aren't the same as bookkeepers, although most people think they are one in the same. A bookkeeper and accountant handle totally different things. You or your property management company usually handles the bookkeeping (rent collection, bill-paying, and basic paperwork), whereas an accountant merely keeps track of what you have done, making sure you are on the right track for allocating expenses, filing proper tax forms with state and federal governments on time, depreciating assets appropriately, and paying applicable taxes and disbursements to your real estate holdings or your investors.

You need to know what to look for when hiring an accountant.

- **Find an accountant who specializes in real estate accounting and in handling real estate transactions.** Ask for a reference from someone you know who owns property.

- **Make sure the person is familiar with real estate law** to some degree, as he or she needs to have a well-rounded picture.

- **Be sure your accountant has the same philosophy you do on taxes and investments.** People tend to be either more conservative or more aggressive with tax write-offs and determining their expected return on investment (ROI).

- **Make sure you know the fee schedule.** Does the accountant charge hourly, or is the cost based on the appointment and the tax returns? Be clear what you are paying for before deciding to hire someone.

- **You can ask the accountant for a few client references.** Any professional will be willing to provide you with a list of references. You need to take the time to call to make sure this is the person you are going to hire.

- **Trust your instincts as well.** You know how you feel about meeting someone new and after talking to him or her — you either feel confident or not.

Moneysaver

Being prepared can save you money. By taking the time at least once or twice during the year to be prepared and to know where you stand financially, you save money by paying less in taxes or knowing what you need to do to pay less in taxes before the year is over.

A good accountant should look out for your best interest. You want someone who is savvy and understands investing and the laws that accompany owning rental property.

Reports to run

When you are using a computer, you probably have the option to run different reports for your accountant to review. You and your accountant will decide which reports and how many, depending on your portfolio. Obviously, managing one unit as opposed to several will make a difference as to how often you run the reports and meet with your accountant.

For example, let's say you own a six-unit building or larger. You would run your rent report on the rental due date, reviewing who has paid and who is still outstanding. The day that you make a deposit or pay bills, it is a good idea to know your account balance, so you would run a report showing your ending account balance at the end of the day. (If you have several properties, you would run the report per property.) It is always a good idea to know where your account stands at all times.

It is best to run monthly detailed reports, as well as year-end financial statement for your accountant and for your permanent records.

- Run a ledger balance whenever you have any financial activity.
- Run a detailed report of all your checking account transactions.

- At the end of the month and after you reconcile your checking account with your bank statement, run a month-end report.

- If you own multiple properties and you maintain one checking account, run a profit and loss statement for each property. This is accurate at any given time if you run all your checks and deposits through a computerized accounting system.

- If you are going in to see your accountant, I recommend doing a cash flow report from the start of that year (or from the acquisition of the property) until the date you are meeting. As an alternative, you could end it at the end of the previous month or quarter end. Run a profit and loss statement for the end date to get the exact income and expenses. Run a balance sheet for that date to get the current cash balance. My accountant likes to see my detailed check register as well. But ask your accountant; he or she may provide a checklist for you.

- You can run a tenant detail statement at any time so that you have details on your tenants such as last rent increase and when the lease expires. This may help for future projections.

You may set up an arrangement with your tax accountant to send either monthly or even quarterly statements for review. I would set this up in advance and determine the cost prior to just doing it. This may be required if you have financing through individual investors, as they want to see that you are handling the investment well.

Meeting with your accountant

When it is time to meet your accountant, be prepared and arrive with your records organized. (If you are paying the accountant an hourly rate, you will save money as well as time.) Some accountants will give you a list of what you should plan to bring in

Backing Up Your System

A very important part of using a computer is the daily working backup. Make sure you take the time each day to back up all data, because you are entering and storing much of your pertinent property information in your computer — and we all know that anything can happen. You need to make sure you have a good backup system and it works! Keep the backup in a safe place — preferably at a different location than your computer.

advance. A good accountant is someone you hear from on a regular basis, not just at the end of the year. If you have an organized filing system along with a property management software program, you will avoid having to scramble around in search of your receipts and paperwork a few days before your appointment. Keep your records accurate and organized all year round. Put receipts and records in their place and in the long run, you will be much happier and your systems will run much smoother.

Just the facts

- Organization will save you time and money.
- Keep your personal income and expenses separate.
- Records from different properties should be kept separate.
- If you are going to keep records manually, there are systems available that will help you keep track of your income and expenses.
- As you grow and add more rental property to your portfolio, adding a computer is a wise choice.
- Shop around for the software package that will work for your needs and call on client references.
- You can collect rent without ever receiving a check.

- Paying your bills automatically can be easy and will save you a great deal of time and postage expense.

- Hiring a great accountant is an important part of owning rental property.

- Meet with your accountant early, not only at the end of each year.

- Be prepared when it is time to meet with your accountant.

- Remember to back up your data.

GET THE SCOOP ON...
Visiting your property after the tenants
are in ▪ Retaining your best tenants as long as
you can ▪ Handling maintenance and complaints
promptly ▪ Doing a contractor's annual walk-
through ▪ Extending the lease ▪ Deciding
whether to raise the rent

Keeping Tenants Long Term

The relationship with your tenants begins the day you first speak to them on the telephone and continues as you meet at the property for the first time. It is important to communicate through the entire process while screening the application and when it is time to sign the lease. The retention of your tenants begins before they ever move in and continues during the life of the tenancy. It is completed after the tenants move out, you have done your exit interview with them, and all monies are accounted for and returned properly.

Make a good first impression

You need to start on the right foot and continue as your landlord/tenant relationship builds into a long-term tenancy. First impressions are one thing, but you as the owner/landlord must continue to keep things running smoothly while maintaining your property and keeping the tenants happy. Don't get me wrong; I am not stating you must do everything your tenants

223

Bright Idea

If you're going to have another tenant on a smaller property assist you in showing and renting the property, be sure to have a flyer with all the details, including the total move-in costs, date the place will be available, and what's expected in applying for the place.

ask, but you want to respond to your tenants promptly and do what is in the best interest of your investment while trying to maintain a good rapport with your tenants. That doesn't mean you must jump with every request made by a tenant or with every complaint that may come in. You need to maintain a good balance and know when you are using good judgment about your tenant's requests.

Keeping tenants happy while running a profitable business is not an easy combination, but over time, you can get quite good at it. Balance what works in your budget and which requests from your tenants are feasible and reasonable.

Keeping your tenants happy works with the long-term plans for your investment. A happy tenant tends to stay longer and keep better care of your investment. If you happen to own a property with more than one unit, you may just find that the happy tenant helps you find another good tenant to live in the unit next door or close by. This can be the ideal situation with a win/win result. In a smaller property such as a duplex or triplex, having the long-term tenant show the unit and be involved in the process can work out to your benefit. It keeps your current tenants happy and feeling like they are involved in the process of deciding who their neighbors may be at the same time that they assist you by showing the property and helping out with the process along the way. If your tenant is a complainer or a whiner, of course, this may not work. Also, you want to make sure that the tenant is familiar with the fair housing laws so you aren't exposed to discrimination suits.

Happy tenants means lower turnover

Turnovers cost you money. Each time a tenant moves, you must go through a long and timely process. What you want ideally is a long-term tenant who is happy, takes care of your property, and communicates when something is wrong or needs to be repaired. Of course, he or she must pay the rent on time. Yes, this is the ultimate goal, the one thing we all want in owning rental property and in our landlord/tenant relationships. But, like anything else, this is not easy and takes work. You must know what to do as the landlord, so that you keep your tenants happy, keep them paying on time, and continue the long-term relationship.

The key to your success as a landlord is having an occupied unit. You need to have a tenant in order to collect the rent, which pays the bills, which keeps things running. And many people have found that by keeping a rent bit under the current market rate, you lower your turnover rate and lower your costs.

Retention does start early on in the process. You need to treat your tenants properly and respond quickly, just as you would want a landlord to respond if you were renting property.

Your tenant is your customer. Remember that in property management, owning property is a business.

What makes tenants happy?

Keeping your tenants happy saves you money in the long run. Happy tenants tend to stay in your rental property longer and don't complain much. Here are some attributes about rental properties that tend to keep tenants happy over the long haul:

- **A place that is a bit under the market prices; a good deal:** Everyone looks for a place that is a good deal and has value. By marketing your property a bit under the going rate you will attract more choices and get a quality tenant. But be careful not to go too far under the market or the opposite will occur. Everyone will think, "What's wrong with the place?"

- **A place with not-too-high rent increases:** Don't be unreasonable and raise the tenant rents too high and too often. If the market is a strong market, explain in a letter what the rental market is for their apartment and let them know you value them as great tenants and you are keeping the property under the market for that reason.

- **A place tenants are proud to live:** Everyone wants to live where they can invite their friends and family over and be proud of where they live. By providing a rental property that is clean and well maintained, you are providing a property that your tenants will be proud to show off.

- **A place that they can move into that's clean:** Again, having a place your tenants can bring people over to and be proud of is important. They want to be able to put their belongings in a clean environment. Be sure old odors are gone and nothing of the past tenants' is left over.

- **A place with well-kept common areas and clean grounds:** For example: clean laundry room, clean pool, well maintained landscape, and well lit parking lot.

- **A place that's safe and well lit:** Make sure the place is well lit and all lights around the outside and inside are in working order. Make sure the tenants feel safe and comfortable in their new home. Let them know that you feel safety is important. Be sure all the smoke detectors are working and that they know how to turn off the water if needed.

- **A place where everything's in working order:** Make sure before your tenants move in that all the appliances work, and the furnace and air conditioning are in working order. In addition, be sure all the windows open and shut that are supposed to and that they all lock. Make sure that all lights are working and everything is in working order prior to giving them the keys to move in.

- **A place that respects tenants' privacy:** This should be easy but for many landlords it is not. Don't go over to the property unannounced (inside or outside); instead, let your tenants know you are coming over prior to showing up. Even if it is inconvenient for you and your schedule, you need to wait and let your tenants know when you are coming and for what reason. This is their home, too, while they pay the rent and live there. Be sure to abide by any local or state law regarding notification to enter.

■ **A place that encourages good neighbors:** Having good neighbors is so important. Don't lose a good tenant due to a bad tenant making noise and causing problems. Take care of the problem, even if that means evicting or asking the problem tenants to leave. Be sure to let the good tenants know you are attempting to solve the problem. You may not be able to explain exactly what you are doing, however, because of privacy issues.

■ **A place where the rental manager truly cares about the property:** From the very beginning, tenants can tell whether they are renting from someone who cares about the property, based on the condition and the reaction to any request before the tenants move in.

■ **A place where the manager responds to reasonable maintenance requests:** Tenants want to know that when they have a problem, it will be addressed and taken care of in a reasonable time.

■ **A place that keeps tenants informed:** No one likes surprises, so keep your tenants informed. If the plumber is really busy and cannot come out for a couple of days, let the tenants know that. If you cannot make a scheduled appointment, show common courtesy by letting tenants know.

■ **A place with fair rules that are monitored and communicated to all tenants:** These are rules the tenants would agree to and sign prior to moving in. It is important that all tenants, especially in a multiple-unit building, follow the same rules and that you as the owner see that they are enforced. There is nothing worse than stating a rule that there is nothing allowed in the carports, and then allowing a few tenants keep a few items in the carports. Other tenants see that, and it will have a domino effect, where if one does it, others will follow.

Being fair and reasonable will keep tenants a whole lot longer. You don't have to make long-lasting friends to have a long-lasting tenant.

Dealing promptly with maintenance issues

When you have rental property, you have to know that there will be maintenance issues that come up. You need to respond to a request for repair or replacement right away. Communication is the key. If your tenants call you and tell you of a problem, you need to at minimum acknowledge the letter or phone call, even if you don't speak to them live when they report the problem.

A tenant should not have to complain several times about the same maintenance issue before getting a response from you or your property manager. By responding and solving the problem quickly, you will keep your tenants happy. Some problems may take a while to fix, however, especially if you have to get two bids for the job. Other times, you may decide not to fix it the way the tenant wants, like getting whole new carpet because a stain is in a non-conspicuous area. Just explain the process and ask for their assistance in getting the matter resolved quickly.

If you have a Web site, having a section for your tenants to send in maintenance problems via the Internet is a great idea.

 Moneysaver

Whenever possible, train your tenants from the very beginning to put all maintenance requests in writing, excluding any emergencies, of course. This will give you a detailed written record. This helps you respond correctly and promptly and assures you are sending the right person out to do the job.

This is something to strive for, and to be honest, Web sites with this feature are quite simple to set up. Even if you don't have a Web site, using e-mail is a great way to get requests, too. That way, you can answer them, even if you get in at midnight. You can also be on vacation and still respond.

Setting up relationships with contractors

If you aren't able to repair things yourself, you need to have a list of contractors whom you can count on to take care of repair items promptly and correctly. They need to be courteous to your tenants. When a call or report of a problem comes in, if I have a rapport with the contractor, I ask the contractor to contact the tenant directly to make arrangements to get into the apartment. That would be my first choice, to have the contractor set up the date and time with the tenants directly and avoid giving the contractor a key to the property. In fact, never give a key to the contractor unless the tenant has given permission.

You need to instruct the contractor to take care of the problem or to call you if it is something major. As you develop a working relationship with your contractors, you'll get a feel for how to work with them.

I usually give the contractor the tenant's number and the tenant the contractor's number to get in touch, basically putting it on both shoulders to take responsibility to get the job done. When the job is completed, be sure to call the tenants to see whether everything is okay and working again. Whenever possible, double-check for satisfaction with your tenants before paying the bill. By making this call or sending an e-mail to follow up with your tenants, you have made them feel like they are important and you care about them and your rental property.

Use the old golden rule: "Treat others as you would like to be treated." Think of how you would like to be treated if you were the tenants with a repair problem. By following up, you have gone above and beyond most landlords. This is a good thing; one that will help you keep your tenants long term.

Keep up with maintenance and replacement

Even if your rental property has had the same tenants for a number of years, you have to keep up with the routine maintenance and replacement. Often, tenants who stay in a property get neglected when the landlord doesn't keep up with the regular maintenance. Carpets wear out, especially the less-expensive carpet found in many rentals. Appliances may break. Often, the attitude of the landlord is to wait until the tenants move out to replace anything. But if you maintain the property while your current tenants are living there, you may just keep them longer and they would certainly be happier.

> 66 If you have a schedule to check routine maintenance while viewing your property annually you not only keep the property up but you also keep the tenants happy. Turnover only costs you money. 99
>
> —Jack D., investor

Sometimes, by doing the smaller things, you can keep your tenants happy. These can include new linoleum, new window coverings, some fresh paint, or some new landscaping.

Some landlords reward tenants with a microwave, a room repainted the color of their choice, or a gift certificate when the tenants have been there for a certain number of years. Of course, let tenants know this up front so they will stay longer in order to get the reward.

Don't get to the point of letting your building run down and think you can appease the tenants by lowering the rent. Don't let your rental property get to the point of looking shabby. Take care of things. Good tenants don't appreciate lower rent and would rather have a well-cared-for home. Nobody feels good paying rent for a dump. Run-down properties don't attract quality tenants.

Respecting your tenants' privacy

Landlords often show up and don't feel they have to inform their tenants. This is a big complaint I hear from tenants. I suggest you

Watch Out!

If a tenant tells you they don't want you entering the property after you provided proper notice, try to work out a new time to enter. Don't enter if a tenant absolutely tells you not to. Then give written notice, but have someone go with you when entering the property.

always let the tenants know in advance that you plan to be on the property, whether you're inside or out. In most states, you must inform the tenants in advance and even in writing prior to entering the premises. Your time of entry should be reasonable and during normal business hours. Never enter if only a minor child is present. Always leave a note if no one is there, so that the tenants know you came in. Remember to lock the doors and leave everything the way you found it.

Be friendly, but not too friendly

Keep in mind that managing your rental property is a business, so you need to run it like a business. This means you can be friendly, but not too friendly with your tenants. Remember they aren't your friends. Friendly tenants can quickly become pests! They feel because you are their friend, they can call you on Sunday or late at night with a minor problem that can clearly wait until the next business day or be communicated through e-mail. For this reason, many landlords don't provide their home address or private telephone numbers. When they are enjoying leisure time, they will not be bothered by a tenant calling to tell them the next door neighbor's stereo is too loud or that their bathroom sink is dripping. What can you possibly do at

> 66 I tried to never create any hostile feelings toward me with my tenants. I always remembered that they were the ones who allowed me to have my rental investment. 99
>
> —Charlie F., retired real estate broker and investor

10:00 p.m.? Exactly my point. Keep things on a friendly business level only. If the owner has created any hostile feelings within the landlord/tenant relationship, the tenants are very likely to vent those feelings by the way they treat the property. It is necessary to have good, positive energy.

Conducting an annual walk-through

You should plan to conduct an annual walk-through once a year, and usually before the current lease expires. Because you know in advance, remember to give plenty of notice. This is a great time to view the care of your property and see what routine maintenance needs to be done. Be sure to check the smoke detectors and change the heater and air conditioning filters, if needed. This is also time to decide whether you want to offer another year's lease.

If the tenants don't plan to be there when you walk through, ask them to leave a note of anything in particular they want you to see or take a look at. Remember to be aware whether your tenants have pets. Often, tenants have animals inside your rental and you want to be sure they don't get out. Be sure not to move or touch any of their belongings when you are doing your walk-through. Respecting their privacy is to respect their space, too. Always leave a note or a business card to show signs you were there.

Increasing the rent

Tenants never appreciate receiving a notice that the rent will be increased. So, what you need to do is to handle the rent increase as best you can.

- Be fair with the rent increase and continue to keep the rent under market value. Let the tenants know what similar properties are renting for.
- Give your tenants plenty of notice so that they can budget and be prepared for the new rent.

- If there is something within reason you can do to your property that would be a benefit for the tenants while maintaining your investment, do it!

- When you do your annual walk-through prior to raising the rent, if you find they are great tenants, send them a letter letting them know how much you appreciate the care they are giving to the property.

- Offer your best tenants another lease with possibly no increase in rent or a very small one. Some people like to know they have another year's lease with no increase and that they will not be asked to move during that year, especially if they have children in school and would have to move in the middle of a school year.

The Unreasonable Tenant

Yes, there are always tenants who love to complain and are usually unreasonable with requests and expectations. They expect you to jump for them and usually come with attitude. You need try to turn them around early on. I find being kind to them helps. If you find that tenants continue to be unreasonable with their requests and attitude, try writing a letter — a really positive letter. If their requests aren't threatening the habitability or safety of your tenant or your rental property, point that out, but be kind. You need to let the tenants know your boundaries early on. Of course, there will always be those tenants who will continue to push until you let them know they are out of line or not being reasonable.

Keep trying to turn them around. If all else fails and you have had it, when the lease comes up for renewal, plan to give them notice to move. Some people are never happy and will not change. Just don't make it retaliatory.

There is nothing wrong with raising your rent to keep up with the current market and the increase of the cost of owning property. Always use common sense and courtesy.

Renewing the lease

Your ultimate goal is to be able to offer the good tenants a new lease, they will want a new lease and have plans to stay. By the time your first lease has expired, you have developed a relationship with your tenants and should know whether you want to offer another one-year lease. This is based on your walk-through, the rental payment history for that first year, and how well you and your tenant are communicating.

Make contact with your tenants prior to the lease expiration about the time you are planning to walk through the property. Don't be afraid to ask about their plans. If they are good tenants and ones you want to keep, ask whether they would like another lease. Let them know what the rent amount will be and whether you plan to do anything to the property.

If the tenants tell you they really want to stay, get the leases drawn up right away and get it to them to sign. You may even take leases with you so that during your walk-through, if you find everything to your satisfaction, you can have them sign right there.

When you write the new lease, make sure you put in the rental agreement that the lease is a carry over from the lease dated (refer to the original date on the lease). Carry over the security deposit and put that it has been carried over from the lease dated (fill in that date again). Let tenants know whether there is a rent increase and that all other terms and conditions

 Moneysaver

Try to have your tenants sign a new one-year lease if the lease has good ending dates. You should try to have the lease end always around the best rental market time.

remain the same. I like to see a new lease drawn up and signed with the new dates and all signatures again. This is a good time to add any requirements that have changed due to laws.

Showing appreciation for tenants

Letting the tenants know you appreciate them is a good thing. Good tenants are to be treasured, so don't take them for granted. When you have a great tenant, one who pays the rent on time, never complains, has maintained a beautiful garden and yard, and is an all-around dream tenant, take the time to show your appreciation.

> **66** A lot of little things can add up over time and make a tenant unhappy. Keep a list of small complaints and make a trip to take care of all of the items once a year. **99**
>
> —Sylvia H., investor and property manager

There really are more good tenants out there than bad ones. Remember the 80-20 rule: About 20 percent of the tenants cause 80 percent of the problems. Don't let the bad ones spoil things for the great tenants.

Here are just some of the ways to retain your quality tenants:

- Follow up on all maintenance requests personally.
- Give a "get out of one late fee" voucher.
- Give good, outstanding service through communication with your tenants.
- Send out a special newsletter.
- Give movie passes, particularly after you have completed a lot of maintenance at the property such that your tenants have been inconvenienced.
- Give a small gift at move-in. You can have something there waiting at the new home, with a nice note to welcome them.

- Give them a gift certificate at move-in from the local pizza parlor. We all know how hard it is to cook when you first move in.

- If your current tenant refers you a new tenant that rents one of your properties, acknowledge it and do something special for your current tenant.

- Maintain the outside common areas or the yard so that the property always looks good.

- Plant new flowers or provide a gift certificate to purchase some for the rental.

- Always let your tenants know that you appreciate their prompt rent payment and care for your property.

Keeping good tenants means paying attention to the needs of your renters and your property. Good tenants are more than those who pay the rent on time and don't complain.

You want tenants who remain long term, pay rent on time, and continue to take good care of your investment. Be a good landlord and keep your tenants happy.

Just the facts

- Retention begins before your tenants move in.

- Turnover costs you more than money.

- A property in great condition will cause fewer headaches while the tenant is living there.

- There are many clear things that can keep your tenants happy and remain long term.

- Respond promptly and keep the best interests of your investment in mind.

- Be reasonable with rent increases and maintain your property and you will have long-term tenants.

- Don't raise your rents too high, as it can force your good tenants to move.

- It is best to conduct an interior and exterior property inspection prior to signing another one-year lease.

- Inform your tenants before going on the property, even if you will be only on the outside.

- Most tenants have reasonable requests.

- Not all tenants are bad tenants. In fact, there are more great tenants than bad ones.

- The ideal long-term tenant also takes care of your property.

- Property with common areas need to have common rules.

- Remember that you aren't a friend to your tenant — this is a business; be professional.

- Not many tenants prefer lower rent versus maintaining the property in a good or great condition.

- Ask tenants whether they plan to extend their leases, and then respond to any concerns.

- Show your tenants that you appreciate them.

GET THE SCOOP ON...
Handling difficult tenants and those who violate rental agreements ▪ Communicating about any problems ▪ Managing late-paying tenants and bounced checks ▪ Recognizing a drug house ▪ What to do about noisy tenants ▪ Dealing with unsupervised minor children ▪ Knowing a tenant's right to repairs ▪ Breaking leases ▪ Handling evictions and other legal notices ▪ Dealing with a tenant who abandons your property ▪ Enforcing a pet policy

Dealing with Problem Tenants

Chapter 13

In a perfect world, a property owner rents to a tenant, and the rent is never late. In this scenario, there are never any maintenance problems nor tenant difficulties. However, this is often not the case. The only way to limit contact with difficult tenants is to employ a property manager (see Chapter 17). Property managers can serve as a buffer between owner and tenant when there are problems, but they can't make difficult tenants go away completely.

If you are the owner and choose to be the property manager, you need to know how to deal with the difficult tenants and the problems that can and will come up. One hopes that with proper screening and following the direction and guidance of Chapter 9, you will weed out the bad tenants who cause you major problems. At some time or another, you will

Bright Idea

Listening to the tenant is a big key to resolution. From the beginning, determine what the unhappy tenant is actually saying. Often, there is something else behind the problem. Listen carefully. Just by asking what he or she wants, you may be able to quickly solve the problem.

come across a tenant or two who will confront you, challenge you, not pay the rent, and just plain become difficult. You need to know what to do.

There are many different types of difficulties that will come up during your ownership and self-management. I think it is good for you as an owner to, at least at first, manage your property yourself so that you can see the day-to-day challenges in the life of a professional property manager.

Handling difficult people or situations does take thought and careful action. Document every conversation. Simply insisting that you have not caused their problems, and that they are being unreasonable, rarely leads to resolution. As a property owner, you need to know what steps to take when faced with a difficult tenant or poor situation.

You never really know what is going on in the tenant's life when you receive that irate, unreasonable call about the broken air conditioner. Remember, you did not cause the air conditioner to malfunction. You are responsible only to listen and assure the tenant that you will do the best you can to solve the problem.

Don't take it personally. The fact that your tenant is being so unreasonable could have to do with his personal life or the lousy day he just had at the job he cannot stand.

He also may have caught you at the end of a tough day, so take a deep breath before returning the call. If you find that you start to get irritable, excuse yourself, take three deep breaths, and return to the conversation. The desired result is to identify and resolve the complaint about the property, not become a counselor or resolve his personal problems. Sometimes, this is difficult to avoid when you have become friendly with the tenant and he has lost his job or had unexpected emergencies occur.

Communication through the entire process is extremely important. Whatever the issues are, it is necessary to keep the residents informed, either by written or verbal communication. When a tenant calls to give me a list of maintenance items that need attention, I kindly request that this list be in writing, via e-mail, with the form I have online, or by fax or mail. If there is a problem and it is not an emergency, be professional and ask for something in writing. You may get resistance, but be persuasive. The way to handle a difficult tenant: Listen, plan a course of action, communicate, follow up, and document everything.

Your level of response will depend on how severe the problem is. Some problems, like non-payment of the rent, continuous late payments, bounced checks, moving in additional occupants, noise and disturbing other tenants, drug sales, and more are all violations of the lease in one form or another. The following sections help you deal with these problems.

What to do when a tenant pays late or bounces a check

At one point or another, you will come across the tenant who calls you to let you know the rent will be late this month. Along with that call or correspondence comes a long story and the excuse. You have to decide how to handle this, taking into consideration the tenant's track record with you. Look at the monthly rental history. Some property managers like to give their new tenant

 Watch out!

Be careful about accepting your rental payments late from your tenants. It can be interpreted that by accepting late rents, you have in fact changed the due date. Also, don't accept partial rents, with the rest trickling in throughout the month. If you do decide to accept a late payment, be sure to put something in writing to your tenants that rent is still due on the first and you will not be accepting late payments in the future.

one free late rent coupon. This can take the stress off, should that one-time emergency arise.

But you don't want to make a habit out of accepting late rent payments and you don't want to begin making exceptions to the rental due date.

No payment

If you have heard nothing from your tenant and your rent is due on the first and late on midnight of the 5th, call your tenant. If you don't reach anyone, leave a message that the rent is due and that as of today you did not receive it. Let tenants know that if you don't hear from them or have the rent by the next day, you will be forced to serve them a legal notice to pay or move. Make sure you follow the exact letter of the law for your state as to how to do this, and know what forms if any need to be filled out as well. In California, we serve the tenant a three-day notice to pay or quit, and we must fill out a proof of service as well. (It is so important to do this paperwork correctly. Check and double-check your work.) If you still don't receive the rent, follow through with a legal notice. It is also a good idea to require the late fees at the same time the rent is paid. You may also want your rental agreement to state that late rents need to be made by secured funds (cashier's check or money order, for example).

I've found that some tenants really believe that you own this property free and clear, are independently wealthy, and will not suffer if rent is not paid for a month or two. Be forthright by explaining your late fees if the mortgage is paid late and that you may have other costs that come out of your pocket if the rent is not paid on time. Sometimes, it is just a matter of educating the tenant. Of course, how this information is received depends on the quality of the tenant.

Bounced checks

Keep in mind that a bounced check means you have no rent and that your tenant is now late. I highly recommend you establish a policy right up front that you don't accept another check to replace the bounced check. It should be policy that you don't redeposit a bounced check as well. (You need to put this into your written rental agreement.) By the time the bank notifies you that the tenants' check was returned, it is almost always past the due date. You have bills to pay and need to be assured that the bounced check will be replaced immediately. Keep in mind that when a tenant bounces a rent check, it makes the rent late, which means you're entitled to a late fee. You should also serve a legal notice at the time the bounced check is received to protect yourself.

Be consistent. Stick to your policies and remember that making exceptions to those policies only gets you in trouble in the long run. It gives tenants the impression that your policies really aren't important, so trying to make another one stick is that much harder.

Handling other violations of the rental agreement

When tenants are in violation of their rental agreement, you need to address the issue right away and in writing. When a tenant is in violation of the agreement, I send the tenant a copy of the written rental agreement and highlight the violations within the agreement, along with a letter and violation notice. The following sections cover some of the common violations.

Additional occupants

You can address this issue in your rental agreement (see Chapter 10). Your lease should state how many residents are approved to live in your property and how long and how often a "guest" can stay. Remember, you should have an application for any tenant living in your property who is 18 years or older (or an emancipated minor) and he or she must sign the rental agreement if living in the property.

Tenants often abuse the guest policy by allowing additional occupants in the rental unit for an extended length of time. To

Bright Idea

Oftentimes, you can tell whether someone is living in the unit when you receive a rent check from someone who is not on your rental agreement but has your property's address on the check. Also, during your drivebys, notice the number of cars parked in front or around your property.

be honest, this is very difficult to monitor. When you are signing agreements with your new tenants, go over the policy about occupants moving in and guests staying a certain length of time. Explain that having additional occupants is a breach of the lease and explain what the consequences are of breaching the lease.

Having too many residents live in your property is very hard on the wear and tear of your unit or home. The bathroom sees a lot of abuse, especially when there is only one. Be careful, however, when you decide how many occupants you will allow in your unit. The U.S. Department of Housing and Urban Development (HUD) has a guideline (not law) of two people per bedroom plus one. If you stay within that guideline, you will most likely not be sued for discrimination. See Chapter 7.

Pets

Your rental agreement should also indicate whether or not pets are allowed. If they are allowed, state the exact type (for example, "golden retriever" versus "dog") and how many. Pets sometimes just appear, and tenants are dog-sitting or keeping the pet while a neighbor is out of town. Your responsibility at this point is to garner the truth. Doing an inspection around the yard and house can usually determine whether this has been a long-term pet or just an overnight guest. Look for large bags of food, hair tufts on blankets/pillows, and scratch marks on doors. Outside, look for holes that have been dug out, as well as pet toys. If you find a pet is in residence, take immediate action by sending a notice to the tenant. Follow up within the week to make sure the pet is not still there.

Keep in mind that some tenants don't think a gerbil or a fish tank is a pet. They are! Both of these can cause a lot of damage, especially if the gerbil is let out a lot or the fish tank is broken.

Be careful. Companion animals aren't pets according to law. They are required to assist the mentally or physically challenged. You cannot refuse to rent to someone because he or she has a companion animal.

Noisy tenants

Tenants live with other tenants. So when you receive a complaint from one of the neighbors or one of your other tenants, kindly thank her and let her know you will call or send a letter to the noisy tenant. However, if the problem persists, tenants have the option of calling the police. You want to encourage tenants to call to let you know of problems but at the same time, let them know there is only so much you can do. You don't want to lose a great tenant due to the abuse of a mediocre tenant, though, so follow up with the noisy tenant. If this is a single-family home, meet the neighbors and give them your contact information. You would much rather get a complaint from the neighbors than from the police department. They will also appreciate knowing that you care about your property and their neighborhood.

> **"** We often put up with a number of violations from a difficult tenant in order to avoid the hassle of rerenting or going through the eviction process. Still, be sure to address in writing any problems with a difficult tenant. **"**
>
> —Roxie M., property manager

You need to send a letter stating that your tenants are in violation of your lease and including the list of violations. I always include a copy of the lease in the letter and highlight the area where they are in violation. If it comes time to evict the tenants or ask them to move, you have written documentation about the problems with your follow up in writing.

Unsupervised minor children

It is a federal law that you must not decline residents because they have children. However, young children are expected to be supervised by an adult. You must walk this line very delicately. Be sure that you have rules that make your expectations very clear.

You usually find out that a young child or children are unsupervised at your rental by a neighbor. The complaint comes from one of your units next door or by someone who just happens to live in the house across the street. Get the complaint in writing, if at all possible. Often, that is not easy so, instead, be sure to document everything. Always write down the nature of the problem, the time and date, who called you to report the problem, and how you addressed it.

Never enter a unit when only minor children are present. Be sure that any contractors you send to the property are also aware of this. It is not unusual in today's culture to find teens or pre-teens at home alone between the time that school is let out and parents arriving home from work.

This issue of unsupervised children needs to be addressed by the parent or guardian, not with the children directly. Try talking to your tenant and following up with a friendly letter providing an overview of your conversation. If the problem persists, you need to give them a written warning according to the letter of the law and your rental agreement. State the nature of the problem and how or what is needed to correct it.

Using your rental as a drug house

It is very important for owners, your property manager maintenance personnel, and anyone else to be able to recognize a rental used as a drug house. Unfortunately, they are now part of our society. In particular, methamphetamine labs or clandestine drug labs are very dangerous, and exposure is normally hazardous. Additionally, drug houses can be located in all economic areas of housing, not just low income.

Property owners or your manager can be liable for ignoring the signs of a drug house and not taking action. Fines and legal fees can be extensive. However, property managers and owners must be careful to avoid discrimination or legal action by wrongfully accusing a tenant of drug activity. Nevertheless, if signs of drug-dealing are evident, it is more perilous to ignore them.

The warning signs

Any combination of the following may be an indicator of a drug house:

- Constant pedestrian traffic, such as many people coming and going at all different hours — often late at night — and staying short periods.

- Constant vehicle traffic, coming and going, parking out front, engines left running, or one or more persons waiting while another goes into the property.

- Extreme security precautions become obvious, such as surveillance equipment, extra motion lights, security cameras, large locks, bars on windows, and dangerous dogs such as a pit bull or Rottweiler.

- Heavy chemical or suspicious odors emanating from the residence.

- Tennis shoes tied together and hanging over the electric lines right outside the house (and never taken down).

- Receiving move-out letters from previous long-term tenants. They may not tell you they are scared.

The tenants may also exhibit suspicious activities, such as never coming outside, looking out windows when people leave, avoiding other neighbors, failing to keep up the yard or house, and having a lot of activity in the garage area, even though the door never opens.

The preceding tips help you recognize a drug house. Now what do you do? There are steps to take for this serious problem.

A suspected drug house — what to do

The signs above are ways to recognize a drug house. I hope you haven't encountered this situation and it will not be part of a future scenario. However, if you do, it is imperative to know what to do and, more importantly, what not to do.

- If you notice any activity or you are contacted by a law enforcement agency or neighbor, call your property management company and attorney immediately for advice and also to warn the property manager of possible danger. You need to follow important legal and practical steps to protect your property. You will also work with the local law enforcement, narcotics division, or narcotics detectives as is appropriate.

- Don't ignore the problem — it could be great risk to you and others in many ways. Act immediately. This is an emergency.

- Contact the neighbors or a neighborhood watch leader, if available.

- Never enter the property if you suspect a drug house or lab.

- Never confront the tenant — you may end up with a lawsuit if a drug problem doesn't exist, or you could put yourself in danger.

- If a problem is occurring right at the moment, call the police or sheriff and make a report.

- Don't call 911 unless there is a life-threatening situation, but definitely do call 911 if you suspect personal exposure to toxic chemicals.

- Bring the information to a public meeting if it has been substantiated. If it hasn't, you have just opened yourself up to a lawsuit for defamation of character.

> **Watch Out!**
>
> Don't attempt to handle a drug problem in your tenant — this could be life threatening. Toxic chemicals can cause great and sometimes permanent damage to the body's system. Toxic chemicals connected with drugs are also highly volatile and can explode at any time.

- Above all, beware of activities surrounding the property. Be careful, document everything, don't attempt to solve this on your own, and seek professional assistance from law enforcement and your attorney.

Tenants' legal rights to repair

In some states, if you fail to properly maintain your rental property in a safe and habitable condition or if the tenant has requested the repairs and has given you written notice, your tenant has the right to repair the maintenance item and deduct the cost of the repairs from the following month's rent.

There are limitations for both you and the tenants. In most states the tenants need to follow the proper procedures in order to repair and deduct it from their rent. There are also limits as to how often the tenants may do this during the tenancy. Sometimes the limits will be in a dollar amount or even a percentage of the rent they are paying.

Your goal as a landlord should be to take care of your property and respond in a timely manner to any reasonable requests or complaints about the condition of the property.

If you don't fix the maintenance item in a timely manner and it falls under this law, you have now lost control of the quality of work that will be performed on your property. You don't want the tenants to make the repairs themselves or hire a contractor who has absolutely no skills to correctly do the job. In addition, the tenant may just hire a very expensive contractor to take care of the problem and will charge you an arm and a leg.

Moneysaver

Negotiate with difficult tenants to move out. Offer to pay for a moving van or pay them a small amount if they are out by a certain date. Return their security deposit if they move out right away. Believe me, this will save you time, money, and aggravation in the long run.

Take care of your property. If you aren't sure if the complaint is legitimate, take the time to meet with the tenant and check it out yourself. This allows you to send the right type of contractor to take care of the problems. You will also be able to note the condition of the property and see firsthand how the tenants are caring for it.

The request from your tenant must be reasonable and affect the safety and habitability of the property. On the other hand, it would be unreasonable if the tenant replaced the carpet inside your rental and sent you the bill.

Many owners, especially if they aren't living in the area, allow the tenants to handle minor repairs. Owners often feel that this will save them time and money if the tenants say they can fix it themselves for only the costs of the part. Be careful, though, as most tenants aren't licensed contractors and often lack the skills to make the repair correctly. Sometimes that minor problem becomes a major problem, costing you more trying to correct the original work performed incorrectly. Your tenants aren't the ones responsible to hire and take care of maintaining your investment property. In the long run, hiring a professional who is licensed, knowledgeable, and properly insured is the right way to go. Take all safety, security, and maintenance calls seriously and take good care of your tenants and your property.

Evictions and the alternatives

There are many reasons that a tenant may get evicted, but most commonly, it will be non-payment of rent. Evictions are expensive, time-consuming, and emotionally draining. If you are evicting based on non-payment of rent, not only do you not have your rental income but also the legal cost and constant worry whether the tenant is going to completely destroy your property.

This is where your homework in the beginning really pays off. When you interview your real estate attorney (see Chapter 1), find out whether a brochure is available that outlines the steps for eviction in your state. Then follow them. Beware of just buying a form and using it. How you fill in the spaces and what information can be used is very important.

Don't delay the action you need to take. Oftentimes, an owner will come to me when a tenant has fallen three or more months behind. Stay on top of the problem at hand, whether it is non-payment of rent or another rental agreement violation.

Types of legal notices

There are many different types of legal notices, and you may be required to fill out a proof-of-service notice that you keep for your records that gives the details of how the notice was served. Check with your attorney as to the type of notice to serve to match the violation of the rental agreement; some common notices are discussed in the following sections.

Pay rent or quit

If you are dealing with non-payment of rent and you have made an effort to collect the funds due, you need to go to the next step. These notices give the tenants from 3 to 15 days to pay (depending on your state) or move. The tenant is allowed the number of days your state allots before going to the next step of the eviction.

Cure or quit notices

This notice is served on your tenant for a violation of the agreement other than non-payment of rent. This is commonly called a "breach of lease" for things like moving an additional person on the property, having a pet on a no pet property without permission, or creating noise or disturbances to others. Parking where they are clearly not allowed or allowing a lawn to die can also be the reason behind giving this notice to the tenant.

Oftentimes, when a tenant is renting a condominium, town-home, planned unit development, or a co-op, there are a set of rules and regulations that the tenants agree to abide by when they sign the lease. There are usually parking rules, pool rules, common area rules, and others that are spelled out in an addendum they sign and agree to. The association management usually lets you know in writing if your tenants are violating the rules. You need to stay on top of this and correct it right away, as there are usually fines associated with it. Your tenant needs to be made aware that they will be responsible for the fines if they don't correct the problem.

Most difficult tenants will call your bluff when you serve them any type of notice, especially a three-day notice to pay or quit. They may be betting that you will not actually start the process, knowing very well just how expensive and extensive the process is to evict them and the length of time it takes.

Be prepared for when the tenants call to say the complaints were made because they aren't liked or "just give me another chance." You need to be firm and remember that this is your property they are putting at risk.

Notice to move

On a month-to-month agreement, you can serve your tenants a notice to move. You must check with your state and local laws to see just how many days you must give a tenant prior to preparing and serving them the notice.

In California, if a tenant has lived in the property longer than 365 days (one-year) and isn't on a lease but is considered a month-to-month tenant, you must give the tenant 60 days' notice to move but you don't have to provide a reason. In fact, you are better off not giving a specific reason. When moving on a month-to-month agreement, the tenants are usually only required to give you 30 days' written notice. Some states require the notice be given at the first of the month while others allow the notice to be at any time in the month. A lot of people believe

Watch Out!

Be careful. If you own property in a city with rent control, such as San Francisco and New York, they have their own laws and you must abide by them. You can usually call and check with a rent control hotline, a local attorney, or a local property manager.

that you must always give notice on the first of the month, and that is not true.

Tenant mediation

Before you opt for a legal eviction, you may consider trying mediation. Most areas have a third party that is neutral and will mediate a resolution or come to an agreeable move-out date with terms and conditions you can all agree on. Usually, you will pay something based on the time involved and a sliding scale of what you can afford. Always get everything you agree to in writing, with specific dates and the consequences if tenants don't move. Type a payment schedule and the conditions in the agreement.

Keep in mind you may have to give back the security deposit or agree to forgive some past rent, but that is all a part of the negotiating process. Go in with options and an open mind. Your goal should be to get your property back so you can make any repairs and sign a good tenant who will pay rent.

Proper service of legal notices

You need to be certain that when serving a legal notice, you do it properly and all your paperwork is complete with the correct information.

You have to pay close attention to the laws in your state for service on any legal notice. Make certain you have proper legal service, as this is something that will come up if you get to the eviction stage. In most cases, there is a separate form to complete that states exactly who served the notice and how. Of course, the preferred form of service is to serve each tenant who is 18 years or older in person. Each adult living at the property should have

Moneysaver

Hire an attorney who specializes in eviction to handle getting your tenant out right away. There are a lot of details to this process and oftentimes, the tenants have figured out how to delay the process. A good, experienced attorney will know what to do and how to do it in a timely manner.

a separate notice in an envelope addressed to that person. However, that is not always easy. In some incidents, after attempting to serve an adult in person you may have to do what is called "nail and mail." This is where you tack the notice to the door or put it in visible sight and also send one through the U.S. mail. Be sure to check with your attorney for the legal requirement before serving any notices. Different states have different requirements and a different amount of days to respond to the notice to pay or quit.

If you serve notice to the tenants in person, the clock starts ticking for the number of days the tenants have to pay the rent, starting the next day.

After you have exhausted all your options and decide to move forward with the eviction, don't delay. I recommend you hire an eviction lawyer who has done this before and knows the process backward and forward. You can attempt to handle the eviction yourself, but remember that with just one mistake, you are back to square one.

In most states, a tenant has a certain number of days, after being served the summons and complaint, to file an answer as to why he has not paid the rent. The reason is usually something that they think justifies withholding their rent. They will even make things up about the condition of the property or state that the property is in need of repairs to make it habitable. All that documentation you've been putting together really pays off here. I've seen many tenants who give up when they realize all the documentation is available and they can't make a case. In California, if the tenant doesn't file an answer, you will have what is known as an "uncontested eviction." This is usually simple and quite routine for most eviction lawyers.

Sometimes tenants will come in with their hard luck story and play on the judge's heart; don't be surprised if the judge grants the tenants a few extra days, especially during the holiday season and if there is a family involved.

On many occasions, a tenant will stay in the property right up to the last possible day before the eviction, and then leave in the middle of the night.

During the eviction, don't attempt to contact your tenants or do anything illegal or that may cause a reaction or a problem. You must continue to care for your property and handle any maintenance problems or requests in a timely manner. Don't threaten or intimidate your tenants.

Try not to take the eviction process personally and don't let your emotions get the best of you. Maintain the property and give your tenant the same service you were previously providing. There is a very serious recourse if you don't, and your tenant files a cross-complaint.

Evictions are never fun and are always a part of a landlord's "war stories." This is why I stress that you want to complete a thorough screening on all of your applicants in advance before renting to the applicants and giving them the keys. Laws vary state to state, and getting possession of your property back relies on your strict adherence to those laws.

Post eviction

As soon as the tenants are out, the first thing I recommend is to secure your property by changing all the locks immediately and making sure the vacant property is locked up at all times. Your tenants are now your previous tenants and if they return to the property, they are trespassing.

When you gain back the property, take a camera with you to take photos of the condition of the property when you first arrive. Hold on to your hat, as you have to be prepared for the

Watch Out!

Oftentimes, tenants leave some belongings in the property and to you it may look like "junk," but be careful. Check with your laws as to what you must do with the property and what you are required to do if they leave anything of any value.

condition in which you will more than likely find the property in. Rarely will the property be destroyed, but it definitely won't be clean and there will probably be a lot of junk left behind.

Handling tenant abandonment

Each state has its own set of laws and guidelines as to what you must do if a tenant leaves personal belongings in your unit, along with their definition of what abandoned property really is.

If items were left behind and your state requires it, try to contact the previous tenants. Ask whether they are out of your property and try to get something in writing that what they left has no value to them and they relinquish all rights to what they left behind. (Keep in mind that this is not easy to get.) Allow the prior tenants to return and take as much of their property away as possible — stay with them at all times, however, and lock up after they go.

Make sure to take some photos and do write down an inventory of what was left.

If you suspect the tenants have just abandoned your property for any reason, some states require a legal notice you can post to the front of the door that is notice of abandonment. Be sure to check with your state laws and follow the letter of the law when doing this.

One of a landlord's biggest nightmares is to discover that the tenants have left the property but have left their personal belongings and what they have left inside is clearly of value. Your requirement as to what to do next will vary from state to state.

Watch Out!

There may be toxic chemicals, oil, paint, or other items left behind that take special handling. Dispose of everything in the proper and legal manner. When you dispose of the items the tenants left, you can deduct this from the security deposit.

Obviously, when you discover your tenants have left personal property inside your rental, try to contact them as soon as possible. If you are unsuccessful in reaching them, have another person as a witness write a statement of what they found in the property in detail and an estimate of value. The estimate of value is what you could get if you tried to sell it — not the value of the item when it was new. A mattress usually cannot be resold, so it has no value. An oil painting of the family only has value to the family — only the frame has any value. Some computer parts are of no value if they are over two to three years old. Take a detailed inventory.

Unfortunately, the next step may not make you too happy. Depending on the state, you may have to obtain indoor storage and secure the items left behind. This can get quite complicated, so I suggest you be very certain you are doing everything legally. You may be required to store the property for a specified number of days before you are able to hold a public auction to sell the belongings. You may have to put any monies collected toward offsetting the debt of the former tenants. Check to see whether any monies you make above and beyond what is owed to you for the past rent, expenses for storage, and cost for the auction belong to the tenant or to you. You may also have to make reasonable attempts to contact the prior tenant to send them their money. Or your property may be in a state that allows you to put all the items on the curb and forget about them. Now you see why having a good real estate attorney who knows eviction procedure for your state is so important (see Chapter 1).

It is very important that you check the laws with this procedure, because personal property left behind can become very
confusing and end up costing you money in the long run if you
don't handle things properly. Check out www.rentlaw.com and
www.landlordportal.com for lists of landlord laws for every
state.

Don't let this chapter scare you into deciding against being
a landlord. Less than 8 percent of all tenancies will end in an
eviction if the proper care is taken when first finding your tenant. However, anything can happen: Your tenant could lose
their job, have major medical problems, go through a divorce,
or have a death in the family. If you are the type of person who
always wants to help out someone in trouble, find a professional
to manage your property (see Chapter 17)!

Just the facts

- Letting a tenant pay rent late may cause you problems in
  the long run.

- You will hear many excuses for why a tenant cannot pay
  the rent. Stick to the terms of the agreement.

- Respond to the problem, not to the emotion.

- Bouncing a check causes the rent to be late.

- You must serve a tenant with a legal notice when they
  don't pay the rent on time.

- Know what the law is in your state for handling non-
  payment of rent.

- Check with your local laws (or your attorney) on how to
  serve legal notices.

- There are many other reasons tenants get evicted, not just
  for lack of paying the rent.

- Reiterate that only approved residents/tenants are allowed
  to stay in your property.

- Define how long a "guest" can stay.

- There are many signs when tenants are using your property as a drug house.

- Act immediately if your property is involved in drugs or any other illegal action.

- Insist that all complaints about another tenant be put in writing.

- There are many laws you must follow when it comes to evicting a tenant from your rental property.

- Tenants have the right to make necessary repairs when it comes to safety and habitability, and they may then deduct it from their rent.

- Don't leave maintaining your property to your tenants.

- Never enter a property with only minor children present, and don't allow contractors to do so.

- Property left behind by a prior tenant can become a major legal problem and a real inconvenience.

- If a tenant abandons the property, take inventory and pictures.

- Less than 8 percent of all tenancies end in an eviction.

GET THE SCOOP ON...
Receiving a tenant's move-out notice ▪ Sending a
move-out acknowledgement ▪ Informing tenants
of move-out procedures ▪ Handling the move-out
evaluation ▪ Determining "normal wear and tear"
▪ Returning all or part of the security deposit ▪
Marketing the property while your tenants are
still paying rent ▪ Handling security deposit disputes ▪ Allowing roommates to stay when a tenant leaves ▪ Knowing what to do if a tenant dies

When Tenants Move

Nothing is ever permanent. All tenants leave at some point. When tenants give notice to vacate your rental property, you need to know exactly what to do, when to do it, and what your local and state laws require of you.

Many owners find refunding the security deposit one of the most difficult tasks to complete to everyone's satisfaction, particularly when there are damages and/or unpaid rent. Property owners are elated when they can issue a full refund because tenants complied with their rental agreement, gave proper notice to vacate, and left the property in excellent condition. However, many times this is not the case, and the damages can range from minimal to large expenditures.

Sometimes, the first notice you will receive is a call from a prospective future landlord or from a mortgage company trying to verify rent. If you receive a call or letter like this, call the tenants to find out whether they are planning to move.

Receiving a notice to vacate

You need to be prepared and have a process in place when your tenants give notice. This includes showing the available unit prior to the tenants' moving out; the move-out notice and the first steps in that process; the pre-evaluation, whether required by law or to evaluate what work will need to be completed at move-out; and coordinating with contractors in advance so that the work can begin as soon as the tenants have turned in the keys, releasing their rights and possession.

Your lease agreement should show your tenants in writing what is expected from them and how they should give notice. The agreement I use states that tenants must give a minimum 30 days written notice after the lease has expired. If the tenants are on a month-to-month agreement, in most states they can give their written notice at any time during the month. Many people believe that a 30-day notice on a month-to-month agreement must be given on the first of the month, but this is not always the case. Check your local laws.

Allow tenants to give you notice via e-mail. If you have a Web site, have a "fill in the blanks" notice to vacate online. Giving notice electronically is simple! You not only have a record of the day and time received, but you can acknowledge the notice immediately.

It is always a good idea to immediately acknowledge receiving the tenants' notice to vacate. I highly recommend you do this by sending something to your tenants in writing. The letter of acknowledgement lets them know when their last day will be based on the notice policy. It also informs them what is expected of them regarding showing the unit, and the move-out process. Appendix 4 gives a sample of the letter I send.

Bright Idea

Refer to the lease and double-check the terms before sending an acknowl-edgment e-mail or letter in reply. If you own more than one property, you can easily confuse your lease agreements. Check and double-check the terms of the agreement and the amount of the deposit.

Showing the unit during the 30-day notice period

If the unit shows well while your tenants are still in your property, you will save valuable time renting the unit. Make arrangements in advance with your tenants to show the units during normal business hours and be reasonable, kind and courteous. Make sure you have in your rental agreement that you're able to show the unit during the last month.

When a roommate moves out

When one of the tenants moves out and the other tenants stay, you need to do a few things to keep your records straight. The tenant moving out needs to provide the notice in writing, indicating he or she releases interest in the security deposit. Occasionally, the tenant moving out thinks you will return his or her share of the deposit. This is not the best way to handle this situation, as you still need to have a security deposit in full in your possession. Let the tenants know that the one vacating will have to get his or her share of the security deposit from the tenant who is staying. Don't get involved with that part. Keep your entire deposit until all the tenants have moved out and turn over full possession. You want to inform the remaining tenants that any new roommates need to complete an application, and all occupants must sign a new rental agreement. You need to keep your records straight, know who is living in your rental property.

Death of a tenant

If a tenant dies in your property, you need to know how to handle the situation. There are a few ways you may find out that a tenant died in your property:

- You have not received the rent check and this tenant pays on time, if not early, every month. When you investigate, you are told by a co-worker, a family member, or another occupant that the death occurred.

- The police get in touch with you and inform you there has been a death in your property.

- Neighbors have not seen the tenant come or go.

- A cat meowing or a dog is barking incessantly inside the property.

If your rental agreement permits your right to enter in the event of an emergency, knock loudly and announce who you are before entering.

When the death has been confirmed and the body has been removed, you must take the necessary steps to protect the tenant's possessions. You should never allow anyone into the unit without legal paperwork that provides authorization to enter. You need to secure the property, which may include changing locks. Usually someone is appointed to take care of the estate or act as the administrator fairly quickly. If you aren't certain what to do, contact your lawyer.

The tenant's estate is still responsible for all unpaid rent. This is a difficult time for all, so you need to be sensitive to the friends and family. However, you need to follow the law so that you don't

---

 Bright Idea

Obtain emergency contact information from your tenants when they move in. It is good to update this information annually when you are doing your walk-through. You need to be able to call someone if there is an emergency or a death.

get blamed if something is missing. Also, the family removing the belongings may not know the terms of your agreement. Be sure you inform them of any conditions of the lease and/or what the expectations are for leaving the unit in a manner that would allow them to get the deposit back.

Some states will require that you disclose the death to any prospective tenant, if the person actually died in the property. If you don't and the tenants find out later — as neighbors will talk — they may have a case for moving out. However, there are certain illnesses — like AIDS — that are protected. You usually cannot tell someone that a person died of AIDS, only that he or she died.

The move-out evaluation

This is a very important step in the security-deposit-refund process and the vacating of your tenants.

What "move out" really means

You need to be clear with the tenants moving out what "completely moved out" really means. Explain to the tenants that all of their possessions must be completely out of the entire property, including the garage. Emphasize that everything — including trash — must be out, the property must be cleaned, and the tenants must turn in the keys. Let the tenants know they will be charged rent until they are out and have turned over possession. All keys should be in your hands before the rent clock stops ticking. This should also be mentioned in your move-out acknowledgment letter.

 Moneysaver

Make sure you put in writing that the tenants are responsible to pay rent on a daily basis until they have completely moved out, everything is out of the unit, and the keys are returned. Tell the tenants where you want the keys returned.

After the tenants are completely out and have returned the keys and relinquished their possession of the property, you need to go and conduct a written move-out evaluation (see Appendix 4). Always bring a camera with you, as you need to be prepared to take pictures if there are damages, something is missing, or there is an area of any controversy. Taking pictures is the best method of proof if there is going to be any discrepancies regarding the damages or charges against their security deposit. If you ever go to court regarding the move-out and charges deducted from the deposit, having photos for the judge will certainly help your case.

> **❝** Always be reasonable and fair when deducting money from a tenant's security deposit. Always attach proof. Send a copy of the bill showing the charges for the damages, along with a detailed accounting in writing. **❞**
>
> —Dana E., property manager

There are different ways to conduct the move-out evaluation, but I always do the move-out after the tenant has completely moved out and no longer has access. I think it is important so that you can take your time when you are conducting the move-out and to not have any distractions while writing down the details. Oftentimes, the tenants moving out will insist on being there, so I kindly let them know I do the move-out on my own as to not miss anything. If they still keep insisting, I remind them again and let them know I am happy to inform them as to what I find. I have had the tenants moving out at the property when I was conducting the walk-through and found that they were trying to divert my attention from some of the damages by talking a lot when I was near something they did not want me to see. They also wanted to come behind me with cleaning supplies to clean anything they had missed — and sometimes even wanted me to wait while they went to the store to get a missing plug or light bulb! Having anyone there during the walk-through is a big distraction.

Normal wear and tear

One phrase triggers a round of laughter at the National Association of Residential Property Managers (NARPM) luncheons or gatherings, and that is, "it [the property] is cleaner than when I moved in." Property managers hear this phrase from nearly every tenant, from those who are clean to one who has lived as a pig in a sty. It is really amazing how a tenant can view filth as "normal wear and tear."

"Normal wear and tear" can elicit very different viewpoints — a tenant, an owner, a property manager, or a contractor. However, there are definite items that don't apply to the phrase. Here are some examples:

- It doesn't apply to filth and dirt, heavy soil, black marks on walls, rips or dye stains on window coverings, bleach or oil on carpets, and so on.

- It doesn't apply to negligence, such as allowing mildew to collect on walls and tubs, or not reporting leak in a roof or toilet leak, and so on.

- It doesn't apply to abuse, such as ripped linoleum from installing a refrigerator, punching a whole in the wall, stained or ripped window coverings, washing the drapes, and so on.

How do I handle the normal wear-and-tear claims? I prepare the property and create a record of good condition before the tenant moves in. My management company then counsels the new tenant on what is expected during tenancy. A rental agreement is signed by both tenant and management that outlines the expectations while living in the property and what is expected at move-out.

Undoubtedly, there will still be tenants who claim many of the items are "normal wear and tear," and property managers and landlords alike will continue to hear this litany. It is not always easy to cope with the tenant who cries "normal wear and tear" when there is actually damage. However, by using common sense, working on the tenant's perspective, and having good documentation, fewer problems arise, and those that do can be handled as needed.

Returning the security deposit

The most practical process for handling security deposits is to start before the tenant moves in. This may sound like an odd approach to take, but the following steps demonstrate common sense tactics for achieving a satisfactory deposit refund.

1. **Complete a thorough tenant screening.** The right tenants in the beginning eliminates most problems regarding a security deposit refund at the end of the tenancy.

2. **Prepare the property for renting and make sure it's in a clean, reasonable condition for the tenant.** For example, it is really difficult to charge for a heavily soiled carpet when it was not professionally cleaned or in good condition prior to occupancy.

3. **Make sure the condition of the property is well-documented before the tenants move in.** With this completed at the beginning of the tenancy, there are grounds for deductions if there are damages at the end.

4. **Make sure your detailed rental agreement complies with all state laws and ensures that the tenants fully understand what is expected of them during tenancy and upon move-out.** Proper documentation includes the details regarding what is due until the end of the tenancy, when the rent is to be paid, and what condition is expected of the property when they move out.

It is not enough to perform these steps before tenancy. These must continue through the entire residency, which means:

- Perform necessary repairs in a timely manner.
- Keep accurate maintenance records.

- Keep accurate financial records on rent, late fees, returned check charges, and repairs that the tenant caused or needed to reimburse for.

- Keep track of any concessions given to the tenants for painting the walls a different color or putting in a garden.

When a tenant gives notice, steps are taken to ensure the last month is uncomplicated and the move-out process continues.

- Date and time-stamp the notice as soon as you receive it. Many agreements require that the tenants provide a minimum of 30 days written notice, beginning from the date the landlord receives the notice. How often the tenant pays rent and the term of the lease may alter this requirement.

- Acknowledge the notice, either by calling the tenants or, preferably, by sending the tenants a letter along with what is expected when they move out. Along with the acknowledgment, send the tenants a set of cleaning guidelines. This helps ensure everyone is clear and on the same page as to what is expected in the move-out process.

- Set up a time to go through the property with or without the tenants so you can make a decision whether to show it during the remainder of the tenancy and to determine what work will be needed before you begin marketing the property for a new tenant.

- Explain that you would like to show the property during the last 30 days. Talk about how the rental showing process works while the tenant is still in the property. The process for showing should have been in your original rental agreement, allowing you to show the property during this time. If it is not, tenants can refuse to allow it to be shown.

- Make sure you have a working key.

- Make sure the property still has that "curb appeal."

- If you place a rental sign at the property while the tenants are still there, include a sign rider up that states, "Don't disturb occupants."

- Make sure to acquire the forwarding address and new telephone number.

- Expect to receive a reference call from the soon-to-be landlord. If tenants are purchasing a home, expect to receive a verification letter from the lenders, which you should complete and return promptly.

- Make sure tenants know where to return the keys, garage door openers, and any other items they are expected to return. Make sure to inform them that they have to be completely moved out and all keys returned, or they are still responsible for the rent.

When a tenant vacates, more steps are taken:

- The property condition is properly documented. You may want to do this with the tenant or on your own.

- A refund and/or statement of condition detailing the deductions is provided in a timely manner, in accordance with your state laws and your agreement.

- Common sense is used. When necessary, compromise on small matters in order to avoid a legal dispute.

Have a process in mind if the tenants ask for extra time in the property. Sometimes, the house they are moving into won't be available as soon as they had expected. Other times, they just don't allow enough time to remove everything and have it cleaned. Whatever the reason, it makes a difference if you already have people scheduled to do work and a new tenant ready to move in soon. If you don't have anything scheduled, the few extra days may be acceptable. Moving is always a highly stressful time, so try to be accommodating, if at all possible. When you receive the move-out notice, find out whether the tenants are waiting for a new house to be built, buying a house, or moving into another rental. Some homework on your part may help both of you be prepared for any delays.

Tenants are never happy when deductions have been made from the security deposit. However, if it is handled efficiently, stressful and/or legal problems can be substantially reduced or may be non-existent. The security deposit belongs to the tenants and should not be considered income to the landlord. State law usually sets a limit as to the total amount you can collect as a security deposit and will dictate what you must do with the deposit and how quickly you must return it after the tenant moves out.

Settling security deposit disputes

Probably one of the biggest items argued in small claims court throughout the country is a dispute arising from security deposit refunds. You as the landlord must have proof of the condition of the property when your tenants moved in and proof of the damages and cost to repair these damages when they move out.

Going to small claims court takes a great deal of time and costs you money. If you must appear in court, be prepared. Have a copy of the rental agreement, a copy of the original move-in inspection you conducted before the tenants moved in, the information you sent them when you received the notice, the photos you took at the time of the move-out, and the written move-out inspection. In addition, have copies of the paid invoices for work you had done because of the tenant's damage. In some states, you cannot charge a tenant for repairs that were never completed. For example, if the tenants damaged the carpet and you had the carpet professionally cleaned but not replaced, you cannot charge the tenants for the cost of replacing the carpet. In others states, you can deduct for a reasonable percentage of the carpet that was damaged. If you are prepared, have your paperwork in order, took photos, and most of all your charges were fair, you should have no problems. Depending on your local court, the judge may be hard on the landlords and always expect the case to be documented and your proof in order. If

Watch Out!

Judges don't take security deposit cases lightly. They expect the landlord and the tenant to have all the necessary paperwork in order and will not tolerate unfair charges. They expect the landlords to know better. Fairness is essential to good business practice.

you want to win, be prepared. This is where your attorney can be of help. He or she will know what a judge will expect. Some localities even have classes to help prepare those who are bringing a small claims case to court.

Another alternative is to use local mediation or arbitration to resolve the problem, rather than getting the courts involved. Just sitting down together with a third party who is not part of the agreement may help resolve the differences. You have the right to be reimbursed for damage your tenants caused, but not the right to take advantage of the security deposit to improve the property or take care of normal wear-and-tear items.

If your tenants move out early, you re-lease the property during the 30-day notice period, and you are receiving rent from the new tenants, you cannot charge the tenants that have vacated for the overlap period. In other words, you cannot receive rent from two different parties for the same time period. Also, some states allow cleaning deposits, which means the tenants pay up-front for professional cleaning. If it is in your agreement up front, there is not a dispute.

Many landlords try to find extra ways to charge the tenant so that they don't have to return all of the security deposit. The security deposit belongs to the tenant.

Just the facts

- Always get the tenant's notice in writing.
- Have a procedure when one roommate is replaced by another.

- Give an acknowledgement of the notice with move-out instructions and procedures.

- There are many steps to take when you receive notice that your tenants are moving.

- Line up the contractors ahead of the tenant's moving out.

- Most states have specific laws to follow regarding security deposits.

- The security deposit belongs to the tenants and is not considered income until it is forfeited for necessary excessive cleaning, rent, or repairs.

- Taking photos of any damage caused by the tenant during will come in handy if you have to go to court; wait until the tenant has completely moved out and turned over the keys before taking pictures.

- There is a limit in most states regarding how much of a security deposit you can take.

- Non-refundable deposits are illegal in most states.

- You need to have emergency contact information for your tenants.

- If a tenant dies, not just anyone has the right to enter the apartment.

- It is important to have the move-in and move-out evaluations completed in detail and in writing.

- In most states, a tenant can give notice in the middle of the month (with a month-to-month agreement).

- Settling a dispute on a security deposit out of court saves time.

- Being fair and reasonable when returning the tenant's security deposit will save you time and money.

PART VI

Expanding Your Business or Selling Properties

GET THE SCOOP ON...
Cashing out though refinancing ▪ Finding
hot properties ▪ Getting the details on a 1031
tax-deferred exchange ▪ Purchasing property
with partners ▪ Looking at bank-owned properties ▪ Buying foreclosed properties ▪ Increasing
your portfolio ▪ Paying down the principal
on your loan

Increasing Your Portfolio of Properties

The hardest part of purchasing investment property is getting your foot in the door. It is scary
and there are a lot of unknowns. If your first
rental property happens to be a single-family home,
you may go into that purchase with the idea of fixing
it up and renting it for at least one or two years. If the
market is right, you can pay off as much of the loan as
possible, and then sell the property, using that property as your stepping stone to move up and purchase
your next rental property, perhaps a duplex or even
four-plex. You also purchase rental property with the
hopes that the value will increase. Sometimes it takes
a few years, and other times it may increase quickly.
A lot of this depends on the market in which you
purchase.

There are many tax and IRS rules to buying and
selling rental properties, so it is important you take

the time to talk with your accountant and know the fine lines that are drawn. Don't get caught paying short-term capital gains and other taxes attached to buying and selling investment property.

Sometimes when you decide to purchase rental property, you decide to join forces with one or more partners. Make sure you are aware of all aspects, as you are just as responsible as the others, whether you own 10 percent, 50 percent, or 90 percent.

Other times, you can purchase properties in foreclosure or distressed properties. If you are ready to purchase, have your down payment ready and be prequalified. You now have put yourself in a great position if a distress sale comes on the market.

This chapter discusses all of these options.

Generating cash to purchase properties

There are many different ways to get cash for a downpayment on another rental property. Refinancing your personal residence or another rental property is common, as is taking out an equity line on existing properties. The following sections help you identify some ways to get cash.

Paying down the loan

Some people like to get a 30-year mortgage but pay down the loan to build up their equity and reduce their debt. You can make an extra payment every year or add an amount — even $50 or $100 — to each month's payment.

 Bright Idea

I have all my mortgages on my properties automatically deducted from the checking account each month. If the loan is due on the 1st and late on the 16th, I have the bank automatically take the payment on the 15th. This gives me time each month to collect all the rents and be certain all checks have cleared.

Moneysaver

By refinancing your personal residence to reinvest in another property, the new loan on your personal home is still a write-off, and the interest is tax deductible. You may also be able to pay off your credit card debt or an auto loan.

Cashing out through refinancing

The way that I first purchased rental property was by using the equity in my personal residence. I had owned a home for a few years and the value had increased substantially, allowing me to take a good-size equity loan. I then used this toward the down payment of the office building I wanted to purchase.

Often, when the interest rates are low like they have been lately, you can refinance your home and use some cash from the equity as your down payment for your next purchase. You may want to ask your Realtor whether he or she can tell you the approximate value of your home at that current time (see Chapter 1). The Realtor who sold you the home may also know the current value and will likely be happy to assist you.

After you have an idea of the value, meet with a mortgage broker or with your banker to determine just how much cash you can count on when you refinance. Tell them that your plan is to purchase another piece of property. As always, it takes planning and meeting with the professional to know what direction to take — purchasing rental property.

Taking on a partner

Often, you are talking to others about purchasing an investment property, and someone you know will say he is looking as well and would love to partner with you on your next purchase.

Watch Out!

The partner you choose may be a close friend but even with a close friend, you don't know all the facts and financial history. You have no idea what his or her credit is like. Be sure you know the entire situation before purchasing rental property with a friend or acquaintance.

You don't purchase property with a partner or partners without an advance plan. You need to be sure you are all clear as to how long you want to keep this property, the price range of that property, who is going to be the general partner, and who is going to manage this property and take care of the day-to-day details. You should really decide on many of these details before jumping in to the purchase; buying a property with a partner is a big step and one that doesn't always work out.

You need to have a plan, a direction, and it needs to be in writing. For example, you need to know how long you plan to keep this property prior to the close of escrow.

After you have identified the property, you should have a rough idea at first of the cash flow. Will you have a negative cash flow and if so, how much and for how long? You need to have a budget and a projection. Don't go into the deal thinking you can talk about it after you close escrow or when something comes up. Always have your agreement with any partner in writing.

Considering bank-owned properties

If you are looking to purchase rental property that the bank owns (a foreclosure), it is important to keep in mind that another investor just like you bought that property at one time and thought he or she would make money. However, something obviously went wrong. It could have to do with the economy in the area where the property is located, or the economy in general, or a problem with the building itself. The important thing here is you need to look at things from all angles. The foreclosure could have absolutely nothing to do with any of the above and was about a problem the owner/investor had.

People get excited about purchasing property that has been foreclosed on, because the property is sold at a great price and well under market as compared to other similar properties sold that in that area. Banks aren't interested in losing money, however. The bank usually works with an appraiser to have the property value determined. They don't have plans to lose money or give away the property.

You need to conduct all of your inspections and have an appraisal done to be certain the purchase is a good one. Fixing up properties is expensive. You need to know what work is needed, the cost involved to get the work done, and the current rental-market value for that property.

In most cases, you have to purchase the property in "as is" condition. Be certain you know what costs are involved all the way around, as well as the true rental income that you can expect for the property when it is in better condition.

If buying a foreclosure interests you, check with the local community colleges and/or community centers. Quite often, a local real estate counselor gives night or adult classes on how to purchase foreclosures. It is quite complex and you have to be sure to follow all the rules, but many investors have watched for these properties and enjoy buying, fixing up, renting, and exchanging.

Tapping into growing markets: Hot spots

Like anything, there are always areas considered the "hot spots" to purchase rental property. Usually, you can ask around to find a Realtor who knows where his or her investor clients are purchasing at any given time.

It is even more of a bonus if one of those hot spots in which you choose to purchase investment property doesn't require you to pay state tax and/or the property taxes are low.

Bright Idea

Find a "hot spot" and take the time to check out the area. Drive around the area to see how much new construction is in the area and how the neighborhood looks and feels. Try to get in contact with another investor your Realtor has worked with in the area before purchasing.

When you find a hot spot, take the time to know all of the anticipated costs. For example, the cost of water or sewer could be much more expensive in that area than you are accustomed to paying.

I had a Realtor friend tell me that she herself is purchasing brand-new properties in a new subdivision during the first phase, and then selling them after all the houses are built. In most cases, if you get in a "hot" market area early on, by the time the property is built and move-in ready, you have made money and can turn around and sell it. Be sure to know the short-term capital gains rules before you begin doing this. Check with your accountant.

Don't be afraid to invest in professional services and hire the best to assist you through the process. You should surround yourself with a good attorney, accountant, professional property manager, banker or mortgage broker and a reputable 1031 exchange company, and even a good handyman or contractor (see Chapter 1). There is nothing worse than purchasing rental property, owning the property for a few years, selling it, and finding out during your tax appointment that you did not handle the transaction correctly and must pay a large sum of money to the Internal Revenue Service (IRS). That is like having to start all over again. Plan and take the time in the beginning so that you don't have any tax implications that could have been avoided and that cost you a large sum of money.

A lot of times, when you buy in an area that is considered a hot spot, rents and values can plummet just as fast as they grew.

Just as in the money and stock markets, investors take bigger risks when the values are rising rapidly. Are you a high or low risk-taker? Answering that question will help you to decide where you want to purchase new property.

Taking advantage of 1031 tax-deferred exchanges

A 1031 exchange allows you to sell an investment property and defer the financial gain into the next investment property, thus avoiding paying tax on the gain. The following sections gives you the details.

Knowing why to make an exchange

Why do investors consider exchanges? There are many reasons that investors may consider performing a 1031 exchange:

- **Property with a large equity:** An exchange would allow the investor to diversify the equity into one or several larger properties.

- **Diversification of holdings:** Acquiring several replacement properties, either in different neighborhoods or of different product types, allows an investor to spread his risk.

> 66 1031s often force investors to make purchase decisions that aren't based on sound real estate analysis. Whenever you factor in a present value tax advantage against something in the future, be careful. 99
>
> —Mark K., Dallas investor

- **Consolidation of holdings:** In essence, an investor with many properties can reduce the management and operational headaches by exchanging several properties into one larger replacement property of equal or greater value.

Moneysaver

It is extremely important to know about tax-deferred exchanges as you begin to buy, sell, and trade properties. There are many rules. Save money and negative tax implications by hiring an expert. If you don't follow the guidelines, you may find yourself writing large checks to the IRS.

- **Cash-flow needs:** By optimizing rental property and exchanging out of non-performing or poorly performing properties, an investor can either increase the overall cash flow or can stabilize the cash flow by entering into a long-term lease with a very credit worthy tenant, such as a large national company.

- **Change of geographic area:** As investors move around the country and acquire real estate, they tend to end up with a collection of properties in different communities.

- **Property with a high land ratio:** A farm or a ranch with acreage but not much rental potential can be exchanged for a more traditional rental property such as apartments.

- **Preservation of equity:** The first discussion of exchanges always centers on saving the taxes and preserving the equity in the property. If an investor doesn't pay capital gains taxes, any of the above scenarios will be enhanced by the use of a 1031 tax-deferred exchange.

Sometimes, your accountant will suggest that you do an exchange because you need a bigger tax write off. Or maybe you are tired of doing maintenance work and want to purchase something newer so you don't have as much work to do.

I've also had people exchange their investment property to another area where they would like to retire, or to where close family has moved. This provides additional tax savings in that the trips to check on your property can probably be deducted from the income. As always, check with your accountant.

To find a good 1031 exchange company, you can check with your Realtor, other investors, or search for "1031 exchanges" on the Internet.

You need to shop around for the intermediary (1031 exchange company) that you want to use. Some charge flat fees, while others charge a percentage of the money they are holding. Some will give you interest on the equity until it is reinvested. So do your homework before choosing a company.

Essential elements of a 1031 exchange

The sale of property held for productive use in a trade or business or held for investment will generally result in a taxable event. However, if the sale is structured as a like-kind or 1031 exchange, prior to the sale, and is linked through documentation and procedures to the purchase of a qualified replacement property, the sale can result in a safe harbor tax deferred exchange.

Key elements in the delayed exchange process are as follows:

- A 1031 exchange is an IRS-approved method to save payment of capital gains taxes.

- A relinquished property must be sold through a qualified intermediary.

- Like-kind property must be acquired for replacement.

- Specific time periods must be met to complete the exchange.

  - From closing of the sale of the first property, the investor has 45 days to identify replacement properties.

  - From the same closing, the taxpayer has 180 days to acquire the replacement property.

- Replacement cost must equal or exceed the net sales price of the relinquished property.

Like-kind property must be acquired for replacement for the transaction to be tax-deferred. The regulations about like kind allow for a broad interpretation of what is "like." Essentially, any real property held for investment can be exchanged for any other real property as long as it is to be held for investment.

Examples of like-kind properties

Consider these examples:

- Vacant land for a rental house
- Farm land for a commercial building
- Motel for an apartment building
- Industrial buildings for timberland
- Apartments for a rental condominium

In addition to property types shown above, like-kind concepts extend to fractional interests or multiple interests exchanged for partial, one, or many properties.

Examples of unlike or non-qualifying properties

Some non-qualifying properties are as follows:

- Cash, stocks, or bonds
- Personal property
- Partnership interests or shares of a REIT
- Stock in trade or inventory
- Personal residence

Selling the property you're giving up

Selling the relinquished property is as simple as placing it on the market. The intermediary will set up an interchange agreement between the taxpayer and the qualified intermediary. They will also provide specific instructions to the closing agent (escrow officer) for the formatting of the settlement statement to accurately reflect the transaction as part of a 1031 exchange. Following the sale of the closing of the relinquished property, the funds will go to the intermediary's escrow account. Holding those funds along with the documentation sequence in a 1031 exchange helps provide safe harbor status for the taxpayer.

Purchasing a replacement property

With the sale of the relinquished property completed, the clock starts ticking on the client's exchange. The exchanger has 45 days to identify replacement property and 180 days to acquire replacement property (or the due date of the tax return, with extensions, whichever comes first).

If you begin delayed exchanges late in the year, April 15 will arrive before the 180th day for completion. The simple remedy is to file for an automatic extension for filing the tax return and thereby change the due date of the tax return to August 15. Under no circumstances should you complete the tax return until the exchange has been completed.

You can begin to search for and negotiate on replacement property prior to the closing of the relinquished property.

After you have found suitable replacement property and have placed it under contract, a similar sequence to selling the relinquished property takes place. The intermediary will accept assignment of the purchase contract and step into the exchanger's shoes to purchase the replacement property. The intermediary will deliver funds held from the escrow account to the closing of the replacement property.

Following the purchase of the replacement property, the final step is to include the required information on the tax return on IRS Form 8824.

> 66 Over the years, I have always sold my worst rentals to buyers motivated to find a deal because of the 1031. People often make mistakes when the pressure of losing the exchange tax benefit forces them to buy less-than-sensible rentals. 99
>
> —Mark K., Dallas investor

Just the facts

- By refinancing your current home, you pay off some or all of your current debt and may be able to get cash out to purchase an investment property.

- Partnerships don't always work. By having your partnership agreement in writing, however, terms become more clear and you have less of a chance for the unforeseen problems.

- There are many "hot spots" to purchase rental properties around the U.S. You don't have to buy close to where you live.

- Foreclosed properties need investigation as to what went wrong.

- Hiring real-estate professionals can save you a lot of time, money, and stress in the long run.

- Your accountant may suggest a 1031 exchange for tax reasons.

- When selling an investment property in a 1031 tax deferred exchange, you must purchase "like kind" in order to qualify.

- Specific time periods must be met to complete the exchange.

- Replacement property must equal or exceed the value of the relinquished property.

GET THE SCOOP ON...
Looking at positive and negative economic
factors ▪ Hanging on in survival mode ▪ What
affects your market ▪ Planning and balancing
your investments ▪ Identifying risks and opportunities ▪ Diversifying your portfolio ▪ Building
a reserve ▪ Shortening the length of your
loan payback time ▪ Watching for the signs of
change ▪ Analyzing the building ▪ Investing in
your investment ▪ Knowing which properties
are performing and which are duds ▪
Assessing your strategies

Surviving the Peaks and Valleys of Real Estate Investing

E very business has cycles, and the successful
investor plans ahead. It is easy to love the
renewal property business when things are
going well and hate the business as it gets more challenging. Remember the lessons of the Great
Depression, the energy crisis, and September 11,
2001, and stand ready to live up to the adage, "When
the going gets tough, the tough get going!"

Reviewing potential economic impacts

There are a number of economic impacts that could
positively and negatively impact your rental business,
and each is discussed in the following sections.

Employment opportunities in your area

Consider the largest employers in the vicinity of your rentals. Is there a healthy diversity in the types of industry that are the mainstay of the economy in your chosen investment area? Learn from and remember the impact of booms and busts like those of the oil industry in Texas, the steel industry in the Ohio Valley, the textile industry in the Southeast, and so on. What would you do if your rental business were located in the neighborhood closest to Enron's or WorldCom's headquarters?

Specialized entities include higher education, the military, and a concentration of government jobs. These sectors frequently expand and contract with broader economic currents as public funds and public preferences change. If a military base were to close or a vast number of its service people reassigned due to war, could your rental-property business survive?

Having investment properties around a university appeals to several investors whose children are now heading to college. Remember that this type of rental is seasonal, however, and usually will require more maintenance and has higher turnover.

Some communities are only for 55+ age bracket. These people may be more stable residents, so find out about the trends in the area you are buying. If this is a favorite retirement area, it may be a good investment.

Supply and demand of housing in your area

There is typically a three- to five-year lag time between the time developers propose housing projects and subdivisions and the time these communities are ready for occupancy. Conversely,

Bright Idea

Consider joining your local chamber of commerce and get involved with the housing committee. Pay attention to what the businesses are doing in the area where you own your investment property. Your local chamber of commerce usually is active in the business community.

there is a lag time between the time these homes are ready for occupancy and saturation (the homes all being filled). Is your business ready to grow from high demand/low supply, and can you make it through the tough times when demand is low and supply high?

Interest rates

In 2003, interest rates hit their lowest point in 40 years, thus producing a window of opportunity for tenants to become homeowners. Just about everyone who could qualify — and some who probably should not have qualified — converted from the rental market to the home-buying market. Are you ready for riskier tenants and higher turnover if this happens again?

Environmental issues

Bad things can happen no matter how well prepared you are. How would you like to have owned investment property near Three Mile Island or the Love Canal?

Proceeding with caution

If you have not dropped this book off the nearest bridge or run screaming from the room, you are probably well suited for the real estate investment business! Just remember that the absolute key to success in any endeavor is to take calculated risks. This means achieving a level of understanding to identify risks and opportunities and planning for long-term prosperity.

So what do you do?

- Pay down your highest rate loans first.
- Buy smart.
- Don't overleverage yourself.
- Diversify your portfolio.
- Watch for the signs of change.
- Use consistent policies and procedures.
- Reinvest every time you sell a property.

- Build a reserve.
- Re-evaluate strategies.
- Constantly evaluate the performance of your properties and get rid of the duds.

The following sections explore each of these ideas in detail.

Pay down your highest-rate loans first

Some investors strive to pay down mortgages more quickly than the original terms of the notes. If you choose to do this, target your highest-interest-rate notes first to save money in the long run. In times of economic weakness, you may think about refinancing the term to lower your monthly payment. You can always pay more principal and shorten the term of the note when the market recovers.

Buy smart

Everyone has an opinion about purchasing investment property. As long as you know there is no cookie-cutter approach, you are ahead of most investors. Cap rates, gross rent multipliers, and return on investment calculations are extremely valuable, but there is more to the total equation.

An analysis of the building includes the structural integrity, present and deferred maintenance needs, aesthetic appearance, functionality, and features and benefits. A financial performance includes rental history, including vacancy rate, turnover rate, cap rate, and finally, the return on investment. An economic analysis includes the political and social forces and the local economy, including crime rates and demographics.

 Moneysaver

Do your homework before you buy. Consider the property's atmosphere, buildings, and financial performance. Atmosphere includes the location, neighborhood, demographics, crime rate, and the economic base. Real estate is all about location, location, location. Make sure to take a good look at the entire area in which the property is located.

Do the research necessary so you know where to invest. Ask around, talk to other investors in the area, drive around the immediate area to see what the neighborhood is like. Good research takes time. Maybe you know the neighborhood is not the best at this time but expect to hold the investment in hopes that it will turn around. As the new owner, many times when you begin improving your property and other investors see that, it starts a trend.

You can tell a lot about the building and the neighborhood by the condition and number of cars around the property. If you see a lot of cars that are run down, old, beat up, and on blocks or look to be non-operational, it is usually a bad sign. Also, are people just hanging around? Is there trash littered on the sidewalk, driveways, and lawns? One approach is to find out the names of other owners on either side and ask to meet with them to discuss a plan to fix up the neighborhood and bring up the quality of tenants.

Visit the local police department and introduce yourself. Let them know that you are a new owner and your goal is to improve the property and to bring in quality tenants. Find out whether they have any recommendations, as some will give you safety tips from a police perspective. Some communities have a program that is in sync with the police department to clean up a neighborhood. The owners and tenants of the properties get together to plan clean-up days, watch groups, and social activities to support one another and keep the neighborhood one they can be proud of.

Decide your goal in owning investment property. It may be to provide housing for your parents or other family members for a short while, and then turn it into a rental. Perhaps it is to help clean up a neighborhood that has your interest. You may want a tax write-off to maximize the bottom line for more income, or it may be to buy that retirement home now that you plan to move into three to five years from now. The type and location of property in which you decide to invest needs to meet your ultimate goal.

Remember that it is okay to take a risk; just know what you are getting yourself into. Negotiate well and prepare for the worst-case scenario.

Don't overleverage

You may have seen paid TV advertisements where a real estate guru tries to sell you a product that will teach you how to make money with no money down. Sounds great, right? After all, if you have nothing at risk what do you have to lose? The answer is your credit rating, income from your primary job or other investments, and possibly even any other assets you own. Fully leveraged investments have no room to absorb economic swings, maintenance projects, vacancies, or any other hidden cost. Downpayments are a good thing.

Lenders have learned over time and experience that they need to protect their investment in your property from failure. The banking industry requires mortgage insurance on any loans exceeding an 80 percent loan-to-value (LTV). They recognize the higher risk associated with a highly leveraged (low down payment) property. Making a loan at 80 percent or less LTV will ensure the success of the bank's investment most of the time. Many institutions are now requiring 25 percent down on multi-family properties or non-owner-occupied properties, so be prepared.

 Bright Idea

Research state and local government laws regarding rental property management, because these vary greatly from one area to another and definitely affect your bottom line. Find out about business licenses, property taxes, special tax assessments, rent leveling calculations, and other laws, as well as restrictions concerning landscaping, exterior color schemes, parking, curfews, and so on.

Watch Out!

If your property is leveraged to the maximum and the market takes a turn and rents decline, or you suddenly have long-term vacancy you mayy experience financial hardship. Be prepared, as rental markets go up and down based on many factors.

When you have selected and analyzed the available properties and have identified the top two or three choices, take a few minutes to think negatively about what would happen to your investment if rents dropped 25 percent or the largest nearby employer were to move its operations or close down completely.

Diversify your portfolio

One strategy for minimizing the effects of a downturn in the economy is to diversify your holdings. As you choose new investments, consider the advantages and disadvantages of each new purchase. Single-family homes and duplexes tend to sell more quickly than multi-family units. Multi-family units however, have the advantage that if a unit sits vacant for a month, you still have some rent coming in. As you build your portfolio, maintain a mix of properties to reap the benefits of each type, while at the same time minimizing the negative effects of economic changes.

In my portfolio, the modest single-family home has statistically out-produced all other types of investment property time and time again. This is attributed to the fact that there is a housing food chain, where the vast majority of tenants begin in a small apartment and move up into a larger apartment, then into a duplex, then into a small single-family home, and then into a larger single family home, and continue renting homes until they are ultimately ready to purchase a home. This natural progression is a result of our quest for more space, more privacy, more bells and whistles, more status, and so forth. This is perfect preparation for the responsibilities of owning a home, which is the ultimate American dream.

Another important consideration in diversification is location. The rule of thumb is that you should not manage rental properties that are more than a one-hour drive away from your home or work because it is too time-consuming to show available units, monitor them properly, and perform maintenance in a timely manner. Within your one-hour radius, though, choose properties in different locations to minimize the effects of business closures, natural disasters, and so on. If you do decide to purchase outside of your immediate area, be sure there is a good property manager you can hire if needed (see Chapter 17).

Watch for the signs of change

The recent recession is frequently attributed to September 11, 2001. However, the economic downturn began long before that date. Early warning signs of a recession include falling interest rates, irregular stock market changes, job layoffs, overbuilding, fewer inquiries from people moving in from another state or location, tenants moving because they need to save money, and so on. You can keep your finger on the pulse of economic changes by watching the newspaper for an increasing number of ads for similar rentals, price changes on similar units, and headlines in the news about changes in jobs and the economy, and by tracking the length of time it takes to get your vacant units rented.

Most small investors and management companies are very slow to change. You can beat the competition by watching for trends and being creative in attracting the best tenants. In a slow economy, investors lament that they cannot afford to take less for a rental unit. However, choosing the wrong tenant or holding out at a high price only increases the problem. The faster you turn your vacancy, the more stable your cash flow will be.

Being in a group of other investors can really help because you aren't on your own to do all the research. You also receive input from others on the trends they are experiencing.

Use consistent policies and procedures

Tenants with poor credit, job instability, questionable landlord references, or criminal histories are turned away from most savvy investors and managers. They frequently look for a private individual from which to rent simply because they cannot get by the qualification process, and typically, they are relegated to paying higher rent as a result of their risk. However, I cannot stress enough how important it is that you set firm qualification guidelines, and then stick to them consistently. Not only does this strategy protect you from lawsuits alleging discrimination, it also keeps you steady in difficult times.

When interest rates recently dropped to the lowest rate in 40 years, tenants evolved into homebuyers at record numbers. In fact, the only tenants left in the market were the ones who could not qualify for a mortgage, and I even saw some tenants qualify for loans whom I had refused to rent to! Even as I saw this mass exodus of tenants, I set firm policies and adhered to them faithfully. If you allow yourself to get desperate and begin accepting any tenant standing upright with green money, your risk multiplies.

Reinvest

Look around your community. Are there poorly cared for areas? Do you see run-down houses, duplexes, or apartment buildings? Do you ever wonder how this happens? Is it just that properties are old?

It is likely that you are seeing rental properties either owned by investors who are in trouble or owned by someone with a philosophy to bleed a property by doing only the minimum maintenance required to keep the property producing income. These investors are also known as slumlords, and they make a lot of money on their investment until the property is sold or bulldozed.

Research in inner cities has shown that if there is graffiti on a building or a broken window that is not repaired immediately, it quickly attracts more abuse. If it is repaired immediately, it is less likely to be vandalized again in the same immediate time period. Whether or not you care about your buildings will be readily apparent, and you will attract the positive or negative by your choice in maintenance philosophy.

> **❝** Plan to keep your properties for a long period of time to obtain the highest rate of return, while at the same time planning for the ups and downs of the market. **❞**
>
> —Susan A., MPM (master property manager) investor and property manager

Protect your investment by monitoring it frequently. Enforce the lease and if there is damage, mandate that the tenant repair it, or repair it yourself and charge the tenant immediately. Get rid of tenants who display a chronic tendency to disrespect your property and their neighbors, or cause negligent damage. Don't allow your property to attract only the poorest-quality tenants.

Quality properties attract quality tenants. If you reinvest in your property by keeping it aesthetically pleasing outside and inside, you will be better prepared to survive and thrive in a down market. As you reinvest, focus first on the curb appeal and second on interior aesthetics. It will not matter how beautiful your property is on the inside if prospective tenants drive by and are turned off by the outward appearance. Cultivate and maintain a clean, manicured, and colorful exterior, and you will out-compete other landlords for the best tenants, even in slow times.

Build a reserve

Plan for upgrades and hidden problems by building a reserve. Just when you think everything is going along nicely, either some major expense comes up or a few of your long-term tenants give you notice to move. You need to plan and be prepared. If you have long-term tenants, you will usually endure a great deal more of expenses, as you will need to upgrade the unit at the time of their move-out. There are several methods for calculating an appropriate reserve to be used for capital improvements and economic changes.

Start by developing a spreadsheet that lists:

Item	Remaining Life	Replacement Cost	Reserve Needs
Roof	10 years	$2,300.00	$230.00/year
Paint	4 years	$1,350.00	$337.50/year
Carpet	5 years	$985.00	$197.00/year
Linoleum	2 years	$375.00	$187.50/year
Appliances	8 years	$1,100.00	$137.50/year
TOTAL ANNUAL RESERVE REQUIREMENT:	$1,089.50/year		

This type of calculation is called the full funding method and will assist you in determining how much money you need to set aside each year to be prepared for replacement costs. In order to keep this calculation current, you have to reinvestigate replacement costs every year. The advantage to using this method is that you will always have the funds immediately available as needs arise. The disadvantage is that you will not be able to leverage that money (that is, spend it) if you are true to your funding plan.

The baseline method uses the same basic calculations, but it trims down the amount required by graphing out cash flow needs so that the funds will be available when needed. The basic premise is that the reserve fund only needs to be large enough to cover expenses as they arise and not drop below a targeted minimum.

Year	Project	Funds Needed	Contribution	Expense	End Balance
2005			$650.00		$650.00
2006	Linoleum	$375.00	$650.00	$375.00	$925.00
2007			$650.00		$1,575.00
2008	Paint	$1,350.00	$650.00	$1,350.00	$875.00
2009	Carpet	$985.00	$650.00	$985.00	$540.00
2010			$650.00		$1,190.00
2011			$650.00		$1,840.00
2012	Appliances	$1,100.00	$650.00	$1,100.00	$1,390.00
2013			$650.00		$2,040.00
2014	Roof	$2,300.00	$650.00	$2,300.00	$390.00
TARGETING MINIMUM RESERVE:	$500.00				
ANNUAL RESERVE REQUIREMENT:	$650.00				

These are the simplest analytical methods to use to determine the level of reserves you should have on hand. Of course, you could just set a policy of x number of months operating and debt service costs. Whichever method you choose is up to you. However, you need to understand the importance of maintaining your properties so that you attract the best tenants, even in a down economy.

Re-evaluate strategies

As markets change, you need to be flexible to change with them. Sometimes, a change in the market necessitates a change in the policy. I decided to accept tenants who showed some risk.

At this point, I created at a policy that I would conduct an interior inspection 30 to 45 days after the tenants moved in to see whether they were good caregivers. Even when tenants know you will be there and clean up for you, a smart landlord can still see whether there is a problem just by looking in corners and under the sofa. Any tenants I identified as having poor property-care habits were immediately flagged for quarterly inspections. Any damage found during inspections was addressed then and there by giving the tenant seven days to correct the problem or be charged for the repair.

Always assess what is working and what is not. Think about the ways to manage the risk and set written policies to address the risk. Being consistent is absolutely crucial, but ignoring trends is certain failure. Set yourself up on an annual schedule of reviewing policies, preferably in mid- to late- May, before the busy summer moving season.

Evaluate property performance (and get rid of the duds)

When you sit down in May to evaluate policies, also evaluate the performance of each of your properties using the same analyses as when you decided to purchase. Compare returns on investment, look at vacancy rates, and obtain information from your Realtor about comparative properties for sale. Meet with your accountant to discuss your tax status and how your investments will improve your position. Is your property producing as it should or would it be wise to sell or exchange it? Always treat your rentals as a business and make good business decisions. Some landlords get personally attached to the properties and lose sight of the bigger picture of the investment.

Opportunities are everywhere. If you miss out on what may have been a great deal, don't give up. The right real estate agent will keep contacting you with everything on the market until your needs and/or goals are matched with the right property.

Don't buy if the property doesn't feel right. Take your time when you are in escrow to be certain this is the right investment for you and that it all makes sense. Better to change your mind before you purchase the property than after, when you are knee-deep in large expenses.

In summary, there are cycles in real estate investing: times of feast and times of famine. Nothing is insurmountable, but there will be times when the going gets tough, and you will need to be tough enough to get going. Savvy investors do their homework before buying and manage risk throughout their ownership by staying current with economic cycles and trends. They respond to change quickly, clearly, and consistently, and prepare ahead of time for the worst. By doing so, everything else in landlording is a nice surprise!

Responding (or Not) to Market Swings

Suppose the rental market is on the rise after you've been struggling for the last two to three years to make ends meet and maintain the property. The normal reaction is to make the same rent adjustments with your tenants as you hear others are doing. This is not the time to be increasing your rents to your steady tenants. Remember that you are in this for the long run and a good tenant is still worth keeping.

On the other hand, rents may be trending down. Don't wait for your tenant to come to you to ask for a rent decrease — go to them. They may not come to you because they may be out looking for a better deal. When you find out, it may be too late. Keep in mind that a turnover costs money and is lost rent revenue.

The market swings are a time for your long-range planning to kick in. Don't just be reactionary.

Just the facts

- All rental markets change, so watch for the signs and be prepared.

- The successful investor plans ahead.

- Keep aware of employment changes in the area of your investment.

- Evaluate what building booms are doing to your property.

- Most banks want at least 20 percent down, if not 25 percent. Overleveraging is not a good idea and can cause financial hardship if the rental market takes a downward turn and there are many vacancies.

- No money down is very risky.

- Diversify your type of investment property.

- When you build up your equity, continue to reinvest.

- Quality properties attract quality tenants and both attract more quality tenants.

- If you plan to pay down your loan/mortgage, pay down the one with the highest interest rate.

- Continue to analyze your strategy.

- Think about and write down your goals in owning investment property.

- Join organizations such as the local chamber of commerce so that you stay current on the employment changes, companies coming in to the area, and perhaps even new building or development that is coming to the area.

- Protect your investment by sticking to your policies and procedures.

- A good plan includes building a reserve for emergencies.

- Get rid of the properties that are problems. Get rid of the duds.

GET THE SCOOP ON...
Knowing what a property management company
does ▪ Getting referrals ▪ Ways to find a professional management company ▪ Interviewing a
management company ▪ Finding other property
management options

Hiring a Professional Management Company

Chapter 17

Throughout the book, I refer to hiring professionals to assist you with the management of
your investment property. Hiring and working
with professional property managers can be an
important part of the success in investing and
expanding your new business. When you can afford
to hire a professional management to do all of the
hard work, you will then begin to really enjoy owning
investment property.

You need to know when it is time to turn your
rental property over to someone who does this each
and every day, who knows day-to-day operations, who
has heard the latest scams, and is familiar with the
latest laws from the government. Most importantly,
you need someone who can take care of your property management needs and the headaches that
come with rental property management and investment property ownership.

Moneysaver

Early on, invest in the time to meet with a professional company, before you make mistakes. I recommend calling a professional company, making an appointment for a consultation and paying for an hour or two of time. Have a list of questions prepared, so as to maximize your time with the property manager.

The right property manager will almost make you forget you own investment property. You need to hire someone who has the skills and the ability to manage your property with the latest technology, attracting quality and long-term tenants.

There are many important factors to consider when hiring a management company. The important thing to know is what to expect from the company managing your rental property and what your responsibility is as the owner during the term of the relationship.

What a property management company does

A property management company plays the role of the intermediary. The management firm steps between you and the tenant, allowing you to be at a distance. A good management company doesn't make decisions based on feelings or personal interests, but instead follows professional policies and procedures and strict guidelines. Often, a property manager's response will be, "We are just the property managers." This lets the tenants know he or she cannot be swayed by emotion and must stick to the rules. Also, it is usually easier for a management company to raise rents based on its industry knowledge of the market, allowing for consistency.

A professional property manager saves you time, work, and stress in the following ways:

- You don't have to clean, paint, or make repairs (or hire someone to do those tasks).

- Emergencies will be handled in the appropriate manner to ensure tenant safety and protect your property.

- You don't have to advertise, take rental calls, and be available to show the available property.

- You don't have to screen applications and be apprehensive about whom to choose.

- You don't have to execute a rental agreement, worry about adding addenda, fill out the move-in inspection report, or worry about the security deposit money.

- You don't have tenants calling at all hours of the day and night.

- You don't have to confront tenants on tough issues like collecting rents or taking care of the property.

- You don't have to collect non-sufficient funds checks (NSF).

- You don't have to serve legal notices or begin eviction proceedings.

- You don't have to schedule and fill out the move-in or move-out inspection report, starting the process all over again with each tenant.

- You don't have to know each and every law that the government is discussing or passing.

- You won't spend time paying bills.

- Professionals will be used for the maintenance on your property.

I am certain there are good reasons for managing your own rental property, but ask yourself whether they worth the hassle and risk.

You don't have to worry about the property or be shocked by its condition when you hire a professional property manager. They are dedicated to selecting quality tenants and keeping your investment in good repair with minimal cost. They want your real estate investment to be successful. One of the last benefits: Your leasing and management fees are usually tax deductible.

Many investors are afraid to end up with a property manager who may not be capable of doing the job. You want to be sure that this person can and will take care of your investment.

When to hire a property management company

Knowing when to hire a professional property management company comes with time and experience. You may prefer to manage your rental property on your own, which is a good thing, especially in the beginning. After a while, though, especially after you've experienced a problem tenant or two, you may consider interviewing, and potentially hiring, a property management company. When you have managed the property on your own for a few years, you will also have a better understanding of exactly what a property management company does.

What to expect and not expect from your property manager

It really helps to know what to expect and not expect from your property management company. Having a clear understanding helps the relationship with your property manager.

Here's what you can and should expect the property management company to be doing:

- Keeping accurate financial records
- Sending monthly and yearly statements
- Sending IRS-required 1099 statements
- Issuing monthly or quarterly newsletters that keep you updated on laws and other changes in the market
- Taking continuing education classes in property management

- Following your instructions concerning maintenance issues
- Keeping you informed of issues on your property
- Responding in a timely manner
- Using professional leases and management agreement
- Maintaining a Web site that list the available rentals
- Marketing your property in several ways (not just in the newspaper)
- Making an annual inspections of your property and details of the inspection provided to you

Here's what not to expect:

- Weekly or monthly updates if everything is going well
- Calls returned the same day, except in an emergency (remember that a property manager's job does require him or her to be near the property at all times)
- That yours is the only property they manage
- A guarantee that the tenant will always pay rent on time
- That there will never be any problems
- That they can rent the property over the current market
- That the company can rent your property even though you haven't maintained it
- That maintenance costs are included in the monthly fee
- That the cheapest property management company is also the best

When the property is just too far away

A good reason to consider hiring a property management company is when your rental property is just too far away. Let's face it: For most people, it is a mistake to buy a rental property one or two hours driving time each way and not hire a management company. At first, the drive may not seem that bad. However, after awhile, that long drive on your day off will get old and tiresome, especially when you have a vacancy. Imagine driving over to show the available rental and no one shows up! Hire a professional.

When the property is too large

As you build up your rental properties and add more inventory, there will come a time when your property or the total number of units you own becomes too much to manage on a part-time basis. It is one thing if you only own a single-family or even a smaller building near you. But if you have a larger building or multiple units, this is the time to look into hiring a professional management company. In this case, a property management company may very well pay for itself.

When you realize how much time you're spending managing your property

When you stop and think about how much time you are taking away from your family, friends, and perhaps your job, you may realize it is time to take the step to hire someone to do it for you.

When you have just had enough

When you are tired of dealing with the late-night calls and tenants who complain incessantly, when you're not raising the rents because you feel bad for the tenants yet your monthly costs are rising, and when you have rented to a tenant for all the wrong reasons, this is the time to call in outside help. In the long run, a property management company will not only save you money but will also keep you out of trouble and they are the ones who take the late-night calls and the first-hand complaints, not you.

Watch Out!

Some real estate companies do management as a token or a favor. Don't take the bait. Hire a company that is not trying to manage properties in several different areas, or selling real estate, or managing associations with a limited staff.

For the majority of investors/managers, the thought of hiring a property manager to care for the property is unheard of. Most of the time, owners believe that managing their property will be easy. In fact, most never think of hiring a property manager until there is a problem. There are so many different types of problems, from slow-paying or non-paying tenants to tenants playing loud music or always complaining about something. Remember the movie *Pacific Heights?* If you have never seen it or forget what happened, view it again. The tenants that drive up in a fancy car and a whole lot of cash may be the ones to ultimately destroy your property after signing the lease. These are the ones that seem so nice and you thought were going to be the "perfect tenants." If your instincts tell you something is wrong, I guarantee your instincts are right.

How to hire a property manager

Choose a property management professional with as much care as you would an attorney or doctor. Friends, neighbors, and co-workers are often good sources for referrals. Try to find out as much as possible about their rental and landlording experience. What kind of service did they receive? Would they choose this particular professional or property management company again? Most of all, make sure you feel comfortable with the person you choose to work with. It is all based on trust.

The National Association of Residential Property Managers (NARPM)

Best known as NARPM, the National Association of Residential Property Managers is one of the best and simplest ways to search and find a really great property management company. NARPM is a professional organization that promotes education, designations, and networking as a resource to empower its members with knowledge and skill. A NARPM member honors and subscribes to a code of ethics and standards of professionalism, while educating its members.

Members are licensed, maintain a high professional standard, and understand the ins and outs of managing rental properties. A NARPM member knows that education is extremely important to his or her business and is able to attend special advanced classes that can earn a coveted residential management professional (RMP) or master property manager (MPM) designation. Associates are able to attend annual conventions, leadership conferences, and local chapter meetings with other property managers. The conventions and conferences are packed with a variety of educational classes, workshops, keynote speakers, and a whole lot of marketing.

Okay, I admit that I'm a little biased. I was fortunate enough to earn my RMP and MPM designations and have attended every national convention, conference, and leadership training since I joined in the early '90s. In addition, my company earned the prestigious certified residential management company (CRMC) designation that required a great deal of preparation along with a thorough policy and procedures manual. You must undergo a detailed and thorough audit and succeed in completing a four-page list of requirements. In order to keep this designation, the company has to be audited every three years.

Bright Idea

When choosing a company, visit the office during normal business hours to see how business is conducted. By visiting the office, you can get a feel for the business and meet the staff who will be involved with the day-to-day operations of managing your property.

Most property managers don't graduate from a college with a degree in property management, as that has not been an area of study until the last few years and still is not widely offered. Most have learned through years of experience and ongoing education provided within the indus-try. A good property man-ager has good common sense, good problem-solving skills, and follows up on day-to-day details. You need a good businessperson who communicates well and has people skills.

You also need to hire someone who is licensed appropriately for your state. Some states don't have any

> 66 When looking for a management company outside of my geo-graphic area, I first searched the Internet, and then left a phone message to see how quickly they responded. I then met with the staff personally. 99
>
> —Willy F., investor and business owner

licensing for property managers; in this case go to www.narpm.net or www.irem.org to see whether there is a professional in the area. NARPM is the National Association of Residential Property Managers, and IREM is the Institute of Real Estate Management. Members of both organizations agree to conduct themselves according to a code of ethics and they are subject to the rules of the professional association. They both offer professional designations that require experience and education to attain. When you choose someone with a des-ignation, you know they look at your property from a profes-sional standpoint and are willing to spend money and time to stay current on local laws and the rental market.

Ways to find a professional property management company

There are many ways to find a company that fits your needs and can manage your rental property effectively and efficiently. Here are just a few ways to find a property management company to hire:

- Ask your friends or co-workers whether they know any residential management company they would recommend in the area of your rental property.

- Drive around the area where your property is located, look for signs, and call on those companies.

- Search the Web (including the NARPM and IREM Web sites, respectively, at www.narpm.net and www.irem.org) for a professional company.

- Let your fingers do the walking and look through the good old-fashioned Yellow Pages.

- Ask your Realtor for a recommendation.

- Look in the local newspaper to see what company does the most advertising.

- Ask your local title company when signing the final papers at closing.

After you have a few recommendations, write a standard list of questions (or see the following section) so you compare apples to apples and ask the same type of questions to each company.

If you are buying a commercial, industrial, or large apartment complex (100+ units), you want to find a property manager with the CPM designation from IREM. IREM provides the same type of professional education and conferences as NARPM, but it caters to the large investment property manager.

Some property managers have earned designations in both associations to be prepared for investors with both types of investments.

Bright Idea

The more friendly, positive, and grateful you are to the property managers and the staff, the better the service. Property managers don't get enough credit or recognition for the hard work they put in for investors. Take the time to say "thank you" and show your appreciation. It will go a long way.

Interviewing a property management company

Be prepared and have a list of questions ready for when you telephone or meet with a property management company. Here are a list of some questions to get you started:

- Why should I choose your company to manage my rental property?
- How long have you been in the residential property management business?
- Do you also sell real estate? (Be sure that managing properties is what they do most and best.)
- How many properties do you manage?
- Do you have a professional designation in property management?
- How will I know when there is a vacancy?
- How do you advertise that vacancy?
- How long will it take to rent my property?
- How do you feel about allowing or not allowing pets, smokers, and/or children? (Be cautious with this. If they say no to children, this could be discrimination, unless it is a 55-and-older community.)
- What is your screening process for prospective applicants?
- How much do you collect at move-in?
- What is the security deposit?
- How much do you charge for monthly management?

- What are your leasing fees and what do those fees include?

- Do you charge a set-up fee and if so, how much will it be?

- Are there any other charges throughout the year? If so what are they?

- What happens if the tenants don't pay their rent on time?

- How much does a basic eviction cost?

- When should I expect my monthly cash-flow report, which details all the activity within that month, showing all rents collected and all of the amounts paid out?

- When do you send my owner-withdraw check, which is the amount of money left over in your rental property account after paying the bills and keeping a small reserve? This is sometimes referred to as a positive cash flow.

- Will I need to change my insurance?

- Who handles the late-night problems/emergencies?

- What happens if the tenants break a lease?

- Do you have a few current clients I can call for reference?

- Who will be my contact person at your office(s)?

- What kind of training does your staff have?

- What type of property management software do you use?

- What is the amount of money you can spend on a repair without contacting me?

- Do you show rentals on the weekends? What are your hours?

- How do you advertise to get renters? Who pays for it?

By sending out some questions or visiting the company's Web site, you will have many of these questions answered in advance, thus narrowing the field. When you go to the property management office, it is to meet the staff in person and to ask a few more questions before making a decision. I think it is a good idea to always meet the owner and staff in person. Make sure you feel comfortable.

Moneysaver

By using technology, you can save a lot of time and money. You can, for example, run a very small ad in the newspaper, directing people to your Web site, which ultimately saves you money. Someone can actually drive by and get a feel for the area without calling you first.

Just the facts

- Self-managing your property in the beginning may help you understand the job at hand in the long run.

- Hire a professional management company so you can enjoy your investment.

- A property manager saves you time, work, and stress.

- Property management fees are tax deductible.

- Use the same care to hire a property management company as you did in finding your accountant and attorney.

- You will get a lot more value when you hire a company that is a member of the National Association of Residential Property Managers (NARPM) or the Institute of Real Estate Management (IREM).

- Some states don't have licensing for property managers.

- Most states require property managers to be licensed, usually requiring that they have or work under a broker's license.

- Hiring a professional company can save you a lot more than money — it can give you peace of mind.

- There are a ton of other services out there that can help you self-manage and market your vacancies if you choose to do that.

- Even though you hire a professional property manager, you still need to know what is happening on a regular basis with your investment.

- Make sure to appreciate your property manager. A little thank you goes a long way, as a lot of people take their property manager for granted. It is a difficult job.

Appendices

PART VII

Glossary

active investor   An IRS classification for a real estate investor who materially participates in running a property.

addendum   a supplementary document.

adjustable-rate mortgage (ARM)   A broad term for a loan in which the future interest rate and terms may change, with that change determined by an index of rates.

adjusted gross income   The income from a piece of property after any adjustments are made for other income, expenses, debt service, or rental losses.

appraisal   The process of estimating the current market value of a property.

average return on equity (AROE)   Each year that you own a property, you can calculate the return on the equity for that year. If you add these up for several years and divide by the number of years, you get the average.

Board of Realtors   An association of Realtors in a given town or district.

buyer's agent   The real-estate agent who locates the buyer and brings an offer to the seller.

cash flow   The amount of money received from rental income each month less the amount paid out in mortgage payments, the purchase of capital assets, operating expenses, and the payment of any taxes.

Cash flow is not the same as profit because it includes nondeductible payments on the loan.

cash-on-cash return   The before-tax cash flow from an investment divided by the investment base (value ÷ loan). Also called return on investment or equity dividend rate.

CC&Rs   Abbreviation for covenants, conditions, and restrictions.

closing   A transaction that takes place when the buyer takes possession of the property and the seller gets the proceeds from the sale.

collected rent   The amount of rental income actually collected.

commercial property   Nonresidential property operated for business use.

commission   An agent's compensation or fee for negotiating a real estate or loan transaction, usually a percentage of the transaction amount.

common area   Space not used and occupied exclusively by tenants, such as lobbies, corridors, and stairways.

comparables   Properties that are similar to the property being considered or appraised. Also known as comps.

comparative analysis   A method of appraisal in which selling prices of similar properties are used as the basis for arriving at the value estimate. This also is known as the market data approach.

condominium   A form of property ownership that combines absolute ownership of an apartmentlike unit and joint ownership of areas used in common with others.

condominium association   A condominium's governing body to which every unit owner automatically belongs.

contingencies   Terms in a contract that qualify the agreement by stating that, for the deal to go forward, one side or the other agrees to meet certain conditions. Typical contingencies include completion of inspections and qualifying for financing.

cost basis   Your basis for calculating the capital gain on a property you own.

CRMC   Certified Residential Management Company, a professional company designation within NARPM.

curb appeal The first impression the front elevation of a property makes on a prospect. The front elevation is the view of the building as you approach it, combining the exterior paint, landscaping, and identity of the property, creating its overall theme.

deduction An expense of property ownership that can be written off against income for tax purposes.

deferred maintenance Ordinary maintenance that is not performed and that negatively affects a property's use and value.

Department of Veterans Affairs The federal government agency that administers GI or VA loans, previously known as the Veterans Administration.

depreciable improvements The value of the structures on a property and capital improvements that the IRS allows you to depreciate.

depreciation As an appraisal term used in the cost approach. This means loss of value due to any cause (physical deterioration, functional obsolescence, or external obsolescence) that negatively affects the value.

depreciation allowance The dollar amount the IRS allows you to deduct each year from the earnings from a property to recover the cost of the investment and capital improvements.

disclosure Releasing or revealing pertinent property information in accordance with governing local, state, and federal laws.

equity The portion of real estate you own. In the case of a property bought for $200,000 with a $133,000 mortgage owing, the equity is the difference, or $67,000.

escrow The process of completing contractually required steps (such as obtaining financing, completing inspections, and paying and transferring funds) and of checking and clearing the title to the property to ensure that all liens have been identified and are satisfied before closing.

estoppel certifications Agreements usually signed by the tenants of a property outlining the terms of their tenancy.

ethics Standards of excellence holding high regard for morals and fairness when performing duties with clients or colleagues.

eviction   To recover possession of a property by a superior claim or legal process.

fair housing laws   Federal laws that prohibit discrimination in the sale, rental, appraisal, financing, or advertising of housing on the basis of race, color, religion, sex, national origin, familial status, mental, or physical disability. Some states have added other classifications, such as source of income, age, and so on.

fair market value   The price a reasonable buyer will pay a reasonable seller for a property that has been on the market for a reasonable period of time.

Federal Housing Administration (FHA)   An agency created by the National Housing Act of 1934 to provide a home-financing system through federal mortgage insurance.

fiduciary   A relationship founded in trust and legally requiring loyalty; full disclosure; full accounting; and the application of skill, care, and diligence.

fixed expenses   The regular, recurring costs required in holding a property, such as taxes and insurance.

fixer-upper   A property requiring repairs, either structural or cosmetic, to gain its full potential market value.

good-faith deposit   A deposit presented by the proposed buyer at the time an offer is made. If the buyer's offer is accepted and the contract is later breached, the good faith deposit may be forfeited.

gross rent multiplier   A factor used for appraising income producing property. The multiplier times the gross income gives an approximate property value.

hard money loans   Loans made by nonconventional lenders. They usually have high interest and high fees.

highest and best use   The use of a property for the most profitable, efficient, and appropriate purpose, given the zoning and other restrictions placed on the land.

HUD   *See* U.S. Department of Housing and Urban Development.

impound account   A trust account in which funds are held, usually by a lender, for the prepayment of property taxes and insurance premiums required to protect the lender's security.

improvements   Any structures or additions to a piece of raw land.

index rate   One of the components used to calculate the interest rate on an adjustable-rate loan.

inflation   An economic condition occurring when the money supply increases in relation to goods. It is associated with rising wages and costs and decreasing purchasing power.

interest-only loan   A loan for which no amortization is required and the entire principal balance is due at maturity.

invest   To commit money or capital in business to earn a financial return. The outlay of money for income or profit.

IREM   Institute of Real Estate Management.

landlord   The lessor or owner of real estate who rents property to another.

lien   A form of security or payment to hold or sell a debtor's property in lieu or payment or obligation.

management fixer-upper   A property with management problems that need to be corrected.

market analysis   The process of placing a property in a specific market, and then evaluating it by those market standards.

master-metered properties   Properties that only have one meter for the utilities of two or more units.

MLS   *See* Multiple Listing Service.

MPM   Master property manager, a professional membership designation within NARPM.

mortgage   A contract that makes a specific property the security for payment of debt.

move-in evaluation   A written evaluation of the interior and exterior of the property done prior to the tenants taking possession.

Multiple Listing Service (MLS)   An association of real estate agents and appraisers that pools listings, shares commissions on a specified basis, and provides data for agents and appraisers in preparing market evaluations and appraisals of real property.

NARPM National Association of Residential Property Managers. Members using this logo agree to conduct themselves according to a NARPM Code of Ethics, and they are subject to the rules of the association. Where required by law, members must hold a real estate license and be in good standing with the organization.

negative cash flow   The condition in which expenses are greater than income.

negligence   Lack of due diligence or care.

operating expenses   Periodic expenditures (not including income tax) necessary to maintain a property and continue the production of effective gross income.

positive cash flow   A situation in which income is greater than expenses.

property management   A service profession in which someone other than the owner supervises a property's operation according to the owner's objectives. It includes fiscal, physical, and administrative management functions.

Realtor   A trademark name of the National Association of Realtors (NAR). Members using this title agree to conduct themselves according to the Realtors' Code of Ethics, and they are subject to the rules of the association.

rent   Money paid periodically (or sometimes services rendered) for use and occupation of a property.

rent control   Laws enacted on a city-by-city basis that dictate the amount of rent or lease terms that landlords can charge or require of tenants.

rent survey   A survey done to find out how much other owners are charging for rent in a given area.

rental agreement   An agreement between a landlord and a tenant that sets forth the terms of a tenancy.

resident manager   An agent of the owner of a building who is employed on a salary to manage the property in which the manager may or may not reside.

residential loans   A loan on a residence or residential units up to and including four units.

return on investment (ROI)   Interest or profit from an investment; before-tax cash flow divided by the investment base (loan value).

RMP   Residential management professional, a professional membership designation within NARPM.

Schedule C   The schedule used to report income and expenses from an investment property for tax purposes.

scheduled rent   The current rent scheduled for all the units in a building.

security deposit   Deposit collected from tenants prior to their moving in that is held by the owner or their agent. It is to be used upon move-out to cover any damages they, their pets, or their guests may have caused, as well as to pay any late fees, rent, cleaning, breaking a lease, or other unpaid charges.

Section 8   The federal government's principal medium for housing assistance. It was authorized by the Housing and Community Development Act of 1974, which provides for new construction and rehabilitation.

Starker exchange   A type of tax-deferred exchange that got its name from the court case with the same name. Also called delayed exchange. Also referred to as a *1031 tax-deferred exchange*.

tax benefits   The tax savings from rental property ownership.

tax-deferred exchange (1031 tax-deferred exchange)   A method of deferring capital gains by exchanging real property for other like-kind property. Also referred to as a *Starker exchange*.

tax shelter   An investment with paper losses that can be used to lower one's otherwise taxable income. In other words, the tax loss from the tax-shelter investment is a write-off against regular salary or other income, thereby "sheltering" that income.

tenant   A person (lessee) who pays rent to occupy or gain possession of real estate.

title company   A company that specializes in establishing the title to real property, including identification of all existing liens on the property. The coverage is paid by a single premium during escrow, and it remains in force as long as the buyer owns the property.

title insurance policy   A special form of insurance issued by a title company to ensure the buyer against any undiscovered liens on the property. The coverage is paid by a single premium during escrow, and it remains in force as long as the buyer owns the property.

title opinion   An analysis of the chain of title of a property in a state where the property owner keeps all the original deeds.

title report   A report that discloses all matters of public record that affect a piece of property.

transfer disclosure statement   A form filled out by the seller of a property to disclose any knowledge the seller has about the property.

turnover   The rate of which one tenant moves out of a property and another moves in. This may mean no loss of rent; however, high turnover rate usually results in added expenses to the landlord.

U.S. Department of Housing and Urban Development (HUD) A government agency established in 1965 to provide federal assistance in planning, developing, and managing public housing.

utility   A public service such as gas, water, or electricity.

vacancy rate   The average percentage of units vacant in a given market area.

value   The worth or usefulness of a good or service expressed in terms of a specific sum of money.

variable expenses   Expenses on a property that tend to be different each month or pay period such as utilities and maintenance.

Resource Directory

The Internet provides a tremendous resource in your quest for more information on managing rental properties. Check out the following:

Name: American Housing Survey

URL: `www.census.gov/pub/hhes/www/ahs.html`

Summary: The survey is conducted by the Bureau of the Census for the U.S. Department of Housing and Urban Development (HUD) to analyze the flow of households through housing.

Name: American Seniors Housing Association

URL: `www.seniorshousing.org/OutsideOf Store/Default.aspx`

Summary: Provides members with research, federal representation, and advocacy in senior housing issues.

Name: Community Associations Institute

URL: `www.caionline.org`

Summary: National organization for condominium, cooperative, and homeowner associations.

Name: Cook & Company

URL: `www.cookcompany.net/Index.htm`

Summary: Leader in training and consulting services for property managers.

Name: Council of Residential Specialists

URL: www.crs.com

Summary: Provides training programs for residential property managers and awards the certified residential specialist (CRS) certification to qualifying professionals.

Name: Department of Housing and Urban Development (HUD), Office of Policy Development and Research

URL: www.huduser.org

Summary: Access to research reports on housing, community, and economic development; HUD income limits; fair market rents; and more.

Name: The Fair Housing Network

URL: www.fairhousing.org

Summary: A not-for-profit organization that offers information and a discussion forum on the issue of homelessness and affordable housing for the poor.

Name: Federal Emergency Management Agency

URL: www.fema.gov

Summary: A former independent agency that became part of the Department of Homeland Security in March 2003; advises homeowners on planning and a variety of disaster-management issues.

Name: Home Rentals.net

URL: http://homerentals.net/Sites/HRN/

Summary: Makes use of the Internet to provide property managers with the essentials: marketing vacancies to residents; marketing services to owners/investors; and managing business operations and communications.

Name: Housing Authority Websites

URL: www.phada.org/linkha.htm

Summary: Links to local, state, and regional housing authority sites.

Name: HUD Property Owners and Managers Survey

URL: www.census.gov/hhes/www/poms.html

Summary: A nationwide sample of housing units that were rented or vacant-for-rent. This survey offers insight into common problems facing property owners and managers within different segments of the rental market.

Name: Institute of Real Estate Management

URL: www.irem.org

Summary: A professional real estate management association that serves both the multi-family and commercial real estate sectors.

Name: Jackson Group Property Management

URL: www.jacksongroup.net

Summary: Premier San Francisco property management company that specializes in residential and commercial properties.

Name: LandlordSource.com

URL: http://landlordsource.com

Summary: Provides property managers and landlords with a variety of tools for daily property management and marketing with practical applications.

Name: Lead Safe USA

URL: http://leadsafeusa.com

Summary: Home of the National Association of the Remodeling Industy. This site gives you valuable information to protect your properties from lead posioning.

Name: Mr. Landlord

URL: www.mrlandlord.com

Summary: Online venue where rental owners can ask land-lording questions and get answers and tips from other landlords.

Name: National Affordable Housing Management Association

URL: www.nahma.org

Summary: NAHMA caters to managers of affordable housing and awards several certifications.

Name: National Apartment Association

URL: www.naahq.org

Summary: America's leading advocate for quality rental housing. NAA offers legislative and regulatory advise to owners and managers of multi-family housing and works to offer safe, affordable, multi-family housing to the public.

Name: National Association of Rental Property Managers (NARPM)

URL: www.narpm.org

Summary: An association for residential property managers that offers designations and provides an effective and professional learning environment for property managers. (I'm the former national president of NARPM and a proud member of the association!)

Name: National Council of State Housing Agencies

URL: www.ncsha.org

Summary: A nonprofit organization that coordinates and leverages federal advocacy efforts for affordable housing, created by the State Housing Financing Agencies.

Name: National Multi-Housing Council (NMHC)

URL: www.nmhc.org

Summary: NMHC advocates on behalf of rental housing, conducts apartment-related research, encourages the exchange of strategic business information, and promotes the desirability of apartment living.

Name: Prandi Property Management, Inc.

URL: www.prandiprop.com

Summary: Premier property management company in Marin County. Specializes in residential single-family and multi-family property. Okay, so this is my company, and I just couldn't resist plugging it!

Name: PROMAS: Real Estate Property Management Software

URL: www.promas.com

Summary: Software for professional property managers, association management companies, and self-managed associations. PROMAS provides integrated accounting and property management reporting functions and is very user friendly.

Name: Property Bridge

URL: www.propertybridge.com/Home.aspx

Summary: Customizable Web-based marketing, management, and online payments platform for residential and commercial property management companies of all sizes.

Name: Thomas

URL: http://thomas.loc.gov

Summary: A service of the Library of Congress, this site allows you to search for legislative information on the Internet.

Name: True Forms

URL: www.trueforms.com/product_index.php?mpage=
trueforms.html

Summary: Leading real estate forms and contracts program.
TrueForms comes with a complete library of state, board,
association, or legal forms. TrueForms Software simplifies
the forms and contracts process by allowing you to download and fill out forms online.

Further Reading

The following books can help you increase your knowledge of property management.

- Griswold, Robert, *Property Management For Dummies*. Wiley Publishing, Inc., Hoboken, New Jersey, 2001.

- Strauss, Spencer and Martin Stone, *The Unofficial Guide to Real Estate Investing*, 2nd Edition. Wiley Publishing, Inc. Hoboken, New Jersey, 2003.

- Taylor, Jeffrey *The Landlord's Kit*. Dearborn Trade (a Kaplan Professional Company), September 20, 2002.

- Weiss, Mark B., C.C.I.M, and Dan Baldwin, *Landlording and Property Management: Insider's Advice on How to Own Real Estate and Manage it Profitably*. Adams Media Corporation, Avon, Massachusetts, 2003.

Important Documents

In this appendix, you find a variety of forms and other documents to use as you screen tenants, rent your property, and manage your business. The following forms are included in this appendix; you can find more information about them in the chapters listed here:

- **Move-In/Move-Out Checklist:** Chapter 5
- **Maintenance Request Form:** Chapter 6
- **Rental Set-Up Sheet:** Chapter 8
- **Phone Questions to Prescreen Tenants:** Chapter 9
- **Rental/Lease Policies:** Chapter 9
- **Application to Rent or Lease:** Chapter 9
- **Tenant Screening Form:** Chapter 9
- **Co-Signer Agreement:** Chapter 9
- **Notice of Denial of Rental Property:** Chapter 9
- **Tenant's Handbook:** Chapter 10
- **Rental-Lease Agreement:** Chapter 10
- **Rental-Lease Addendum:** Chapter 10
- **Lead-Based Paint Disclosure:** Chapter 10
- **Mold Notification Addendum:** Chapter 10
- **Roommate Addendum:** Chapter 10
- **24-Hour Notice to Enter:** Chapter 12

- **Change in Terms of Tenancy Form:** Chapter 12
- **Pet Addendum:** Chapter 13
- **Proof of Service:** Chapter 13
- **Tenant Notice to Vacate:** Chapter 14
- **Roomate Notice to Terminate:** Chapter 14
- **30-Day-Notice Acknowledgment:** Chapter 14
- **Security Deposit Refund:** Chapter 14

Move-In/Move-Out Checklist

OK = Okay; S = Critical safety issue; I = Needs immediate attention;
W/N = Work needed at some point

EXTERIOR				
FRONT ELEVATION	**OK**	**S**	**I**	**W/N**
1. Driveway				
Concrete/asphalt/gravel				
Oil Stains/rust				
2. Exterior garage door condition				
3. Inoperable vehicle? Y/N____				
4. Lawn landscaping				
Tree/shrubs/trim				
Sprinklers				
Leaks				
Type				
Trash/debris				
Retaining walls				
5. Front fence				
Gate				
6. Paint				
House				
Trim				
Foundation vents				
7. Walkway				
Exterior light				
Doorbell				

FRONT ELEVATION *(continued)*	OK	S	I	W/N
8. Roof				
Gutters				
Downspout				
Eaves and vents				
Spark arrester				
9. Chimney				
Fireplace caulking				

BACK ELEVATION	OK	S	I	W/N
1. Deck				
Cover				
2. Patio				
Cover				
Screening				
3. Lawn landscape				
Tree/shrub trim				
Sprinkler				
Leaks				
Type				
Trash/debris				
Retaining walls				
4. Fences				
Gates				

BACK ELEVATION	OK	S	I	W/N
5. Paint				
House				
Trim				
Foundation vents				
6. Pool/spa				
Cover				
7. Roof				
Gutters				
Downspout				
Eaves and vents				
8. Chimney				
Fireplace caulking				
Spark arrester				

INTERIOR

ENTRY	OK	S	I	W/N
1. Screen door				
2. Front door				
Double-key deadbolt				
3. Floor: Wood/tile/vinyl/carpet				
4. Entry closet door				
5. Lighting fixtures				

LIVING ROOM	OK	S	I	W/N
1. Paint				
2. Wallpaper				
3. Floor: Wood/tile/vinyl/carpet				
4. Window/screens				
Window coverings				
5. Fireplace/hearth				
6. Light fixture				
7. Ceiling fans				
8. Wet bar				
9. Sliding door				
Screen				

DINING ROOM	OK	S	I	W/N
1. Paint				
2. Wallpaper				
3. Floor: Wood/tile/vinyl/carpet				
4. Windows/screens				
Window coverings				
5. Sliding door				
Screen				
6. Fireplace/hearth				
7. Light fixture				
8. Ceiling fans				
9. Wet bar				

FAMILY ROOM	OK	S	I	W/N
1. Paint				
2. Wallpaper				
3. Floor: Wood/tile/vinyl/carpet				
4. Window/screens				
Window coverings				
5. Sliding door				
Screen				
6. Fireplace/hearth				
7. Light fixture				
8. Ceiling fans				
9. Wet bar				

KITCHEN	OK	S	I	W/N
1. Paint condition				
2. Wallpaper condition				
3. Floor: Wood/tile/vinyl/carpet				
4. Windows/screens				
5. Window coverings				
6. Sliding door				
Screen				
7. Sink				
Caulking				
8. Faucet				
Pipe leaks				

KITCHEN *(continued)*	OK	S	I	W/N
9. Electrical: GFI				
10. Countertop condition				
Tile/Formica/other				
Grouting				
11. Cabinets: Visual condition				
12. Appliances				
Hood				
Cooktop				
Oven				
Microwave				
Refrigerator				
Dishwasher				
Garbage disposal				
Trash compactor				
13. Light fixtures				
14. Pocket or other door				

HALLWAY	OK	S	I	W/N
1. Floor: Wood/tile/vinyl/carpet				
2. Smoke detector				
3. Carbon monoxide detector				
4. Light fixtures				
5. Wall heater				

HALLWAY	OK	S	I	W/N
6. Linen closet/cabinet				
7. Closet door				
8. Furnace				

STAIRWAY	OK	S	I	W/N
1. Banister				
2. Floor: Wood/tile/vinyl/carpet				
3. Smoke detector				
4. Carbon monoxide detector				
5. Light fixtures				

MASTER BEDROOM	OK	S	I	W/N
1. Paint				
2. Wallpaper				
3. Smoke detector				
4. Light fixtures				
5. Windows/screens				
Window coverings				
6. Closet doors				
7. Entry door				
Patio screen door				
8. Floor: Wood/tile/vinyl/carpet				
9. Door stops				

MASTER BATH	OK	S	I	W/N
1. Paint				
2. Wallpaper				
3. Light fixture				
Fan				
4. Sink				
Faucet/pipes				
Caulking				
5. Countertop				
Tile/Formica/other				
Caulking/grouting				
6. Electrical: GFI				
7. Medicine cabinet				
8. Towel bars				
9. Toilet paper holder				
10. Mirrors				
11. Toilet				
Leaking				
Loose base				
12. Tub				
Fixture				
Caulking/grouting				
13. Shower				
Leaking				
Caulking				

MASTER BATH	OK	S	I	W/N
14. Enclosure				
Caulking/grouting				
15. Floor				
Water damage				
Discoloration				
16. Doors				
17. Window/screens				
Window coverings				

SECOND BEDROOM	OK	S	I	W/N
1. Paint				
2. Wallpaper				
3. Smoke detector				
4. Light fixtures				
5. Windows/screens				
Window coverings				
6. Closet doors				
7. Entry door				
Patio screen door				
8. Floor				
9. Door stops				

SECOND BATH	OK	S	I	W/N
1. Paint				
2. Wallpaper				

SECOND BATH *(continued)*	OK	S	I	W/N
3. Light fixture				
Fan				
4. Sink				
Faucet/pipe				
Caulking				
5. Countertop				
Tile/Formica/other				
Caulking/grouting				
6. Electrical: GFI				
7. Medicine cabinet				
8. Towel bars				
9. Toilet paper holder				
10. Mirrors				
11. Toilet				
Leaking				
Loose base				
12. Tub				
Fixture				
Tile/Formica/other				
Caulking/grouting				
13. Shower				
Tile/Formica/other				
Leaking				
Caulking				

SECOND BATH	OK	S	I	W/N
14. Enclosure				
Caulking/grouting				
15. Floor: Wood/tile/vinyl/carpet				
Water damage				
Discoloration				
16. Doors				
17. Windows/screens				
Window coverings				

LAUNDRY ROOM/GARAGE	OK	S	I	W/N
1. Doors				
2. Walls/ceiling				
3. Light fixture				
4. Plumbing leaks				
5. Electrical: GFI				
6. Floor: Wood/tile/vinyl/concrete				
7. Venting				
8. Exhaust fan				

GARAGE/CARPORT	OK	S	I	W/N
1. Entry door				
2. Water heater				
Safety code				
Leaks				
Fire hazard				

GARAGE/CARPORT *(continued)*	OK	S	I	W/N
3. Furnace				
Fire hazard				
4. Light fixtures				
5. Storage area				
6. Auto sprinkler controls				
Location: Internal/external				
7. Oil stains				
8. Auto garage door opener				
Safety issue				
9. Garage door condition: Interior				
10. Side door				
Window				

GENERAL	OK	S	I	W/N
1. Pets				
Damage				
2. Smoking				
Damage				

Maintenance Request Form

Date: _____

Assign to: _____

Phone: _____ Cell: _____

Address of Tenant: _____

Tenant's Name: _____

Phone: (H) _____ (W) _____ (C) _____

Entry ok_____ Call to schedule_____ Where to pick up key_____

Vacant_____ Lock box_____ Move-in date_____

Special Instructions: _____

_____

_____

Work Requested: _____

_____

_____

Scheduled Date: _____ Time: _____

Recommendations from Contractor: _____

_____

Estimated cost: $_____

Estimated completion time: _____

Charge To:

Occupant_____ Management _____ Owner (approved)_____

Job complete: _____

Approved by: _____

Signature

Rental Set-Up Sheet

Listing property manager: _____

Date listed: _____

Property address: _____

_____

Apt. # _____

Owner: _____

Ph. # _____

Does owner need to approve applicant? Yes / No

Type of property: House / Condo / Townhouse
Apartment(s) / Duplex / Tri- or four-plex

Rent amount: $_____
Security deposit: $_____
Total move-in: $_____

Bedrooms: _____
Baths: _____
Date available: _____
Lease term: _____

Utilities Included: Water / Garbage / PG&E / Pool
Garden / Other Inc / None _____

Type of heat _____

Average monthly utilities cost _____

HOA rules and regulations _____

Association _____

Features: Yard / Deck / Patio / Fireplace / View
Private / Hot tub / Pool / Skylight(s)
Other features: _____

Parking: Street / Assigned spot(s) / Carport
1-car garage / 2-car garage / Parking slab

Pets: Yes / No
Type: _____

Smoking: Yes / No

Appliances furnished: Refrigerator / Microwave /
Garbage disposal / Dishwasher / Trash compactor

Stove: Gas / Electric
Other:_____

Laundry facilities: On-site / In unit
Hook-ups: (gas or electric) / None
Location: _____

Keys, do we have? Yes / No

Garage door opener: Yes / No
How many _____ Location: Home _____ Office _____

Any additional keys _____

Who is in the property? Owner / Tenant / Vacant
Name:_____

Home #:_____

Cell #:_____

Work #:_____

Move-out date: _____

Multiple listing info: _____

APN # _____

Thomas Bros. coordinates _____

Cross street _____

Sub division _____

Year built _____

Square footage _____

How many stories _____

Floor types _____

Ad in paper?   Yes / No

Date in paper? _____

By whom? _____

Description: _____

_____

_____

_____

_____

_____

_____

Directions: _____

_____

_____

_____

_____

_____

_____

Additional comments or recommendations for putting this property into move-in condition:

_____

_____

_____

_____

_____

_____

_____

_____

_____

_____

_____

_____

_____

_____

_____

Phone Questions to Prescreen Tenants

My name is _____. To whom am I speaking?

_____

- How did you hear about my property?

  _____

- What size rental are you looking for? How many people will be living in the property? (*Note:* Federal fair housing laws state that a rental should allow a minimum of two people per bedroom, plus one.)

  _____

- Is the monthly rent a price that will work for you?

  _____

- What is your present occupation? Are the other applicants also employed?

  _____

- Where are you currently living?

  _____

- Is there any particular reason as to why you've decided to move?

  _____

- When will you need to move in? Do you have a specific date in mind?

  _____

- Do you have any pets? If so, what kinds and sizes? (Be sure to get some details about the pets and ask if they would be able to provide references for them.)

  _____

- Are you comfortable that the first month's rent and the security deposit are due in full prior to moving in?

  _____

- Have you driven by the property? (Always ask them not to disturb any of the current occupants.)

  _____

- When can you meet? (Get the full name and cellphone number of the person whom you will be meeting.)

  _____

  _____

Rental/Lease Policies

Please read the following policies. If you feel you meet the guidelines for qualifying, we encourage you to submit an application. Only one application will be processed at a time and applications will be processed in the order received. **An incomplete application will not be considered.**

APPLICANTS

- Each person 18 years of age or older must complete and sign an application, and only the applicants may reside in a property.

- If a co-signer is necessary, the co-signer must also complete and sign an application. The acceptance of a co-signer is not normal policy and is subject to individual approval or denial by the owner.

- To be processed and considered, a $25 non-refundable processing fee must accompany all applications. If your application is not processed, this $25 processing fee will be refunded.

- Applications aren't considered if they contain missing or false information.

PROCESSING FEES

- $25 processing fee (per applicant)
- $200 holding deposit (if approved, the holding deposit will be credited to the security deposit)

CREDIT CRITERIA

- The owner will obtain a credit report for each applicant and co-signer 18 years of age or older. Reports supplied by applicants will not be accepted.

- Discharged bankruptcies are acceptable.

INCOME CRITERIA

- Applicant's gross monthly income must be three times the amount of the monthly rent.
- Income will be verified from copies of the prior month's pay stubs provided with the application.
- Self-employed applicants must provide their most recent tax return and three months of bank statements.
- Unverifiable income will not be considered.

IDENTIFICATION

- Photo ID must be provided at the time lease/rental agreement is signed.

CONDITION OF MOVE-IN

- Hours for lease signing are Monday through Friday, between 9:00 a.m. and 4:00 p.m., and Saturday by appointment.
- All utility and garbage accounts, where applicable, must be transferred into the resident's name as of the date of possession.
- Security deposit and first month's rent (prorated) are to be paid in cashier's check or money order before keys are provided.

(Daily rate will be charged if keys are delivered prior to date on lease/rental agreement).

Note: Some properties do not allow pets.

If you feel you are qualified for the property after reading the attached rental/lease policies, please follow these instructions:

1. Your application will not be processed without the correct funds and all documentation attached.
2. Fill out the application completely and legibly. Each person 18 years of age or older must submit an application. Emancipated minors must fill out an application. One person per application, please.

3. Include one check for $25 for each person 18 years or older who will be residing in the property. This includes married couples as well as singles. **This fee is non-refundable!** (Refundable only if application is not processed.) Include a separate check for $200. This holding deposit is required to hold the unit during processing. **This must be a separate check from the application fee.**

4. Reliable and legal documentation and telephone numbers are required to verify all income.

5. If employed, you will need to submit a copy of your last year's W-2 and 2 (two) of your most recent pay stubs.

6. If self-employed, you will need to submit a copy of your last 2 (two) years of income tax returns and documentation of the current year (i.e. P & L, receipts, etc.).

7. A copy of a photo ID, for example, driver's license, military ID, and so on, must be submitted.

If you have any questions, please feel free to call us at _____
_____.

Thank you for your application.

Application to Rent or Lease

Designated property address _____

Requested date for lease/rental _____

How did you hear of this property? _____

1. <u>Personal Information</u>

Name _____

Social Security No. _____

Present address _____

City _____

State _____

Zip _____

Residence phone / fax _____

Drivers license no. _____

2. <u>General Information</u>

Other occupants _____

Number _____

Relationship _____

Animals _____

Number _____

Type _____

Smoker: Yes / No

Car make _____

Year _____

Model _____

Color _____

License plate no. _____

3. <u>Employment Information</u>

If employed less than two years, please give same information on prior occupation

Present occupation _____

Business phone _____

Employer _____

Supervisor _____

Self employed d.b.a. _____

Title _____

Employed from _____ to _____

Type of business _____

Monthly gross income (salary) _____

Prior occupation _____

Business phone _____

Employer _____

Supervisor _____

Self employed d.b.a. _____

Title _____

Employed from _____ to _____

Type of business _____

Monthly gross income (salary) _____

Do you plan to run a business in the residence? Yes / No

If yes, what type? _____

Do you own any liquid filled furniture (such as a water bed)? Yes / No

Describe _____

Do you have a Section 8 Housing Voucher? Yes / No

4. **<u>Housing References</u>**

   Current address _____

   _____

   _____

   From _____ to _____

   Landlord / agent_____

   Phone_____

   Address_____

   Reason for moving_____

   Current rent _____

   Prior address _____

   _____

   _____

   From _____ to _____

   Landlord / agent _____

   Phone _____

   Address _____

   Reason for moving _____

   Rent _____

5. **<u>Credit</u>**

   Bank _____

   Address _____

   Phone number _____

   Checking? _____ Savings?_____

   Account numbers _____

   Credit reference _____

   Highest amount owed $_____

   Acct. # _____

   Address _____

   Phone _____

6a. <u>Personal Reference</u>

Name _____

Address _____

_____

Phone _____

Length of acquaintance _____

Emergency contact information _____

6b. <u>Personal Reference</u>

Name _____

Address _____

_____

Phone _____

Length of acquaintance _____

Emergency contact information _____

_____

7. <u>Other</u>

Have you ever filed a petition of bankruptcy? _____

Have you ever been evicted from any tenancy or had an
eviction notice served on you? _____

Have you ever willfully and intentionally refused to pay
any rent when due? _____

Have you ever been convicted of a misdemeanor or felony
other than a traffic or parking violation? _____

Are you a current illegal abuser or addict of a controlled
substance? _____

Have you ever been convicted of the illegal manufacture
or distribution of a controlled substance? _____

If yes to any of the above, please indicate the date of
occurrence and briefly explain: _____

_____

_____

_____

Applicant represents that all the statements are true and correct and hereby authorizes verification of the following items including, but not limited to obtaining a credit report, and agrees to furnish additional credit references upon request.

This application is for qualification purposes only and does not in any way guarantee the applicant that he/she will be offered this property. Processing fees are non-refundable. Applicant understands that property manger can and will accept more than one application on this rental property and property manager in its sole discretion will select the best-qualified tenant. Any application with missing information will be returned.

_____

Applicant's signature   *Date*

Tenant Screening Form

Applicant's name: _____

Property applying for: _____

Accepted: **Yes** / **No**

If declined, reason: _____

Applicant notified of results? **Yes** / **No**

1. **Current Address**

   Verified? Yes / No

   Person spoke to: _____

   Title: _____

   Any relation to applicant? Yes / No

   Rent/mortgage amount: $ _____

   If owned home, was it sold or closed? Yes / No

   How long did applicant live there? _____

   Was Rent paid on time? Yes / No

   Was late: # _____ **times.**

   NSF checks: # _____ **times.**

   Notices served: # _____ **times.**

   For? _____

   Was notice given to move? Yes / No

   Did applicant take good care of the property? Yes / No

   Did applicant maintain yard? Yes / No

   Would you rent to applicant again? Yes / No

   Comments:_____

   _____

   _____

   _____

2. <u>**Former Address**</u>

Verified? Yes / No

Person spoke to: _____

Title: _____

Any relation to applicant? Yes / No

Rent/mortgage amount: $ _____

If owned home, was it sold or closed? Yes / No

How long did applicant live there? _____

Was Rent paid on time? Yes / No

Was late: # _____ times.

NSF checks: # _____ times.

Notices served: # _____ times.

For? _____

Was notice given to move? Yes / No

Did applicant take good care of the property? Yes / No

Did applicant maintain yard? Yes / No

Would you rent to applicant again? Yes / No

Comments:_____

_____

_____

_____

3. **Do addresses match-up to credit report?**

Current address? Yes / No

Former address? Yes / No

Any address given that conflicts with the residence information on the application? Yes / No

4. **Does current address match with driver's license?**

Yes / No

5. **Employment History**

   Verified? Yes / No

   Is employment verified on credit report? Yes / No

   Employment: _____

   Person spoke to: _____

   Title: _____

   Any relation to applicant? Yes / No

   How long applicant at job? _____

   Applicant's position: _____

   Applicant's monthly income: $ _____

   Comments:_____

   _____

   _____

   _____

Completed by: _____

Date: _____

Have we received?

$200 deposit/$25 credit check? **Y** / **N**

W2s and/or paystubs? **Y** / **N**

Photo ID? **Y** / **N**

Co-Signer Agreement

The parties to this agreement are _____ herein called co-signer(s), and owner. Co-signer(s) acknowledges that he/she has read the residential lease agreement and addendum for the property at _____, between the owner, and _____, herein called "resident," dated _____, and understands its terms.

Co-signer(s) agrees to personally guarantee the payment of any monetary damages suffered by owner including but not limited to actual attorney's fees incurred in the enforcement of said residential lease rental agreement. Co-signer is not entitled to service of any statutory notices required by law to be provided occupants.

This co-signer(s) agreement shall continue in full force and effect for the entire term of resident's tenancy, including any extension and any rental increases in effect during such tenancy.

_____

Co-signer   *Date*

_____

Owner   *Date*

Notice of Denial of Rental Property

Date: _____

To:

_____

Applicant(s) name

RE: Your application to rent the property at:

_____

Rental address

We have carefully reviewed your rental/lease application and regret that we are unable to approve it. The reason(s) for our decision is/are indicated below.

_____   1. You do not meet the minimum income and/or stability requirement of our rental policy. If you have any questions, please contact the undersigned.

_____   2. The employment references, which you provided, did not return verification. If you have any questions, please contact your references directly.

_____   3. The landlord references, which you provided, did not return verification. If you have any questions, please contact your references directly.

_____   4. Adverse retail credit information was reported by:

    _____ Equifax, P.O. Box 105873, Atlanta GA 30374

    _____ Trans Union, P.O. Box 390, Springfield, PA 19064

    _____ Experian, P.O. Box 2002, Allen TX 75013

You have the right under Section 1785.16 to dispute the accuracy or completeness of any information in a consumer credit report furnished by the consumer credit reporting agency. If you have been denied rental housing in whole or in part because of information obtained from a person other than a consumer credit reporting agency, you may within 60 days of this notification submit a written request to the user of said information requesting disclosure of the nature and substance of said information.

_____   5. Other

_____

_____

_____
Owner   Date

Tenant's Handbook

Welcome to your new residence. We would appreciate it if you would let us know your new phone number as soon as possible. Remember to also have all the utilities placed in your name (where applicable), effective the first day of your lease.

The following information is designed to answer frequently asked questions, and to minimize confusion related to caring for the property and interacting with our management company.

Please review this document and keep it on file for handy reference.

Your property manager: _____

Address: _____

_____

Phone number: _____

Paying rent

Rent is due on the 1st of each month and may be mailed or delivered to our office. Make checks payable to _____ _____ and send to the address above. Rent may be paid by personal check, money order, or cashier's check. **Please do not send cash.** *Remember:* Late charges are assessed on the 6th of each month.

- Please put your name and rental address on your check/money order to ensure that you are properly credited with the payment.

- Be sure checks/money orders are completed with names of payer and payee. The management company is not responsible for cash or incomplete money orders left on the premises.

- Rent delivered to the management company should be deposited in our rent dropbox during office hours or put through the mail slot in the door after hours.

Maintenance

- If a maintenance issue should arise, you may complete a maintenance request form and fax your request to _____, or call your property manager's assistant. We ask that you submit maintenance requests in writing to avoid confusion and to ensure that we have a clear record of your request.

- When making a request, be specific about the problem and remember to include your name, address, and the best number(s) to reach you.

- Tenants must be prepared to schedule time and make themselves available to let a contractor or repair person into the property, or give permission for the management company to provide a key for the contractor to enter in their absence.

- Tenants are responsible for securing any pets that the contractor may encounter on their visit to the property.

Emergency Maintenance

- If you have an emergency that cannot wait until the next business day and it is before or after our regular business hours, you can page us at _____. Be sure that you are using a phone that accepts incoming calls.

- An emergency is a fire, flood, or any dangerous or hazardous situation.

- An emergency is not an annoying sound, outdoor sprinklers going off in the middle of the night, and so on.

Locked Yourself Out?

- The management company keeps extra keys for each property. During regular business hours you may come by and borrow a key that will need to be returned to our office within 72 hours. After business hours, keys aren't available and you will have to call a locksmith.

- It is a good idea to leave a spare set of keys with a friend or neighbor. However, if you hide the keys and they are discovered, the locks should be changed and it will have to be at your cost.

- Be sure to carry all of your door keys (handle and dead-bolt) with you. When contractors are authorized to enter a property to make a repair, they are required to secure the premises when they leave. That includes setting the dead-bolts or locks whether you set them or not.

Care and Use Maintenance

The following information has been gathered in response to requests from residents looking for guidelines at move-in and move-out times. If you have questions about the use and care for items not on this list, please call the management company.

Most of our properties have care manuals for appliances, and so on, provided by the owners. Please refer to them first whenever there is a problem. Answers are often found in these guides.

Please report unsafe or hazardous situations immediately.

FURNACE and WALL HEATER MAINTENANCE

- All tenants are responsible for cleaning or replacing the furnace filter at least once a year, preferably at the beginning of the fall or winter. Problems caused by failure to clean/replace the filter may be the tenant's responsibility.

- Dust can accumulate at furnace vents as well as at fan vents. A small broom brushed across the vent openings will clear away any dust and help the furnace or fan operate efficiently.

- Prior to the heating season, please arrange to have the gas company check your furnace/heater to be sure that it is in good operating condition. If they identify needed repairs, notify the management company immediately. This is a complimentary service. The gas company can be reached at _____.

GAS WALL HEATERS

- If your residence has a gas wall heater, it is prudent to turn off the gas at the unit when the heater is not needed. On any gas appliance, new or older, if the pilot light goes out you may detect a gas odor, which should dissipate in a few minutes after airing out the room. If the odor persists call the gas company immediately.

POWER, FURNACE, and HOT WATER HEATER OUTAGES

- If the power goes out in your unit or house, first check to see if the whole area is without power. If it is out in the area, chances are the gas company already knows about it, but you can try calling them to report it.

- If the power is only out in your house/unit, check the circuit breaker box. One or more circuits may be tripped, and you may see the switches in the off position. If no switch is off, turn each switch off and then on again to reset the circuits. If this doesn't solve the problem, call the gas company.

- If either your furnace or water heater is not working, call the gas company first to have them check it out and/or relight the pilot. If there are additional problems, they will inform you as to what needs to be repaired. Call the management company with the information they provide you.

DRAINS

- Avoid letting food, hair, and excess soap get down the drains.

- Clogged drains caused by hair, grease, and soap are the tenant's responsibility. Some dishwashers will clog from food left on the dishes when put in the machine.

- An excellent drain cleaning/clearing solution recipe is 1 cup salt, 1 cup baking soda, 1 cup vinegar, followed by eight cups boiling water. We recommend performing this treatment monthly to avoid build-up.

■ Hardware stores carry "hair catchers" to place in sink and tub drains that significantly help keep drains free of hair.

GARBAGE DISPOSALS

■ Always run water while the disposal is operating to avoid damage to the unit. Let the water run long enough to grind all the material in the disposal. Then let the water run for 10–15 seconds after turning off the disposal. Learn to recognize the sound the machine makes when completely free of garbage.

■ Disposals are designed to grind up organic items only. Exceptions include: banana peels, artichoke leaves, celery stalks, flower stems, coffee grounds, bones, or any item that is particularly tough. Never put paper, plastic, glass, aluminum foil, or grease in the disposal.

■ Always be sure to check the power switch (usually under the sink), try the reset button (somewhere on the machine), and remove all contents before calling for maintenance. *Remember:* Problems caused by users are the tenant's responsibility.

REFRIGERATOR COILS/DRIP PANS

■ Keep coils on refrigerators (especially sub-zeros) free of dust.

■ Coils need free air flowing around them to operate efficiently. Failure to keep coils clean may cause the appliance motor to burn out. The replacement of a burned out motor due to dirty coils may be the tenant's responsibility.

■ Some refrigerators have drip pans under them. If not kept clean, the pans can start to develop a strong odor. Please take the time to get acquainted with the appliances in your unit.

FIREPLACES

- Please burn only hardwoods in the fireplaces and wood-stoves to minimize to buildup of creosote, and so on in the chimney. Creosote buildup is a fire hazard.

- Be sure a fireplace screen is in place when a fire is burning to prevent hot ashes from burning the floor or floor coverings.

OVEN RACKS and PANS

- The easiest way to clean oven racks and pans is to put them in a heavy-duty garbage bag (do this outdoors), add 2 cups of ammonia and seal the bag. Let it sit for a couple of hours, and then carefully open the bag (without inhaling the strong odor). Remove racks and pans and the grease will wipe off with very little effort.

PLUMBING FIXTURES

- Never use abrasives on brass or gold fixtures.

- It is best to wipe fixtures clean after each use.

- If brass needs to be polished, please use a product specifically designed for use on brass.

- Many homes and apartments have low-flow toilets. We strongly recommend that you keep a plunger nearby. Low-flow toilets tend to clog or back up if too much paper, and so on is flushed. Tenants must be prepared to plunge the toilet to clear clogs and avoid damage from overflows.

WATER DAMAGE

- Tenants must take care to avoid water damage caused by allowing water to sit on counters and floors.

- Care must be taken to ensure that shower curtains are inside the tub, and that shower doors are completely closed when taking a shower. Water on tile floors can seep through the grout and cause dry rot on the floorboards below. Water can also seep around the edges of vinylleum and damage the flooring below. We recommend putting a mat, towel, or rug on the floor to step on when exiting the tub or shower.

- Water can easily be splashed into the space behind the faucet in the kitchen or bath and damage the counter surface. Please be sure to keep these areas dry to prevent damage.

SLIDING GLASS DOORS, SCREEN DOORS, and SHOWER TRACKS

- It is imperative that dirt and debris regularly be cleaned out of sliding door tracks. Rolling over dirt, leaves, and pine needles that frequently accumulate in the tracks can damage the wheels on sliding doors, especially the heavy glass sliders. Please make it part of your cleaning routine to clear the tracks.

- Please don't use oil or WD40 to lubricate slider doors or screens. It only attracts dirt and gums up the wheel mechanisms.

- In order to retard the growth of mold in the tracks and at the bottom of shower doors, keep the tracks clean. Use an old toothbrush and do a regular monthly cleaning; it's much easier than doing one major cleaning at move-out time!

MOLD

- Bleach is the best product for removing mold that forms around the edges of showers, tubs, on tile walls, around metal windows, and anywhere there is moisture. The easiest way to remove mold is to cut paper towels in half and fold them into one-inch strips. Dip each strip into the bleach bottle and hold your finger against it as you draw it out. Lay the bleach-soaked strips directly on the mold and leave them there for several hours. It works like magic. Remember to use rubber gloves, and air out affected rooms.

HOUSE PLANTS

- Be sure drip pans are kept under all plants. Water runoff will stain or damage most surfaces.

KITCHEN COUNTERS

- To avoid costly damage from nicks and cuts in counter tops, use a cutting board at all times.

CERAMIC TILE, MOLDED TUB, and SHOWER WALLS

- Dilute one part white vinegar in five parts water for cleaning all ceramic tiles and molded fixtures.

- Never use scrubbing cleansers like Comet or AJAX on molded fixtures, as these products will permanently scratch the surfaces.

MINI BLINDS

- When cleaning mini blinds, don't soak them; the finish may bubble and peel. Spray them with a mild soap and water solution and wipe them. Weekly dusting or wiping can save a lot of work later.

SMOKE DETECTORS

- Tenants are responsible for keeping fresh batteries in smoke detectors. We recommend changing batteries at the beginning and end of daylight saving time.

WOOD DECKS/PORCHES

- Potted plants and flowers add beauty and appeal to a property. If you have planters or pots, raise them off the deck a few inches to allow airflow beneath the pot, and to prevent water runoff from rotting the deck.

HARDWOOD FLOORS

- Never use a mop for cleaning or applying oil. Use a soft cloth only. It is best to sweep and dust regularly.

- Kitchen areas only: Once every three months clean floors with a small amount of vinegar in water.

- Periodically clean floors with Murphy's Oil Soap, following the directions on the label.

- Use throw rugs in front of the sink and the stove to protect these areas from water and grease.

MARBLE and GRANITE

- Never use any acidic or abrasive cleaning products, including vinegar. It is best to use warm water and a sponge with a small amount of dishwashing liquid such as Dawn or Joy.

- Marble is a porous material. Be careful that water runoff from plants is not left standing on the surface. It will permanently stain the marble.

UTILITY and SERVICE DIRECTORY

_____

_____

_____

In case of emergency, dial 911.

LOCAL POLICE and FIRE DEPARTMENT TELEPHONE NUMBERS

_____

_____

_____

Rental-Lease Agreement

LANDLORD: _____

TENANT(S): _____

_____

PROPERTY ADDRESS: _____

_____

1. **RENTAL AMOUNT:** Beginning _____, 20____
   Tenant agrees to pay Landlord the sum of $_____
   per month in advance on the _____day of each calendar
   month. Said rental payment shall be delivered by Tenant
   to Landlord or his designated agent to the following
   location:

   Rent must be actually received by Landlord, or designated
   agent, in order to be considered in compliance with the
   terms of this agreement.

2. **TERM:** The premises are leased on the following lease
   term: (please check one item only) _____ month to month
   (OR) _____ until _____, 20___.

3. **SECURITY DEPOSITS:** Tenant shall deposit with landlord the sum of $_____ as a security deposit to
   secure Tenant's faithful performance of the terms of this
   lease. The security deposit shall not exceed two times the
   monthly rent. After all the Tenants have vacated, leaving
   the premises vacant, the Landlord may use the security
   deposit for the cleaning of the premises, any unusual wear
   and tear to the premises or common areas, and any rent
   or other amounts owed pursuant to the lease agreement.

   Tenant may not use said deposit for rent owed during the
   term of the lease. Within 21 days of the Tenant vacating
   the premises, Landlord shall furnish Tenant a written
   statement indicating any amounts deducted from the security deposit and returning the balance to the Tenant. If

Tenant fails to furnish a forwarding address to Landlord, then Landlord shall send said statement and any security deposit refund to the leased premises.

4. **INITIAL PAYMENT:** Tenant shall pay the first month rent of $_____ and the security deposit in the amount of $_____ for a total of $_____. Said payment shall be made in the form of cash or cashier's check and is all due prior to occupancy.

5. **OCCUPANTS:** The premises shall not be occupied by any person other than those designated above as Tenant with the exception of the following named persons: _____

_____

If Landlord, with written consent, allows for additional persons to occupy the premises, the rent shall be increased by $100 for each such person. Any person staying 14 days cumulative or longer, without the Landlord's written consent, shall be considered as occupying the premises in violation of this agreement.

6. **SUBLETTING OR ASSIGNING:** Tenant agrees not to assign or sublet the premises, or any part thereof, without first obtaining written permission from Landlord.

7. **UTILITIES:** Tenant shall pay for all utilities and/or services supplied to the premises with the following exception: _____

_____

8. **PARKING:** Tenant ___is not ___is (check one) assigned a parking space. If assigned a parking space it shall be designated as space #_____. Tenant may only park a vehicle that is registered in the Tenant's name. Tenant may not assign, sublet, or allow any other person to use this space. This space is exclusively used for the parking of passenger automobiles by the Tenant. No other type of vehicle or item may be stored in this space without prior written consent of Landlord. Tenant may not wash, repair,

or paint in this space or at any other common area on the premises.

Only vehicles that are operational and currently registered in the State of California may park in this space. Any vehicle that is leaking any substance must not be parked anywhere on the premises.

9. **CONDITION OF PREMISES:** Tenant acknowledges that the premises have been inspected. Tenant acknowledges that said premises have been cleaned and all items, fixtures, appliances, and appurtenances are in complete working order. Tenant promises to keep the premises in a neat and sanitary condition and to immediately reimburse landlord for any sums necessary to repair any item, fixture or appurtenance that needed service due to Tenant's, or Tenant's invitee, misuse or negligence.

Tenant shall be responsible for the cleaning or repair to any plumbing fixture where a stoppage has occurred. Tenant shall also be responsible for repair or replacement of the garbage disposal where the cause has been a result of bones, grease, pits, or any other item which normally causes blockage of the mechanism.

10. **ALTERATIONS:** Tenant shall not make any alterations to the premises, including but not limited to installing aerials, lighting fixtures, dishwashers, washing machines, dryers or other items without first obtaining written permission from Landlord. Tenant shall not change or install locks, paint, or wallpaper to said premises without Landlord's prior written consent. Tenant shall not place placards, signs, or other exhibits in a window or any other place where they can be viewed by other residents or by the general public.

11. **LATE CHARGE/BAD CHECKS:** A late charge of 6% of the current rental amount shall be incurred if rent is not paid when due.

If rent is not paid when due and landlord issues a 'Notice To Pay Rent Or Quit', Tenant must tender cash or cashier's check only. If Tenant tenders a check, which is dishonored by a banking institution, than Tenant shall only tender cash or cashier's check for all future payments. This shall continue until such time as written consent is obtained from Landlord. In addition, Tenant shall be liable in the sum of $10 for each check that is returned to Landlord because the check has been dishonored.

12. **NOISE AND DISRUPTIVE ACTIVITIES:** Tenant or his/her guests and invitees shall not disturb, annoy, endanger or inconvenience other tenants of the building, neighbors, the Landlord or his agents, or workmen nor violate any law, nor commit or permit waste or nuisance in or about the premises.

Further, Tenant shall not do or keep anything in or about the premises that will obstruct the public spaces available to other residents. Lounging or unnecessary loitering on the front steps, public balconies or the common hallways that interferes with the convenience of other residents is prohibited.

13. **LANDLORD'S RIGHT OF ENTRY:** Landlord may enter and inspect the premises during normal business hours and upon reasonable advance notice of at least 24 hours to Tenant. Landlord is permitted to make all alterations, repairs and maintenance that in Landlord's judgment is necessary to perform. In addition Landlord has all right to enter pursuant to Civil Code Section 1954. If the work performed requires that Tenant temporarily vacate the unit, then Tenant shall vacate for this temporary period upon being served a 7 days notice by Landlord. Tenant agrees that in such event that Tenant will be solely compensated by a corresponding reduction in rent for those many days that Tenant was temporarily displaced.

If the work to be performed requires the cooperation of Tenant to perform certain tasks, then those tasks shall be performed upon serving 24 hours written notice by Landlord. (Example: removing food items from cabinets so that the unit may be sprayed for pests.)

14. **REPAIRS BY LANDLORD:** Where a repair is the responsibility of the Landlord, Tenant must notify Landlord with a written notice stating what item needs servicing or repair. Tenant must give Landlord a reasonable opportunity to service or repair said item. Tenant acknowledges that rent will not be withheld unless a written notice has been served on Landlord giving Landlord a reasonable time to fix said item within the meaning of Civil Code Section 1942. Under no circumstances may Tenant withhold rent unless said item constitutes a substantial breach of the warrantee of habitability as stated in Code of Civil Procedure Section 1174.2.

15. **PETS:** No dog, cat, bird, fish, or other domestic pet or animal of any kind may be kept on or about the premises without Landlord's written consent.

16. **FURNISHINGS:** No liquid filled furniture of any kind may be kept on the premises. If the structure was built in 1973 or later Tenant may possess a waterbed if he maintains waterbed insurance valued at $100,000 or more. Tenant must furnish Landlord with proof of said insurance. Tenant must use bedding that complies with the load capacity of the manufacturer. In addition, Tenant must also be in full compliance with Civil Code Section 1940.5. Tenant shall not install or use any washer, dryer, or dishwasher that was not already furnished with the unit.

17. **INSURANCE:** Tenant may maintain a personal property insurance policy to cover any losses sustained to Tenant's personal property or vehicle. It is acknowledged that Landlord does not maintain this insurance to cover

personal property damage or loss caused by fire, theft, rain, water overflow/leakage, acts of GOD, and/or any other causes.

It is acknowledged that Landlord is not liable for these occurrences. It is acknowledged that Tenant's insurance policy shall solely indemnify Tenant for any losses sustained. Tenant's failure to maintain said policy shall be a complete waiver of Tenant's right to seek damages against Landlord for the above stated losses. The parties acknowledge that the premises are not to be considered a security building which would hold Landlord to a higher degree of care.

18. **TERMINATION OF LEASE/RENTAL AGREEMENT:** If this lease is based on a fixed term, pursuant to paragraph 2, then at the expiration of said fixed term this lease shall become a month to month tenancy upon the approval of Landlord. Where said term is a month to month tenancy, either party may terminate this tenancy by the serving of a 30 day written notice.

19. **POSSESSION:** If premises cannot be delivered to Tenant on the agreed date due to loss, total or partial destruction of the premises, or failure of previous Tenant to vacate, either party may terminate this agreement upon written notice to the other party at their last known address. It is acknowledged that either party shall have no liability to each other except that all sums paid to Landlord will be immediately refunded to Tenant.

20. **ABANDONMENT:** It shall be deemed a reasonable belief by the Landlord that an abandonment of the premises has occurred, within the meaning of Civil Code Section 1951.2, where rent has been unpaid for 14 consecutive days and the Tenant has been absent from unit for 14 consecutive days. In that event, Landlord may serve written notice pursuant to Civil Code Section 1951.2. If Tenant does not comply with the requirements of said notice in 18 days, the premises shall be deemed abandoned.

21. **WAIVER:** Landlord's failure to require compliance with the conditions of this agreement, or to exercise any right provided herein, shall not be deemed a waiver by Landlord of such condition or right. Landlord's acceptance of rent with knowledge of any default under agreement by Tenant shall not be deemed a waiver of such default, nor shall it limit Landlord's rights with respect to that or any subsequent right. If is further agreed between the parties that the payment of rent at any time shall not be a waiver to any unlawful detainer action unless Landlord in writing specifically acknowledges that this constitutes a waiver to the unlawful detainer action.

22. **VALIDITY/SEVERABILITY:** If any provision of this agreement is held to be invalid, such invalidity shall not affect the validity or enforceability of any other provision of this agreement.

23. **ATTORNEY FEES:** In the event action is brought by any party to enforce any terms of this agreement or to recover possession of the premises, the prevailing party shall recover from the other party reasonable attorney fees.

    It is acknowledged, between the parties, that jury trials significantly increase the costs of any litigation between the parties. It is also acknowledged that jury trials require a longer length of time to adjudicate the controversy. On this basis, all parties waive their rights to have any matter settled by jury trial.

24. **NOTICES:** All notices to the tenant shall be deemed served upon mailing by first class mail, addressed to the tenant, at the subject premises or upon personal delivery to the premises whether or not Tenant is actually present at the time of said delivery. All notices to the landlord shall be served by mailing first class mail or by personal delivery to the manager's apartment or to:_____

_____.

25. **PERSONAL PROPERTY OF TENANT:** Once Tenant vacates the premises, all personal property left in the unit shall be stored by the Landlord for 18 days. If within that time period, Tenant does not claim said property, Landlord may dispose of said items in any manner Landlord chooses.

26. **ADDITIONAL RENT:** All items owed under this lease shall be deemed additional rent.

27. **APPLICATION:** All statements in Tenant's application must be true or this will constitute a material breach of this lease.

28. **ADDITIONAL TERMS:**

29. **ENTIRE AGREEMENT:** The foregoing agreement, including any attachments incorporated by reference, constitute the entire agreement between the parties and supersedes any oral or written representations or agreements that may have been made by either party. Further, Tenant represents that Tenant has relied solely on Tenant's judgment in entering into this agreement. Tenant acknowledges having been advised to consult with independent legal counsel before entering into this Agreement and has decided to waive such representation and advice. Tenant acknowledges that Tenant has read and understood this agreement and has been furnished a duplicate original.

Landlord/Agent   *Date*

Tenant   *Date*

Tenant   *Date*

No representation is made as to the legal validity or adequacy of this agreement. If you desire, consult with an attorney before entering this agreement.

Rental-Lease Addendum

Tenant(s): _____

Address: _____

_____

Deductions from Security Deposit

Tenant understands and agrees that the Interior carpets (if applicable), and remaining areas throughout the residence were professionally cleaned prior to the Tenant moving in, and will be responsible for said costs after Tenant moves out. Tenant is to leave the property in the same condition as found upon move-in. Other deductions could include, but are not limited to, the following that are deemed "beyond normal wear and tear":

- Any necessary cleaning, i.e., carpets, appliances, bathrooms, floors, walls, windows, window coverings, etc.

- Any damage or needed repairs caused by neglect or abuse by tenant.

- Removal and disposal of Tenant's personal items, property, or unwanted and abandoned items left behind.

- Touch-up prep. Repair needed to any walls or ceilings.

- Pest control spraying (if tenant had a pet).

SMOKE DETECTOR

Tenant is aware of a working smoke detector in the premises and is solely responsible for its upkeep and battery replacement, if applicable. Tenant agrees to notify the property owner or agent for the owner, if the smoke detector does not work.

HEATER FILTERS

Tenant shall vacuum and/or replace the heater filters twice each year, where applicable.

NOTICE TO VACATE

A minimum of a 30-day written notice to vacate is required from all tenants, whether in the last 30 days of multiple-month lease agreement, or on a month-to-month basis. The 30-day notice is effective 30 (thirty) days from the date received in our office. All rent will continue to be due and payable in full. Tenant(s) will allow the showing of the property during this 30-day notice period of time, with the appropriate advance notice as per terms of the Lease, or otherwise agreed upon.

BREAKING A LEASE

In the event a tenant breaches (breaks) this lease before the lease period is over, Tenant shall be responsible and liable for all expenses incurred to re-lease the property. Expenses will include, but are not limited to:

- Rent amount for any remaining unpaid days/months before the expiration of the Lease.
- Real estate commissions for a new similar lease.
- All advertising costs.
- Any other costs directly relating to the re-leasing of the property.

UTILITY CHANGE-OVER

Tenant is responsible for all utility charges (unless otherwise agreed upon in advance in writing). Tenant must also change over all utility billing into their name (Tenant) and mailing address, to be effective upon the commencement (move-in) date stated on their Lease.

VEHICLE CARE

If a tenant parks a vehicle on the property the vehicle must be in good working order and registered. The storage of inoperable vehicles and/or any vehicle maintenance is not allowed on the property. Exceptions are held to the temporary use of jumper cables or the repairing of a flat tire.

INSURANCE

It is the Tenant's responsibility to obtain insurance for personal property and liability.

LEGAL ISSUES

If Tenant is served a 60-day notice to terminate tenancy for any reason, and does not vacate property within said 60 (sixty) days, Tenant agrees to pay any and all legal costs incurred by the property owner and/or agent for the owner. (Only applies to a month/month rental agreement).

MOVE OUT

Upon vacating the property, Tenant must return all keys to owner or agent for the owner, and will continue to be financially liable for rent until all keys are returned. Tenant agrees to pay for lost or not returned keys. During the final 30 days of tenancy, Tenant will allow the showing of the property to prospective renters or purchasers. Owner or agent for the owner will provide reasonable notice to Tenant before any showing hereunder.

Tenant _____   _Date_

Tenant _____   _Date_

Owner _____   _Date_

Lead-Based Paint Disclosure

Housing built before 1978 may contain lead-based paint. Lead from paint, paint chips, and dust can pose health hazards if not managed properly. Lead exposure is especially harmful to young children and pregnant women. Before renting pre-1978 housing, Tenants must disclose the presence of known lead-based paint and/or lead-based paint hazards in the dwelling. Lessees must also receive a federally approved pamphlet on lead poisoning prevention.

Landlord's Disclosure

(a) Presence of lead-based paint and/or lead-based paint hazards (check (i) or (ii) below):

    (i) _____ Known lead-based paint and/or lead-based paint hazards are present in the housing (explain).

    _____

    _____

    _____

    (ii) _____ Landlord has no knowledge of lead-based paint and/or lead-based paint hazards in the housing.

(b) Records and reports available to the Landlord (check (i) or (ii) below):

    (i) _____ Landlord has provided the Tenant with all available records and reports pertaining to lead-based paint and/or lead-based paint hazards in the housing (list documents below).

    _____

    _____

    _____

    (ii) _____ Landlord has no reports or records pertaining to lead-based paint and/or lead-based paint hazards in the housing.

Tenant's Acknowledgment (initial)

(c) _____ Tenant has received copies of all information listed above.

(d) _____ Tenant has received the pamphlet *Protect Your Family from Lead in Your Home.*

(e) Tenant has (check (i) or (ii) below):

    (i) _____ received a 10-day opportunity (or mutually agreed upon period) to conduct a risk assessment or inspection for the presence of lead-based paint and/or lead-based paint hazards; or

    (ii) _____ waived the opportunity to conduct a risk assessment or inspection for the presence of lead-based paint and/or lead-based paint hazards.

Agent's Acknowledgment (initial)

(f) _____ Agent has informed the Landlord of the Landlord' obligations under 42 U.S.C. 4852(d) and is aware of his/her responsibility to ensure compliance.

Landlord Initials _____   *Tenant Initials* _____

Certification of Accuracy

The following parties have reviewed the information above and certify, to the best of their knowledge, that the information they have provided is true and accurate. Penalties for failure to comply with Federal Lead-Based Paint Disclosure Laws include treble (3 times) damages, attorney fees, costs, and a penalty up to $10,000 for each violation.

_____   _____
Landlord/Agent   *Date*

_____   _____
Tenant   *Date*

_____   _____
Tenant   *Date*

Mold Notification Addendum

This agreement, made and entered into between _____
_____, "owner" and _____,
"resident." Resident is renting from owner the premises located
at _____.

It is our goal to maintain the highest-quality living environment for our residents. Therefore, know that the owner/agent
has inspected the unit prior to lease and knows of no damp or
wet building materials and knows of no mold or mildew conta-
mination. Resident is hereby notified that mold, however, can
grow if the premises are not properly maintained or ventilated.
If moisture is allowed to accumulate in the unit, it can cause
mildew and mold to grow. It is important that resident regularly
allows air to circulate in the apartment. It is also important that
resident keeps the interior of the unit clean and that they
promptly notify the owner/agent of any leaks, moisture problems, and/or mold growth. Resident agrees to maintain the
premises in a manner that prevents the occurrence of an infes-
tation of mold or mildew in the premises. Resident agrees to
uphold this responsibility in part by complying with the following list of responsibilities:

- Resident agrees to keep the unit free of dirt and debris
  that can harbor mold.

- Resident agrees to immediately report to the owner/agent
  any water intrusion, such as plumbing leaks, drips, or
  "sweating" pipes.

- Resident agrees to notify owner of overflows from bathroom, kitchen, or unit laundry facilities, especially in cases
  where the overflow may have permeated walls or cabinets.

- Resident agrees to report to the owner/agent any significant mold growth on surfaces inside the premises.

- Resident agrees to allow the owner/agent to enter the unit
  to inspect and make necessary repairs.

- Resident agrees to use bathroom fans while showering or bathing and to report to the owner/agent any non-working fan. If there is no fan, resident agrees to open window.

- Resident agrees to use exhaust fans whenever cooking, dishwashing, or cleaning.

- Resident agrees to use all reasonable care to close all windows and other openings in the premises to prevent outdoor water from penetrating into the interior unit.

- Resident agrees to clean and dry any visible moisture on windows, walls, and other surfaces, including personal property, as soon as reasonably possible. (Note: Mold can grow on damp surfaces within 24 to 48 hours.)

- Resident agrees to notify the owner/agent of any problems with the air conditioning or heating systems that are discovered by the resident.

- Resident agrees to indemnify and hold harmless the owner/agent from any actions, claims, losses, damages, and expenses, including, but not limited to, attorneys' fees that the owner/agent may sustain or incur as a result of the negligence of the resident or any guest or other person living in, occupying, or using the premises.

The undersigned resident(s) acknowledge(s) having read and understood the foregoing, and receipt of a duplicate original.

_____   _____
Tenant   *Date*

_____   _____
Tenant   *Date*

_____   _____
Owner   *Date*

Roommate Addendum

JOINT AND SEVERAL LIABILITY

- Each roommate named on the lease or rental agreement acknowledges that he/she is jointly and severally responsible for the performance of this entire agreement whether or not he/she continues to physically occupy the premises.

- Each roommate named on the lease or rental agreement is bound for the term of the lease unless released by all parties concerned, which includes the owner, as well as the remaining residents on the lease. In the event that one roommate vacates and is replaced by another, the new roommate must fill out a rental application and sign a new lease or rental agreement in order to release the departing roommate from any further obligation on the contract.

- Roommates agree to pay the monthly rent in the form of one check for the total amount of the rent each month, due on the 1st of each month.

- In the event any roommate wishes to move out of said property, a 30-day written notice in advance is required, releasing his or her interest in the security deposit to all other remaining roommates of this property.

SECURITY DEPOSIT REFUNDS

- No security deposits will be returned to any roommates until the owner is in full possession of the property and all roommates have vacated upon lease expiration. No refund or rent pro-ration will be made to any departing roommate when other roommates are still in possession of the property. Such amounts that he/she believes are owed to him/her must be worked out between the roommates themselves.

- No person other than those on the lease or rental agreement are allowed to move into this property at any time, for any reason, unless approved by the owner in advance and in writing.

UNAUTHORIZED OCCUPANTS

- Occupancy of the premises by an unauthorized party prior to the written consent and approval of the owner will be considered a material breach of the rental agreement and may subject all residents to immediate termination of the tenancy.

- There will be a lease re-write fee of $75, to be paid by the lessees for any new Lease or Rental agreement required due to a roommate change.

We, the undersigned, do hereby agree to the terms of this agreement.

_____

Tenant   _Date_

_____

Tenant   _Date_

_____

Owner   _Date_

24-Hour Notice to Enter

Pursuant to this state's civil codes, owner hereby gives notice to: _____, and all persons in occupancy of the premises located at _____, that owner, owner's agent, or owner's employees will enter said premises on or about _____, 20_____, during normal business hours for the reason set forth in the checked item(s) below:

- ❑ To make necessary or agreed repairs
- ❑ Decorations
- ❑ Alterations or improvements
- ❑ Supply necessary or agreed services
- ❑ To exhibit the rental to prospective or actual purchasers
- ❑ To exhibit the rental unit to prospective tenants
- ❑ To exhibit the rental unit to workman or contractors
- ❑ Pursuant to court order
- ❑ To inspect waterbed or liquid-filled furniture
- ❑ To test the smoke detector
- ❑ To verify resident has abandoned premises
- ❑ Other comments: _____

_____

_____

_____

Owner   *Date*

Change in Terms of Tenancy Form

_____
Date

_____
_____
_____

Dear _____,

We are very happy to have you as our tenants, and we hope that we can continue a good relationship in the year to come. However, we are forced to keep our rents near market rates.

Please make note of the following change in terms of tenancy:

Effective _____, your rent will increase $_____ a month. Currently your rent is $_____ per month, and the rent increase will make your new rent $_____ per month.

In the event rent is not received in our office within six days after the due date, tenant agrees to pay a late charge of 6% of the monthly rental amount, with a minimum of $50.

All other terms and conditions in your lease remain intact and unchanged. Please keep in mind that we are here to assist you with any problems, concerns, or maintenance issues you may have.

Thank you,

Property Manager

Pet Addendum

This pet agreement is hereby attached to and becomes part of the residential lease rental agreement between

Resident: _____

and owner: _____.

Dated: _____

Regarding property at: _____

A deposit of: _____

Description of pet: _____

Witnessed:

That, whereas the said resident desires to keep a pet in the premises demised under the agreement herein, and whereas the said residential lease rental agreement prohibits the keeping of said pets without the permission of the owner, now, therefore, in consideration of the rental reserved herein on the mutual terms and conditions and covenants of the residential lease rental agreement herein, the aforementioned pet in his demised premises subject to the following terms and conditions:

1. Resident agrees to pay owner additional deposit and rental monies as stipulated above in accordance with terms of the residential lease rental agreement.

2. Tenant(s) must provide proof of renter's liability insurance, prior to move-in.

3. That the pet will not be permitted to cause any discomfort, annoyance, nuisance or in any way to inconvenience or cause complaint from any other resident and the resident does hereby covenant that upon receipt of notice from the owner of a complaint by another resident, that action will be taken immediately to remedy the cause of the complaint to the satisfaction of the owner.

4. The aforementioned pet will not be permitted to commit any damage or nuisance or in any part of the demised

premises or elsewhere in or on the property; the resident agrees and covenants to be financially responsible for any and all damage, loss, or expense arising out of his keeping his pet in or on the premises.

5. Resident further agrees that if the pet is a dog, it will not be permitted outside resident's premises unless restrained by a leash.

6. For failure or breach of any of the terms and conditions set forth above, the owner reserves the right to revoke permission to keep the pet in the premises and to terminate the residential lease rental agreement herein and to hold the resident responsible for the remainder of the unexpired term thereof.

7. The cleaning/security deposit will be returned to the resident at termination of the pets tenancy on the following basis:

   ▪ Manager or owner will inspect premises.

   ▪ All monies not needed for cleaning and/or repairing necessitated by the pet's occupancy will be returned to the resident within three weeks of the inspection date.

   ▪ If the cost of cleaning and/or repairing exceeds the amount of the deposit, resident agrees to promptly pay owner for such excess.

_____
Tenant   _Date_

_____
Tenant   _Date_

_____
Owner   _Date_

Proof of Service

I, the Undersigned, being at least eighteen (18) years of age, served a THREE-DAY NOTICE TO PAY RENT OR QUIT, of which is a true copy, on the below named tenant, in the manner indicated below:

Tenant: _____

Address: _____

_____

_____

1. I personally delivered a copy to the tenant at _____ _____on (date) _____, at _____ o'clock ____ AM ____ PM

2. The tenant was absent from his or her residence and business address. I personally delivered a copy to _____ _____, a person of suitable age and discretion at tenant's residence or business address, on (date) _____, at _____ o'clock ____ AM ____ PM and mailed a copy addressed to the tenant at his or her place of residence.

3. There being no person at the leased premises, I affixed a copy of the notice in a conspicuous place on the property on (date) _____, at _____ o'clock ____ AM ____ PM and mailed a copy to tenant at the leased premises.

I declare under penalty of perjury under the laws of the State of California, that the foregoing is true and correct.

_____

Signature   *Date*

Tenant Notice to Vacate

I, (tenant) _____

_____

_____

intend to vacate the premises that I currently reside in located at:

_____

_____

_____

on the _____ day of _____ 20_____.

My forwarding address and telephone number will be:

_____

_____

Submitted this _____ day of _____ 20_____.

_____   _____
Tenant   *Date*

_____   _____
Tenant   *Date*

Roommate Notice to Terminate

Name: _____

Address: _____

SECTION I

I hereby give notice to terminate my residency from this property on _____ (date). I understand that I must forfeit all keys to the current tenants on the rental agreement upon vacating the unit.

    Each of these remaining roommate(s) _____ _____ continue to live in this unit and will be held accountable to the terms of the rental agreement.

    I hereby release the entire amount of the security deposit to my former roommate(s).

    I am leaving the property for the following reason: _____ _____

SECTION II

All remaining roommates, having undersigned, indicate that they understand and agree that the rental agreement is hereby revised, removing the above-named tenant from the agreement and releasing this tenant of any responsibility for the agreement terms. The agreement is now binding and holds fully liable all of the undersigned roommates.

_____
Remaining roommate   *Date*

_____
Remaining roommate   *Date*

_____
Owner   *Date*

30-Day-Notice Acknowledgment

Date: _____

Tenant: _____

We understand that you have turned in your 30-day notice to vacate, which was served to us on: _____, and that you will be out of the premises by: _____

After you have vacated the premises and have returned all keys to us, the following steps must be taken to ensure that your security deposit is returned to you in a timely manner within three weeks.

HOW TO LEAVE RESIDENCE

Upon vacating the premises, be sure to leave the residence, all appliances and surfaces, clean, empty, and neat, just as you found it when you moved in.

KEYS

You must return all keys that pertain to the residence (for example, doors, storage, mailbox, etc.) to our office on or before the scheduled move-out date. You may put the keys through the mail slot at any time. (They must be put in a marked envelope for identification purposes.) You will continue to be liable and responsible for rent until we receive all keys.

PERSONAL BELONGINGS/ITEMS

All personal belongings and items (for example, furniture, clothes, and so on) must be removed from the premises on or before the scheduled move-out date. Any items left or abandoned in the premises after your move-out will be removed and discarded at a cost to you.

MAINTENANCE ISSUES

Please inform us of any maintenance items that you are aware of in the residence (for example, non-functioning oven, stove, lights, fans, plumbing, and so on).

PRE-INSPECTION

Under state law, you may request to have a pre-inspection walk-through up to two weeks prior to vacating the property. The request must be in writing and will be performed at a mutually agreeable appointment time during normal business hours.

FORWARDING ADDRESS AND PHONE NUMBER

This is very important. You must inform us of your new address and telephone number so we can forward your security deposit refund and any other correspondence to you.

It has been nice having you as our tenant, and we hope that we may be of service to you again in the future. Please feel free to call us with any questions that you might have. Thank you.

_____

Owner   *Date*

Security Deposit Refund

Date _____

Resident's name _____

Rental address _____

Date paid thru _____

Lease expiration date _____

Date notice given _____

Move-out date _____

Reason for moving _____

All keys returned? _____

Forwarding address _____

Remarks _____

DEPOSITS

Security Deposit $_____

Key Deposit $_____

Pet Deposit $_____

Other Deposits $_____

TOTAL DEPOSITS $_____

DEDUCTIONS

Repairs $_____

Cleaning $_____

Keys $_____

Miscellaneous $_____

Insufficient Notice $_____

Unpaid Rent $_____

Other $_____

TOTAL DEDUCTIONS $_____

Numbers

A